Tough Stuff from the Bible, Tendered Gently

PAIDEIA
PRESS

Tough Stuff From the Bible
Tendered Gently
■ Encouraging Faith Manifestos
For People with Open Ears ■

Calvin G. Seerveld

Biblical Prophetic Oracles

Paideia Press
Jordan Station, ON Canada

Copyright © 2024 Calvin G. Seerveld
ISBN: 978-0-88815-352-4

Fragmentary portions of this book may be freely used by those who are interested in sharing the author's insights and observations, or purposes of the Reformational Publishing Project (www.reformationalpublishing-project.com), so long as proper credit is visibly given to the author and Paideia Press. Others, and those who wish to use, reproduce, or store larger portions of text, must seek written permission from the publisher.
Scripture translations are the author's responsibility.

Typescript preparation of pre-digital documents /proofreading:
Mary Martens
Book design / page makeup and typography:
Steven R. Martins & Paul Aurich
Cover design / typographical formatting assistance and editorial troubleshooting: Peter Enneson
Cover Image: John Tiktak, "Woman and Child," c. 1960-1969; stone, 16 x 5.6 x 8.8 cm;
Collection of the Winnipeg Art Gallery Twomey Collection, with appreciation to the Province of Manitoba
and Government of Canada, 2060.71.
Photo: Ernest Mayer, Courtesy of WAG-Qaumajuq

Library and Archives Canada Cataloguing in Publication
    Title: Biblical Prophetic Oracles/ Calvin G. Seerveld
    Names: Seerveld, Calvin, author.
    Description: Series Statement: Tough stuff from the Bible, Tendered Gently; 2 includes index.
    Identifiers: Canadiana 20240348346 ISBN: 978-0-88815-352-4 (softcover)
    Subjects: LCSH: Bible–Meditations. LCSH: Bible–Criticism, interpretation, etc. LCSH: Christian life–Biblical teaching. LCSH: Spiritual life–Christianity. LCGFT: Meditations.
    Classification: LCC BS491.5 .S445 2024 DDC 242/.5—dc23

Printed and published in Canada by
Paideia Press, P.O. Box 500,
Jordan Station, Ontario L0R 1S0, Canada

Other books by the author are listed at:
http://www.seerveld.com/tuppence.html

Dedicated to my parents
Lester Benjamin Seerveld (1907–1990)
and Letitia Elizabeth Van Tielen (1905-1981)
who by their Bible-reading
and non-judgmental, low key vibrant chrisitan faith
formed me into a studious, cheerful and
curious follower of Jesus Christ

---

and to Inès' mother
Ruth Huber (1905-1991)
who kept her family alive during
de honger winter (1944–45)

My fishmonger Father who served as a perennial elder of the Christian Reformed Church, and was a leader in developing the Christian School of West Sayville, Long Island, New York.

My Mother who early fostered my musical talent and bent for poetry

---

Generous Oma, whose multi-lingual and deep European cultural knowledge enriched our North American children's lives.

Cover Image
and Acknowledgements

JOHN TIKTAK WAS ABLE to craft a piece of weather-beaten stone into a statue of immense tenderness, *Woman and Child* (c.1960-1969). The partially bowed, but head up, plodding woman is carrying her child onward, snug on her back, probably with a long way to go.

I was privileged to hold this little artwork in my hands for a short while deep in the vault of the Winnipeg Art Gallery. You could feel the love in the smoothly cut contours of the figures, both respect for the stone and admiration for the care being imaged.

Inuit Tiktak's burden-bearing Mother helps me imagine how the Older Testament prophetsthe wise poetic Isaiah, the intrepid defeated Jeremiah, the outrageously outspoken Ezekiel—how these sorry prophets bore God's people on their backs, so to speak, trying to bring them on to safety. As Isaiah puts it, "The LORD lifted them up and carried them along all those days long ago" (63:9).

This indigenous Canadian carved stone art also echoes Psalm 131, where I, in spite of the evil all around me, may be calmed down, close to my Lord, the LORD God! "like a weaned child near the neck of its Mother." Such is the good steadying news of the Bible.

THIS COLLECTION OF SCRIPTURAL meditations, spoken to all sorts of people, were heard in gatherings dating from 1976 to 2021. This is Book 2 in a projected series which may become four, along somewhat the same lines. But each book selects different kinds of biblical texts. This Book 2 deals mostly with Prophetic Oracles. Next to come are Artful Wisdom passages, like Judges 5, Psalms, Proverbs, and a few Pauline letters. The whole series represents a lifetime of struggling to hear the call of God on how to live in response to God's great deeds in history.

The same faithful persons who began this project with me have given of their life time too to its continuation. Mary Martens and Peter Enneson continue to constitute the reliable team which puts the written text and songs and illustrations together. Whether (at age 93 years) I live to see its completion myself is up to God, but this collecting of earlier **spoken** meditations has become for me, despite its faults, a joyful "ending of life" endeavour. I gladly thank Paideia Press and its staff for supporting and orchestrating the publication.

Table of Contents

	Foreword	1
1.	**God is calling us to be an apprenticed company of Pregnant Priestly Leftovers** Isaiah 11:1-10 with Revelation 5	13
2.	**Restorative Just-doing is the key to finding True Restfulness with God** Isaiah 28:1-22 and 30:15-18	27
3.	**On doing Creatural Justice to Weeds in God's World** Isaiah 28:23-29	49
4.	**God is impatiently waiting for our faithful Restorative Just-doing and hope-filled, politically aware prayer** Isaiah 30:1-3, 8-21; 31:1-3; 32:15-18 and Philippians 4:4-7	61
5.	**The nature of prayer to which God says "Yes": check out Hezekiah in Isaiah 36-39** Isaiah 38:1-6, 9-20; 39:1-2, 5-8; 36:11-15; 37:7, 14-20, 37-38, and Mark 11:20-26	81
6.	**In the Older and Newer Testament of the Bible comes the Good News: NOTHING can pry God's people out of the loving grip of God's hand** Isaiah 42:18-43:21	103
7.	**A Good Deed of Spilled Perfume, despite the poverty all around us** Isaiah 53:2-5, Malachi 1:10-13, Mark 14:1-11	121
8.	**God's calling us to become Melchizedek mature in our faith** Isaiah 54:1-3 and Hebrew 5:4-6:12	131

9. **Biblical Reformation among God's people: confession of our sin, and being clothed in Christ's redemptive deeds**   155
   Isaiah 59-60, Psalm 33:12, 18-22

10. **The Incredible Generosity of God for us ungrateful pixilated people: becoming a listening, faithful tzaddiq**   183
    Ezekiel 18, Matthew 20:1-16, Romans 4:4-8

11. **The LORD God is a prodigal God who gives grace to sinners even before they are historically ready to be delivered from their captivities**   199
    Ezekiel 33:1-20, 34:1-16, 20-31, with Luke 15

12. **The Sorrowful Pottery-making God revealed in Jesus Christ and our Psalm 2 task**   223
    Jeremiah 18:1-20:6 with Psalm 2, Joel 2:12-14, II Timothy 2:11-13

13. **The Rechabite Alternative, and Following Jesus Christ First!**   243
    Jeremiah 35, Mark 11:17-31, Luke 9:57-62, and Mark 8:31-35, 38

14. **Beasts in God's World and our daily Psalm 2 Responsiblity: tough merciful just Rule expecting Jesus Christ's return**   259
    Daniel 7:1-18, 27

15. **The Older and Younger Generation of Christ's followers may expect the Wisdom of Moses and the Energy of Elijah to unite them in service during the last days**   285
    Malachi 3:13-4:6, Luke 1:16-17, Jude 1:24-25

    Index of Scriptural passages freshly translated   299

    Psalms and Hymns   300

    List of illustrations   301

Foreword

WE NEVER HAD A TV in our home while the children were growing up. My lame excuse was "we don't want the whole blasted world of politics and rough culture afoot in our living room." A home deserves to be a sanctuary.

When our three teenaged children (without TV exposure) left home for college they had learned to make music—piano, clarinet, flute and drums, had hobbies in film, dance, and literature, had run track, swum in the Atlantic Ocean, and seemed well-spoken. My European wife and I had missed, with no TV, it's so, a lot of American pop culture exposure in the twentieth century, although living on the outskirts of the city of Chicago in the '60s, I took guitar lessons in Old Town, we both subscribed to regular drama productions at the Goodman Theatre, visited regularly the Art Gallery of Chicago, and we witnessed at close hand the riot of the 1968 Democratic Convention in the downtown city— Ines and I had precariously attended a Black Panther 'Support Huey Newton' rally[1]—and faced various racial

---

[1] Admission was free, but—it was announced later during the proceedings—you had to make a monetary contribution to get out of and leave the meeting. The scrutinizing persons at the exit were big men.

incidents in Roseland. But ours was basically a quiet-book culture.[2]

In all those years of bearing and raising children, from 1959 to 1972, the local Church was like a spare tire for us. Well kept in the trunk of the car.

I PERSONALLY MET GOD working through all-night shifts in my study, preparing philosophy lectures and brief chapel messages at Trinity Christian College for first year beginning students. Peter Smith's woodcut, "Working Late," catches

---

2   During sabbaticals in England and Germany (1973 and 1980) we had been briefly exposed to European TV programs, and later turned down the gift from our eldest now married daughter to accept her 14 inch black-and-white machine in 1992. Our media-savvy son finally bought us a regular TV for our Toronto home in 2015 AD.

the quasi monastic, almost imprisoned solitude and quiet intensity of those long nightly struggles to translate and interpret Scripture for young persons who were on the cusp of relinquishing parental authority. Can you *Take Hold of God and Pull* as the deceiver Jacob once did, in a 10-12 minute chapel bite, book-ended by a psalm or hymn and a brief prayer, and make it stick for a restive audience?

You realized later it was not normative, that some of us faculty had found our "Church" in the workings of this brand new Christian college of total 32 students, where the teaching faculty were also the administration! There was no president. No traditional protocols. So it was a heady experience. Do you begin a German class with a *Vater Unser?* What does Vollenhoven's book, *De Noodzakelijkheid eener Christelijke Logica* (1932) (*The Necessity of a Christian Logic*) mean for understanding Aristotle's syllogisms? Teaching *To Kill a Mockingbird* with Christian sensitivity should not turn an English Literature seminar into a catechism class!

WHEN OUR FAMILY MOVED to Toronto in 1972, the difference and the relation of "Kingdom of God" activity and the task of "The congregated Church" became more clear. You struggled to form a **Christian Labour Association of Canada** with an "open shop" policy (=You don't have to be a union member to work in this labour unionized factory), but the Christian labour union did not become an Anglican or Reformed church. **Patmos Art Gallery Workshop** was a collective of artists professing a redemptive spirit, not a church with elders, pastor and deacons. **Citizens for Public Justice** was organized as a community, united to bring justice to the unorganized poor in the land, but CPJ was not a church with Sunday services and the Apostles' Creed.

And the Church, ἐκκλησία, was a congregation of faithful and sinful forgiven believers trying to follow Jesus Christ, who met regularly to hear God's Word proclaimed, and to develop a prayerfully educated outreach of loving communal service to one's neighbours, local and foreign. The **churchly communion** was to be at the rejuvenating center of one's many life activities, infusing a justifying merciful spirit into our mundane daily life and even our professional activity.

The Christian Reformed Church in Canada was very different from the irrelevant church experience we had had in the '60s USA. The predominantly post-war Dutch immigrants making up the Christian Reformed Church in Canada were accustomed to solid preaching, Older and Newer Testaments together, and wanted to hear God's challenging Word of remonstrance, visionary projects, and comfort. "Abraham Kuyper" was not just an identifying "every inch" slogan back then as it sometimes is today, but Kuyperian non-church societal reform, especially **Christian schools**, was what you as a Reformed Canadian believer gave money for, even before groceries.

In Canadian Reformation services you sang Genevan psalms in syncopated unison led by an inspired organist, sometime using a trumpet stop, that gave muscle to your faith in the Lord. (The Genevan psalms had been trashed in the USA by setting them in all "even" whole notes which persons then sometimes tried to sing slowly in four-part harmony, stifling the exciting Genevan bounce and vigour.) Many Canadian CRC pastors had Jean Calvin in their blood and had undergone the reality of Nazi Gestapo fear firsthand in Europe—which gives a special kind of backbone to your personal trust in God that rubs off in giving a new generation counsel. Many immigrant parishioners had been professionally educated in Holland, but now had to make a living in Canada as farmers and hired workers; so Sunday and church services became a free day, to tap back into faith roots, rest from labour, and spend time visiting other displaced persons.

As a non-Dutch American doctoral student in the '50s Netherlands, I had promised my Dutch professor Vollenhoven not to dabble in "preaching." "There are lots of preachers," Vollenhoven had said, "but not many teachers of a redemptive philosophy; so give your time to teaching philosophy." But when Professor Vollenhoven passed away, I thought maybe my promise could be waived. Given the opportunity by the Toronto CRC "Classis" (a group of CRC churches in the Ontario geographic area) to be examined and tested on Bible knowledge and confessional reliability—I had never gone to seminary—I received permission to "bring the Word" as an approved person, upon occasions when needed. That opportunity has been an extraordinary blessing in my life.

OLDER TESTAMENT BIBLICAL PROPHETIC oracles are not ambiguous conundrums like those the ancient Greek oracle at Delphi delivered. The standard Older Testament prophets' formula was: **"Thus says the LORD God!**

Stop slaughtering cows as sacrifices for me. Do you people think I want meat to eat? I want you folk to give the poor enough food and sing me a song of thanksgiving." There is nothing ambiguous about God's forthright directives spoken clearly and directly to people by God's beleaguered prophets.

Prophets are not priests. Prophets were not "establishment" figures. Prophets were indeed advisors to Judah and Israel's kings, but unlike jokers at court were not usually appreciated for their God-sourced penetrating critique of royal ruling policies: Ahab and Jezebel tried to kill the bold Elijah for denouncing their idolatries (I Kings 19:1-10). Ahab had the prophet Micaiah imprisoned and put on a bread and water diet because the prophet would not approve his plans for war (II Chronicles 18:1-27). King Jehoiakim publicly burned Jeremiah's critique from God against his pro-Egyptian political decisions written down by the scribe Baruch (II Kings 23:34-37, Jeremiah 36); and King Zedekiah later incarcerated Jeremiah in a deep earthen pit of mud (Jeremiah 37:11-38:6).

Fascinating and important for us today is that the Older Testament takes seriously the embedded life of God's people in the socio-political culture of their day. God expected the people of God to interact with the nations of the world to whom God was foreign. For example, God of the Angels wanted Amalek King Agag put to death because of his atrocities toward God's people (I Samuel 15). God loved the city of Nineveh (and its cows, Jonah 4:11), and by exception sent the Jewish prophet

Jonah there, who couldn't stomach an Assyrian, to bring these unbelievers to repentance and relief (Jonah 3:1-4:3). God told a later generation of God's punished people to seek the welfare of godless and repressive Babylon! so that God's exiled people there could benefit from Babylonian culture (Jeremiah 29:1-14, v.7).

The LORD God Yahweh was the special protector of the children of Abraham and the covenanted progeny of David, but God is the Creator of **all** peoples, and as Creator of the world cares for God's animals, forests, seas, and mountains too. Once one realizes the Older Testament God is vitally interested in the saving potential of Egyptian agriculture, the incessant turmoil of Canaanite military skirmishes, the temporary Babylonian world domination before the Medes and Persians took over control, and that Melchizedek, Joseph's Pharaoh Amenhotep II, General Sisera, Nebuchadnezzar, Ahasuerus with Hamish, and Cyrus enter into the LORD's historical plans, then one is more likely to recognize the Newer Testament's mention of Herod, Pilate, Festus and Rome is more than a background scenario to Christ's birth.

Psalm 2 carries over into the task of the Church post-Pentecost. God's anointed (baptized) sons and daughters (Heidelberg Catechism, Q&A #32) may have to break and reshape the political bonds they live within. The Newer Testament is more than a Jesus-saves-individual-you-from-hell story, as the final book of Revelation makes clear with Armageddon and the return of Jesus

Christ with his angels to **rule** the new earth (Revelation 21-22). The Older and Newer Testament biblical landscape has a cosmic panorama underneath the salvific message: historical reality is a war against societal idolatry, deadly seduction of new generations, and the foolishness of adult pride in high and low places. The Bible speaks to how God's presence provides comfort and buoys perseverance in daily lives of believers **and** unbelievers.

And it is especially prophets who speak God's cheer amidst foreboding to the public at large. Prophets don't predict events. Biblical prophets tell what God has done, is doing, and will do later in response to our human obedience and obstinacy. True prophetic voices admonish, encourage, and make godly counsel known that points to a redemptive Way to go in difficult and complicated circumstances. More than Yes or No, a good prophetic word stirs up imaginative horizons with primal certainty that Jesus Christ's incredible sacrifice in history makes our life past death possible. Biblical prophetic oracles ready anybody who hears their word with expectations of shalom.

Isaiah, it seems to me, is one of the richest and most provocative books in the Bible. Imagine God addressing the assembled World Council of Churches' presidents and vice-presidents this way: "Greeting to you, O representatives of Sodom and Gomorrah!" (Isaiah 1:10-20)

There is not only plenty of rhetorical irony that bespeaks God's hurt, but soaring poetry in Isaiah (chapter 40), and still unfilled promises for today that rival those in the Newer Testament book of Revelation (chapters 60-61, 63:6-66:25). You always need to keep reading Isaiah's chapters because a wave of curses condemning Israel's apostasy (chapter 24) is nevertheless followed up by expressions of God's sure and unforgettable love for God's "chosen ones" (chapters 25-27). There are 11 chapters with God's judgments on the failings of pagan nations—Assyria, Philistia, Moab, Syria, Ethiopia, Egypt, Babylon and Arabia (chapters 13-21, 23) before the prophet warns Israel about the destruction of Jerusalem (chapter 22). The prophet Isaiah exemplifies what the apostle Peter had difficulty learning: "God does not show favouritism to anybody, but in every nation (ἔθνει, ethnicity), whoever stands in awe of God and works for what is truly just (δικαιοσύνην), is acceptable to God" (Acts 10:34).

Every biblical prophet seems to revel in his or her idiosyncrasy. Cowboy Amos is not impressed by the put-down he received from King Jeroboam's head priest Amaziah, and responded with a curse that Amaziah's wife would become a prostitute (Amos 7:10-17). The ecstatic prophet Ezekiel is sometimes so outlandish—his vision of the valley of dry bones that come to breathe and live (Ezekiel 37:1-14)—I suspect he was autistic. The poetic Jeremiah knew how to lament his woes and mourn the LORD God's coming punishment for God's people: Jeremiah was brave rather than morose, and he could still testify that "The steadfast covenantal love (*chesed*) of the LORD never ceases; God's mercies never end, but are new every morning" (Lamentations of Jeremiah, 3:22-23). The highly educated, multilingual statesman Daniel could interpret dreams, and his enigmatic prophetic vision has apocalyptic reach and power that speaks to our human struggle against beastly 'powers' to this day (Daniel 7).

I SHOULD MENTION THAT I have become aware that a person could exhort behind the pulpit for 30-45 minutes in the 1970s. Reformed Church goers then wanted interpretations of Scripture to chew on and were willing to hear out longer expositions of Scripture. Attention span today seems more limited. A 20 minute sermon is about what people expect now. So #9 below with a two chapter Isaiah text will seem too long for most people today; back in 1976 it was a festive, celebrative occasion for a gathering of all the Toronto metropolitan Christian Reformed congregations.

I realize too that my occasional use in parentheses of a key Greek or Hebrew biblical word may seem hoity-toity to some. But I ask those who are monolingual to be generous toward those knowledgeable of the original biblical languages, just as it is right for the educated to make difficult matters intelligible to those who are untrained in foreign languages and involved reflection. We should avoid both high-fallutin prose and dumbed-down simpleminded talk.

- If you don't ever dare to splurge because your neighbour is stuck in poverty, read #7.
- If you feel like a "leftover," read the first chapter.
- Try #3 if you don't know how to pray for (or against) Putin, Trump, or Trudeau.
- May a very sick person pray for 15 more Hezekiah years of life? See #5

- Should you not be afraid of the addictive power of Daniel's scary Beasts in chapter 14?
- Not "righteous," not "pious," not "orthodox," but learn the rich Hebrew word **tzaddiq:** a man or a woman of God with the attractive demeanor of Jesus Christ—but #10 is a little difficult.

   Calvin Seerveld, Toronto
   August 2023 AD

1

God is Calling us to be an Apprenticed Company of Pregnant Priestly Leftovers

TEXTS: Isaiah 11:1-10 with Revelation 5

I WILL READ FIRST the great passage from Isaiah 11:1-10, about the restoration promised for the world when the shoot from the stump of Jesse, the Messiah Jesus Christ, comes into the world again, and the nations, the *goyim*, the unbelieving peoples all around, shall look to this One upon whom the Spirit of the LORD descends: the peoples of the world shall seek direction from this odd shoot out of a stump.

Isaiah 11:1-10

THERE SHOOTS A SPROUT out of the stump of Jesse!
A new growth out of the old roots, and it will bear fruit!
The Spirit of the LORD God shall rest upon him:
    the spirit of wisdom and insight,

the spirit of considered counsel and restful strength, a
    knowing spirit;
a spirit of standing in awe of the LORD God shall
    settle down upon him,
and he will be just glad to be awe struck before the
    LORD God!
He shall not judge by what his eyes see,
and shall never decide a matter on what his ears hear.
No, **he shall rule the cowering, defenseless ones protectively,**
and speak law, judge with fairness, for the poor hurt ones of
    the land.
He shall stop dead in their tracks, by the blow of his mouth,
    the ruthless violent ones,
and kill off the wicked by the breath of his lips.
So, right-dealing fits snug to his loins like a girdle,
and trustworthy faithfulness clings to his hips like tights.

Then strangely,
wolf will become a guest of the lamb,
and leopard will lie down next to the kid goat;
calf and sinewy young lion and choice fat cattle
all together will be tended by a little boy;
the heifer and bear will associate peacefully
and their young shall gambol together;
lions shall eat pieces of straw like oxen—
and a breast-fed baby shall be able
to drool and goo right on top of a poisonous snake's hole;
a weaned child shall be able to stretch out its little hands to
    a nest of vipers.
There will be no damaging, ruining, taking place anymore
    in all the strongholds of my holiness! says the LORD,
because knowledge of the LORD God shall fill the earth like
    the water waves cover the sea!
And on that Day, the stump of Jesse, which had been standing

around only as a warning sign to peoples of the earth:
on that Day, unbelievers will look it up, turn to the root of Jesse
 questioningly listening—
and the places where the One coming lodges shall be a
 stunning glory.

Now we read a vision the apostle John had of a worship service in heaven (chapters 4-5 of *The Revelation of Jesus Christ* given to John). God is on the throne surrounded by a rainbow, four "Living Creatures" ("Animals" according to Eugene Peterson's paraphrase; a special body-guard of unusually strange, important angels, in my judgment), each with six wings full of eyes, plus 24 elderly (Senior citizen) angels, seven fiery torches—there they all are, worshipping and singing day after day:

> Holy, holy, holy, is the LORD God Almighty
> who was and is and is to come!

We pick up the action in Revelation 5.

Revelation 5

Then I saw (says John) in the right hand of the One seated on the throne a papyrus scroll written on both sides sealed closed by seven seals. And I saw a mighty angel proclaiming with a loud voice, "Who is worthy to open the scroll and break its seals?" And no one in heaven or on the earth or under the earth was able to open the scroll or look into it. So I began to weep bitterly that no one was found to open the scroll or look into it. But one of the Senior angels said to me, "Don't cry. Look! the lion from the tribe of Judah, the root of David, has overcome [ἐνίκησεν] (all obstacles) so as to be able to open the scroll and its seven seals."

At that point I saw in between the throne and the four Living Creatures among the Senior angels a Lamb standing there as if it had been slaughtered, and it had seven horns and seven eyes, which represent the seven spirits of God commissioned (to observe) all the earth world. And the Lamb came and took (the scroll) from the right hand of the One seated on the throne. When the Lamb had taken the scroll, the four Living creatures and the 24 Senior angels fell down in front of the Lamb, each one holding a little harp and little golden bowls full of various **incenses, which are the prayers of the saints.** And they sang a fresh new song (5:9-10):

> You are worthy to take the scroll and break open its seals,
>   because You were sacrificed,
> and in your blood bought back for God (persons) from every
>   tribe and language and people and nation,
> and **You have made them to be a ruling authority (kingdom)**
>   and priests for serving our God,
> **and they shall come to reign on the earth.**

Then I looked and heard the voiced sound of many angels surrounding the throne and the Living Creatures and the Senior angels, and their number was ten thousand of ten thousands, thousands of thousands, singing with an enormous sound of voices:

> Worthy is the Lamb that was sacrificed
> to receive the power and wealth and wisdom and strength
> and honour and glory and blessing!

Then I heard every creature in the sky and on the earth and underneath the earth and on the sea, and everything in them all singing:

> To the One seated on the throne and to the Lamb
> be blessing and honour and glory and strength
> for ever and ever, ever and ever....

The four Living Creatures said, "Amen!" And the Senior angels fell down and worshipped.

This is the Word of the Lord!
Thanks be to God!

AN APPRENTICED COMPANY OF PREGNANT PRIESTLY LEFTOVERS

THE PICTURE OF PEACEFUL violent animals cared for by a Holy Spirited "Prince of peace" (Isaiah 11) followed by an upbeat heavenly Hallelujah worship service happening (Revelation 4-5) sets the horizons for the good news today.

The first time Jesus Christ came to earth was to save sinners, including turning around God's people. The next and last time Jesus Christ comes to earth is to judge sinners and bring his Rule to completion on a new earth with those whose names are written in the Book of Life, and then everyone will see that scroll of world history that only the bloodied Lamb could open in heaven.

Today we are living in between those two comings of Jesus Christ on earth. Right now, Jesus is in heaven getting ready to come back. So how then does Scripture say we should live on earth in the meantime, if we have been "reborn by water and the Holy Spirit" (John 3:5)

A simple answer is found in that new song the angels are singing in heaven right now, praising the Lamb, the baby Jesus Christ who grew up to have his blood shed on earth, but was raised from the dead and ascended into heaven, to make us "to be a 'kingdom,' a rulership, **a community of ruling <u>priests</u> to serve God, to be those who shall eventually come to reign over the earth."**

We are called today to be apprenticed priestly rulers, and to exercise that calling in a sure hope. That's the message in a nutshell this morning straight from God's Word (Revelation 5:9-10).

Early fruit of the stump's shoot

ISAIAH 11 ALWAYS GIVES me hope, because it turns the world as we meet it right side up. That the wolf takes refuge with the lamb and lions eat straw like oxen is another way of saying the first shall be last and the last shall be first, and the meek shall inherit the earth. It is certain that the time is coming when, as Isaiah 11 puts it, the babies of believers will be able to crawl among poisonous snakes unharmed, and as the prophet Zechariah puts it (Zechariah 8:5), boys and girls who are holy will be able to play friendly road hockey on Yonge Street, and elderly women and men will be able to sit outdoors on their porches in the worst sections of Detroit or New York without getting shot. That's a promise, say Zechariah and Isaiah, when Jesus Christ comes back to earth triumphant!

Particularly wonderful about this hope Isaiah 11 provides is that God works the miracles of God historically where nobody would look for them: a shoot comes forth from what looks like a dead stump.

That was true the first time Jesus Christ came to earth too. After the Babylonians got through with the house of Israel, even though the Persians let the Jews struggle back to build up a dinky "new" Jerusalem, the line of David indeed looked like a dead stump of Jesse (as Psalm 89 hollers). Yet later God went to the least important part of that covenanted stump, Bethlehem, Ephrathah (Micah 5:2), to have a shame-faced virgin give birth there to a mere baby who was set "for the fall and rising of many in Israel" (Luke 2:34), who brought righteous, protective judgment to the poor hurt ones of the land, and challenged Sadducee and Pharisee leaders. Also, as Isaiah 11:10 says, wise wealthy persons from unbelieving foreign nations came looking, "Where is the King of the Jews?" (Matthew 2:1-2)

Wherever Jesus Christ walked on earth that first time, the Spirit of reconciling wisdom and the fruit of right-doing got started. Christ healed those who had had strokes and were lame; the Lord purged people of their cancerous leprosy so they could live normal lives again; Jesus healed people of nervous emotional breakdowns and cast out devils by a word of command (Matthew 8-9). Christ talked with a half-breed Samaritan woman of easy morals at a well in the midday sun (John 4) and went for Sunday dinner with bookie tax-collector Zacchaeus (Luke 19:1-10), to pull these outcasts redemptively into the community of believers.

But Jesus' own people didn't want him and Christ's gentle rule; so they hung him on a Christmas tree. And when Jesus Christ died there, that death ripped to shreds the unholy veil of their legalistic, self-righteous temple of worship.

Faithful leftovers

GOD STILL WORKS TODAY within the lines of Isaiah 11's prophecy awaiting fulfillment. It is so that wolves still eat lambs; the poor and weak are still exploited by crafty ones in power. Evil does happen; good people are ruined, and the sick do not have all their diseases healed; the Lord is not with us so you can touch the hem of his garment. Jesus went back to heaven, and the Satan was cast out of heaven to mess up God's earth world (Revelation 12:7-12, I John 5:19).

But God is still preparing for the surprising coming of Christ again by using leftovers.

Many years ago my Dad told me jokingly, when you are looking for a wife, check out whether she can help you make a good meal from leftovers. (I followed that advice, also because Inès had very long hair down her back and she could read Greek.)

I've thought about that when I realized God works God's majestic, inscrutable purposes historically on earth with leftover people, shoots from stumps, a remnant of covenanted ones often returning from some exile or other, like refugees. Not because the leftovers are more holy, but precisely because they are leftovers, and God prefers to work with what is fraught with woes and weak to show the Lord's strength.

The apostle Paul was very sensitive on this point, because he knew as unbeliever Saul he was very much a leftover and out when the "natural" branches would be lopped off the olive tree. In Romans 9-11 Paul agonizes to get leftover Jews to be for Jesus, as well as the "wild" shoots of humbled believing Gentiles. And in I Corinthians 1-2 Paul extends the leftover policy to affirm that God has chosen what is stupid to the Greek, a stumbling block to the Jew, and what is narrow-minded and parochial to the secularist Romans, in order to confound the conceited, shame the privileged, and boggle the imperial efficiency experts.

Because God works with leftovers there is hope for me and you. We are the leftovers from all the people rushing to make a buck so they can take a brief expensive cruise vacation and come back to overwork again, chasing promotions and bigger income so they can pay more income taxes, always busy with getting ahead competitively. We are the leftovers here—right?—far from the madding crowd? If so, there's something mournful about it, but peaceful, and hopeful, if we are faithful to the Lamb, buoyed by the vision of Isaiah 11 and Revelation 5, living as a faithful remnant in a biblical hope.

A biblical hope has certainty

"Hope" according to the Bible is not something uncertain as it was for the pre-Christian Greek culture which saw ἔλπις (hope) as the last irritant to escape from Pandora's box of troubles: "hope" was a falsifying delusion to keep you going, a fake promise. Biblical hope in God's promised conclusion, however, is a sure thing; you can count on its certainty, says the Bible (Hebrews 6:13-23). To live in biblical hope is to be truly expectant, pregnant, you could say, in permanent advent, especially if you are more than 80 years old. And the pregnant followers of Jesus have **the labour pains of ruling as priests together on earth** as we wait for the bridegroom to return from heaven—that's how we are to be living day in and day out, says Scripture.

The priestly Way of ruling and living

Revelation 5:10 says, on the final day Christ's believing followers, after judging the angels! (I Corinthians 6:3), will rule with merciful justice and imaginative wisdom and happy glory over the earth. So, before Christ comes back the next time, good ruling is characterized by being "priestly," that is, permeated by faith (not sight), by upbuilding love (not recriminating judgment), and long-term generational wisdom (not hard-boiled success).

Already in Exodus 19:3-6, when the LORD God was bringing God's people up out of Egyptian bondage, God told Moses God's people were being called to be a company of "priestly rulers and a holy nation." That did not mean everybody had to become an authorized priest like Aaron or join the special tribe of Levites, become a cleric. God was commissioning a whole people to be a special witness on earth. And later, when the 70 elders were touched by the Holy Spirit to help Moses administer rule among the complaining people of God in the wilderness, and some legalists felt left out of ruling, Moses said, "would that all God's people were prophets" like Eldad and Medad (Numbers 11:16-30, v.29). Scripture suggests that **the quality of a consecrated prophetic and priesthood office could be open to everyone.**

Later Psalm 110:4 made clear in describing David's royal prerogatives that he should be a priestly king not in the butchering line of Aaron or Zadok, but in the order of Melchizedek; that is, with a mysterious unmediated authority from God and access to God that breathes the fruit of just-doing full of mercy. And then Jesus Christ as a high priest, by the bloody sacrifice of himself! turned the priesthood God bestows on those whose sins are forgiven (Revelation 1:6) into one of pouring out magnanimous restorative justice and saving good news for unbelievers (Romans 15:16).

So "Priestly Rule" in the Bible means a diaconal ruling, governing as a servant, not as a boss, **ruling as a mediating help,** like a hospital chaplain giving courage and solace to those near death, like a political statesman or womanly judge—imagine!—who **ministers to the poor and disenfranchised** without trumpeting one's accomplishments, or like a teacher or writer or musician who **washes the feet** of students, stiff people, slow readers, an audience with hearing aids, washes their feet with healthful insight and joy. Priestly Rule asks us to fight and govern with the gentle-forceful liberating sword of God's Word and Spirit (Ephesians 6:17) so we bring a circle of rescue to those who are lost and the actual beginning of shalom to the broken-hearted and defenceless (Isaiah 61:1-4). Priestly Rule asks you to overcome evil by doing **good** things even for your enemies (Proverbs 25:21-22, Romans 12:14-21)

Priestly Rule is exercised by those quiet, believing, often leftover people of God who know how to **pray for others**—Did you hear *Revelation* 5:8? The prayers of the saints are like bowls of incense lifted up to the triumphant Lamb in heaven. After the temple of God's people in Jerusalem was destroyed in 70 AD, physical sacrifices had to become "spiritual sacrifices" (I Peter 2:5): intercessory prayer is reflective "spiritual sacrifice" of yourself; that's the kind of love-your-neighbour "obedience" God wants (Matthew 12:6-7). "Bowls of incense" means that a brief honest prayer of trustfully asking for God's mercy to lift up your neighbour smells like good perfume to God!

I suppose a lot of our routine prayers are more like deodorant. But praying—children learning to pray unaffected prayers, elderly persons who have time unretired people lack, to pray—those who can read or sing a psalm sensitively with somebody who is sick or discouraged—that's genuine praying: unhypocritical heartfelt stumbling praying in faith is exercising the priestly rule Revelation 5 says God calls us leftovers to be busy with as persons in between the first and final coming of Christ, even if it doesn't seem productive of tangible results. Believing parents, like St. Augustine's mother, who pray fervently in hope for their wayward children and grandchildren, and children who pray without ceasing for their wayward parents and grandparents, **shall be heard** by the Lamb; that is when it gets quiet in hallelujah boisterous heaven today (Revelation 8:1), so God can focus on the pleas mediated by the Holy Spirit.

A pregnant, therefore hopeful and expectant Priestly Rule is the Way Christ instituted for us to walk during the second Advent after our Saviour's blood was shed for our sins. "You are a selected (chosen) peoplehood (γένος), a royal priesthood, a holy community (ἔθνος), God's own people, so that you may proclaim (ἐξαγγείλητε) the mighty deeds of the One who called you out of darkness into God's wonderful light" (I Peter 2:9).

Bear each other's burdens cheerfully

IF THERE BE ANYONE here who is not really an adopted child of God, but just a sometime fellow-traveller with the Church, you need to talk to someone who is a faithful leftover, to an elder or Pastor Thyra of this congregation, so you may hear the simple message of "repent and trust the forgiving God revealed in Jesus Christ" to save you from your misery or false confidence in your addicted or discombobulated self, from your hidden selfishness, so you may be kept safe past the coming again of Christ or past your breath-be-gone sleep, whichever comes first.

And if you have been born "of water and the Spirit," have been baptized and are believing the Word of Isaiah 11 and Revelation 5, then be comforted, because the troubles and suffering we are "graciously given"! (as Philippians 1:29-30 puts it) cannot compare, says Romans 8:18, with the glory of reigning with the triumphant Lamb. A good Way to complement prayer as a priestly ruling practice is to actually bear another's burdens cheerfully, carry the load for a while which is buckling over your neighbouring fellow, especially the trials of other faithful leftovers (Galatians 6:2, 10). That means something different than commiserating with other also-rans: "to bear one another's burdens" means a communal jubilation of a cloud of witnesses still running the race set before them (Hebrews 12:1-2), happily hearing the singing in heaven we may echo here on earth.

That is the enabling imperative to carry with us leftover pregnant people from this worship service, because our Lord who became flesh and blood, who died, was resurrected, ascended, and is right now sitting in heaven at the right hand of God, is worthy to receive power and wealth, wisdom and might and honour and glory and blessing and is poised to come back unexpectedly sooner than you think to a place very near you.

Closing Prayer

Thank you, Lord, for the vision of peace acoming on earth, including among the nations. Call us today to be faithful leftovers leading the way in praise and merciful ordering of our creatural activities. Help us to appreciate the glory of little deeds that supply the needs of our neighbours, as we grow fortitude to bear each other's burdens cheerfully, praying for Jesus Christ to give us a hug and come back soon!

Along with the four Living Creatures near God's throne, let all the believers here who will, say AMEN!

19 January 2020
First Christian Reformed Church
Toronto, Ontario

2

Restorative Just-Doing is the Key to Finding True Restfulness with God

Texts: Isaiah 28:1-22 and 30:15-18

The important book of Isaiah in the Bible is hard to understand, because we don't normally take the time it needs to live into its 66 chapters, to get the historical setting fresh in mind, or respect the poetic density of the writing—what a vocabulary Isaiah has! We usually pick up the Bible and want our 'biblical thought for the day' simple. But Isaiah, Hebrews would say, is more complicated than a simple glass of milk. God's Word found as the book of Isaiah, is a multiple course meal with meat, potatoes, vegetables and a tangy sauce (Hebrews 5:11-14).

Do you chew and eat the Bible, or just drink it down?

Most people remember Isaiah 40 ("Comfort ye! comfort ye!") and Isaiah 53 ("a man of sorrows and acquainted with grief") because of the *Messiah*; maybe some remember

Isaiah 6 ("Here am I, LORD, send me") or Isaiah 61 ("The Spirit of the LORD God is upon me...to bring good news to the poor,"—Jesus' text when he preached in his home town of Nazareth).

But Isaiah as a book is difficult to follow because the repetitious chapters are not in strict chronological order, and it's a little bit like Shakespeare's late plays where there are multiple shifts of scenes, one different thing after another: different speakers—sometimes Isaiah, sometimes God, sometimes the enemy, quotes from angelic voices, poetic paragraphs, proverbs thrown in, songs, ironic sentences which mean just the opposite of what they seem to say. And you always need to be careful to read enough or you will get the wrong idea, because sections speaking God's judgment on sin are suddenly juxtaposed with promises of God's blessing for those who repent of chasing other gods and restart obeying the LORD's leading: **Yes,** you people will be devastated! **But,** a few who trust in Me shall be saved....

Like Phillip with the Ethiopian eunuch who was browsing through the book of Isaiah around chapter 53 in his chariot (Acts 8:26-40), I should like to try to serve up to you today chapter 28. You probably don't read Isaiah 28 regularly, which makes fun of the drunken leaders of God's people—can that be edifying? What's the point of Isaiah 28 for our Willowdale CRC congregation and any visitors here this morning?

If you read chapters 15-19 of II Kings or II Chronicles 27-28 during this past week, you know a little bit of the historical background to Isaiah 28. Let me mention just a few things before we read the chapter:

The Assyrian empire centered in Nineveh was the superpower of Isaiah's day. Little Ephraim (Bible shorthand for the Ten tribes of Israel) with its lovely capital of Samaria, and the kingdom of Judah to the South with Jerusalem as its capital—God's divided people, since Solomon died—were fairly well off until around 750 BC, when they started to get embroiled in the political maneuvering alliances of the time.

Syria with Damascus as capital, and the Babylonians, the Edomites and Philistines, got tired of paying heavy taxes in silver and gold every year to Tiglath-Pileser (ruled 746-727 BC) and then Shalmaneser (ruled 727-722 BC) of Assyria. This is the Assyria after Jonah had been there (cf. II Kings 14:25), a godless country which had nevertheless repented! so the LORD God had relented in punishing Assyria (Jonah 3).

Israel under King Pekah (ruled 735-730) teamed up with General Rezin of Syria to invade brother Judah. King Ahaz of Judah (ruled c. 735?-728?) paid Tiglath-Pileser of Assyria to go after Syria and Israel. Tiglath-Pileser besieged Damascus and finally captured it in 732 BC and had Pekah of Israel killed and put Hoshea on the puppet throne in Samaria c. 730 BC.

While Assyria was preoccupied with other conquests, Hoshea of Israel made a pact with Egypt, so he dared break with paying tribute to Assyria. So Shalmaneser of Assyria came and besieged Samaria for three years—Israel's supposed ally Egypt was a no-show—until finally in 722 BC

Samaria was destroyed, and follow-up Assyrian strongman Sargon (ruled 722-705 BC) ravaged the countryside of Israel, deported most of the people to the far reaches of his Assyrian empire, and settled Chaldeans and others with their own strange religion in the land of Israel. Judah under weak-kneed King Ahaz had to keep on paying off Assyria to stay somewhat intact.

Such is the setting of Isaiah 28.

IN THE FIRST SECTION, the prophet poetically foretells the disaster coming to Israel and Samaria from Assyria in 722 BC, because they had disobeyed the LORD God who brought them up out of and away from Egypt ages ago, and they have gradually merged into serving Canaanite idols; Israel never listened to cowboy prophet Amos or Hosea but are living a self-indulgent life of relaxed leisure.

This is the Word of God from Isaiah 28:

Isaiah 28:1-6

The prophet foretells Isreal's (ten tribes) disaster coming from Assyria in 722 BC; cf. II Kings 17.

WOE TO THE splendid crown the drunkards of Ephraim wear!
 [=10 tribes of Israel]
Woe to the fading flower of its impressive beauty
 [=lovely city of Samaria]
which has graced the head of this fertile valley where the leaders
 are besotted with wine.
That's right! My Lord has a strong-armed power (coming)
 [viz. Assyria]
like a downpour of hailstones, like a destructive hurricane,
 a downpour of water, a ravaging tidal wave

> which smashes down to the ground with [terrible] force—
> the splendid crown the drunkards of Ephraim are wearing
> shall be trampled under foot,
> and the fading flower of its impressive beauty
> which has graced the head of this fertile valley
> will be like a first-ripe fig before the summer harvest
> which when somebody sees it, grabs it in the hand,
> and gulps it down.
> In that same Day (when Samaria is destroyed)
> the LORD God of the Army of Angels will be self
> a beautiful jeweled crown, an impressive crown,
> for the leftovers of God's people
> [=land of Judah after Samaria is taken, later the returning
> exiles from Babylon—God always seems to work with
> leftovers, remnants of the faithful].
> The LORD God shall be a spirit of just-doing for whoever
> sits in the place where judges administer civil judgments;
> the LORD God shall be a resource of strength for whoever
> must turn back the battle near the gate [of the city].

So vv. 1-6 is a prophecy about the tribes of Israel which will be demolished by Shalmaneser of Assyria in 722 BC.

THEN ISAIAH TURNS IN chapter 28:7, as it were, to address Judah, probably a little bit later than Samaria's destruction in 722 BC, after Hezekiah has become king of Judah following Ahaz. Judah's King Hezekiah was considering the strong advice of some of his court advisors to adopt a pro-Egypt foreign policy and thumb his nose at Assyria too. This is why I asked you to read Isaiah 20, where God told Isaiah to walk around Jerusalem stripped to his underpants for three years, to be a living visual aid along with his sermons on how God's people will look if they trust Egypt! against Assyria as they revelled in their prosperity, forgetting to live as the LORD asked them to.

Isaiah 28:7-13

[Isaiah's interactive prophecy to priests/prophets on Judah's coming disaster in 701 BC with Assyrian Sennacherib; cf. II Kings 18-19]

AND NOW (BELIEVE IT or not) these fellows too (just as over
    there in Israel) reeling with wine, dizzy from liquor—
the priest and charismatic prophet! totter around drunk,
    befuddled from the wine—
they stagger around from the strong drink,
their vision is blurred, they are irresolute in making decisions;
all the tables—that's right!—are full of vomit,
    no place without excrement!
"Who will [this guy Isaiah] teach 'knowledge' to? (they say)
Who does he expect to explain 'the God-message' to?
    [Who does he think we advisers to the king are, anyhow!?]
Kids weaned from milk! just off the mother's breast!?
    Chalechacha, chalechacha!
    Ladidaqab, ladidaqab!
    Bitty botty, bitty botty!"
    [mimicking, making fun of Isaiah's exhortations to them,
    as if his sermons were nonsense]
Well, (says Isaiah) the Lord will [soon] be speaking
    to this people (Judah)
    with derisive lips and in a foreign tongue (Assyrian!)—
those to whom the Lord once said,
    'This is resting: giving rest to the weary—
    that is true restfulness.'

but [these leaders] were not at all even willing to listen!
So the LORD God's Word for them will now indeed be:
>'Chalechacha, chalechacha!
>Ladidaqab, ladidaqab!
>Bitty botty, bitty botty!'

[Isaiah throws their taunts about God's counsel
right back in their faces]
so that [these intoxicated leaders of God's people] will go away,
trip over backwards, break [their necks],
become trapped, be taken captive....

IMAGINE ISAIAH LAYING THIS out to the priests, charismatics, and now in vv.14ff to the educated nobles, like the MPs and Senators in Ottawa, you might say, sprawled in the temple courtyard after a sacrificial feast with too much wine, Isaiah standing there in a jock-strap—this is the Bible reporting what is serious to God!

Isaiah 28:14-22

[Now Isaiah challenges Judah and Jerusalem's civic, political rulers]
SO, HEAR THE WORD of the LORD God,
>you scoffers who rule this people living in 'Jerusalem'!
>[the tone is about the way rural Ontarians or Western
>Canada might say "Toronto," or the way people in the CRC
>denomination sometimes refer to "Grand Rapids"]

So, hear the Word of the LORD God,
>you scoffers who rule this people living in 'Jerusalem'!
>[become the fashionable city!]

Because you have said,
>"We have ceremonially entered into a covenant with Death,
>we have made a pact with the Underworld
>[these are code words for 'Egypt': Isis & Osiris are the

Egyptians gods of fertility, Death and the Underworld; so this was the cute way Judah's advisors were saying, make overtures to Egypt! to save us from Assyria, who had just wiped Samaria off the map];
    when the overwhelming scourge (=Assyria) flashes through,
        it shall not come our way
            for we have made deceptive (political) deals our refuge,
        and have taken shelter in (diplomatic) trickery":
therefore, thus says my Lord, the LORD God
    "Don't you see! I have laid a stone,
        a tested stone as foundation in Zion,
        a precious cornerstone,
        a sure founding foundation.
    Whoever holds firmly on to this will never be shamed!
    And I (says the LORD God) **will instate just-doing as the measuring line, and tried-and-true dealings as the plummet."**
Hailstones shall sweep away the refuge of (political) deception,
and flooding waters shall wash away the shelter (of diplomatic trickery).
Then your 'covenant with Death' will be wiped out,
and your 'pact with the Underworld' will not remain standing;
whenever the overwhelming scourge [=Assyria] indeed flashes through,
    you shall be trampled down by it (leaders of God's people in Judah).
As often as the scourge comes through, it shall seize you;
yes, the scourge will come through morning after morning,
    day in and night out,
and it will be sheer terror to understand its 'God-message.'
Remember the old saying? (says Isaiah)
    'The bed is too short to stretch yourself out on it,
        and the bed covering is too narrow to roll yourself up in it.'

Yes, the LORD God shall rise up as God did on Mount Perazim,
> [referring to King David's overcoming the Philistines
> and their idols, II Samuel 5:17-21]

and the LORD God shall storm in as God did in the valley of Gibeon,
> [referring to God's smashing the Philistines again for David,
> I Chronicles 14:13-17]

to get the Lord's deed done—strange is God's deed!
to get the Lord's work working—God's work is barbaric!
> [God uses cruel disbelieving Assyrians to punish
> God's own beloved folk—'barbaric'! says Isaiah]

So now (you leaders of God's people in Judah),
> you had better not scoff lest your bonds be made the tighter;
> for I have heard of complete destruction as a final decision from
> my Lord, the LORD God of the Army of Angels ("hosts")
> —destruction upon the whole land…
> [referring maybe to what just one of God's angels did?
> killing 185,000 Assyrian soldiers in one night, in order to
> spare "the leftovers"? or maybe Isaiah had heard hints
> from God about the 586 BC terror when Jerusalem would
> be razed to the ground by Babylonians, as had happened to
> Samaria under the Assyrians?].

This is the Word of the Lord!
Thanks be to God!

ONCE YOU CATCH THE rhetorical fireworks in Isaiah, you can much better understand the temper and bite of Jesus' interaction with us Pharisees, in Matthew 15 [that's for tonight's service, with the rest of Isaiah 28].

But the point right now with Isaiah 28 is that once you sort out the paragraphs and get the historical setting, it's quite clear what's going on:

God's Word is spoken to the leaders of northern Israel and southern Judah that they and their people are going to be swept away by ruthless political, cultural forces, Assyria **or** Egypt, because they are an unjust society, ignorant of the LORD God's order to bring peace to people, neglecting to hold onto the only genuine security there is—the temple **whose cornerstone is God's stern presence aching to be merciful.** So God's beloved, careless people are going to be brutally killed and exiled by unbelievers, thanks to God— that's strange, Isaiah dares say (v.21), terrible, barbaric!

But you people of God ought to know (v.20) you can't stretch out to rest peacefully on the all-too-short bed of buying security with silver and gold and backroom deals that try to cut you more time to live a life of dissolute leisure! You can't fool God by keeping up the temple ceremonies (Isaiah 1) while you avoid hearing and doing God's prophetically preached Word; sooner or later the falsity of putting up a good front and knowing how to get around on the worldly scene, but living secretly obsessed by power, possessions or pleasure, will do you in. God's people will be hung out to dry, just a few leftovers (v.5) for God sorrowfully to start over with again in history.

That's the story Isaiah 28 tells.

LET ME COMMENT ON the key verses of 16 (cornerstone/rock), 17 and 6 (the plumb line of just-doing), and 12 (true restfulness).

(1) That Almighty God is the Rock of salvation, the cornerstone on which the faith of God's Older Testament-ed people rested, is a lived truth throughout the Bible (I

Samuel 2, Psalms 18, 31, 95, I Corinthians 10:1-4) with which v.16 resonates. God is the Rock who always comes through and will rescue us even from ourselves! Israel and Judah, the split Jewish nation to whom Isaiah prophesized, rejected God's gift to live daily out of the LORD God of the Angels' powerful grace, and decided instead—the leaders and the people—historically to try to work out their own political, military, economic and societal salvation their own work-righteous way. Instead of becoming outstanding righteous children of God, the sons and daughters of Abraham stumbled over the precious cornerstone of God's free giveaway of shalom.

The apostle Paul in Romans 9:27-33 and Simon Peter (with his 'rock' confession to Jesus—"You are the Messiah, the Son of the living God!" [Matthew 16:13]) in I Peter 2:4-8 both quote v.16 mixed with Isaiah 8:14 to update this crucial matter: the cornerstone of God's presence has become Jesus Christ in the flesh. So Israel and Judah not only were packed off, dispersed, to remote parts of the world powers of their day whom they had tried to trick and ingratiate themselves with, but also forfeited their select status as rightful heirs of God's promises, testify Paul and Peter in the Newer Testament.

You don't have to commit political suicide or become an economic hermit to honour God as the Rock of your salvation, but Isaiah 28:16 reveals, in the context of the whole Bible story, that there is a certainty **and** jealousy to the LORD God's being the foundation of us human creatures' deeds in a world culture fraught with insecurities, aggressive uncertainties, and permissiveness. But whoever waits on the LORD in sheer faith and determined obedience will never finally be left in the lurch, says Scripture (Psalms 118, 130).

(2) I will institute the plumb line of just-doing, says the LORD God in v.17. (A plumb line is a strong string with a weight on the bottom which when held free in gravity gives you an exact vertical line, it's never crooked.) Tried-and-true dealings in society are what I expect, says God, from prophet, priest, king, teacher, farmer, weaver, money-lender, nurse, musician, baker and candlestick-maker. Not the stuff I see you people conducting on the national and international scene of powerbrokers and greed, says God: my rulers, leaders, judges, must be *tzaddiq*. *Tzaddiq* is a rich word which means trustworthy, reliable, sterling, those without guile who come through in the clutch, who simply actually do what's right, are chastely straight as a plumb line.

I will give the faithful leftovers of my people, says God in v.6, the spirit of being *tzaddiq*, of doing justice not only in settling claims and counterclaims with imaginative, enriching equity, but also the strength to fight crookedness, the perseverance, staying power one needs to withstand evil, whether it be misleading (pro-Egypt) advice, outright extortion, or malignancy in your body (cf. II Kings 20:1-7).

The plumb line of justice the God of Isaiah institutes turns our secularized idea of justice inside out/upside down. We think justice means: give me my equal share! give me what I rightfully have coming to me, calculated mathematically, counted up with interest. No, says Scripture, the LORD God as Rock and refuge provides the justice of *tzaddiq* (Deuteronomy 32:4). God in Jesus Christ was doing justice! says the letter of I John 1:5-2:6. "If we confess what we do wrong," says Scripture there (1:9), "the Lord is faithfully *tzaddiq* **in forgiving us our sins** and setting us free from the guilt of committing injustice!" Can you believe that?

This means that whoever truly follows Jesus Christ's way of "doing justice" (2:6), does not justify oneself and seek one's own interests but instead, you restore in good measure what the neighbour lost even if it be to your own hurt (cf. Psalm 15)! "Just-doing" the way God does it, is to justify the other; you make good for the other in order to respect yourself. That is the spirit of justice, says vv. 17 and 6, God will instill in the LORD's "leftovers."

(3) Verse 12 holds Isaiah's God-breathed critique of the restlessness of the leaders of God's people. Currently, King Hezekiah's cabinet, full of militarists, is spoiling for a war with Assyria, while the poor people of Judah have hardly caught their breath from the recent invasion of Syria and Israel, who are now themselves gone the way of all flesh which lives by the sword (Matthew 26:51-53). Why must there constantly be wars and rumours of war not only in the nations at large but also in the church? (cf. James 4:1-10)— conniving restlessness! Verse 12 also hints at why the Land of Promise to which the LORD God brought God's people after 40 years of wandering around in the Arabian desert did

not turn out to be a land of milk and honey and Sabbath rest: the people of God turned their back to God, and busied themselves in the distracting rat race-pursuit of godless happiness (cf. Leviticus 26, Deuteronomy 11 and 28).

The good news of v.12 is this: do you want to come to rest from the turmoil in your life? that is, do you ache for peace within the rough-and-tumble of political campaigns, making a living, mixing it up with evil? Then you are to give a rest to someone else who is worn out—that brings on true restfulness, says v.12. If you have the faith-grit to support a sister or brother or neighbour who just can't take the pain or disappointment anymore, or the strain of the endless stupid demands put upon them by their circumstances, and you are able to alleviate the trouble somehow, to reassure, give a hug of hope, pray and enact the Lord's blessing down upon their embattled or tattered lives, then you will experience yourself God's merciful, calming presence.

Jesus picked up v.12, maybe you remember, when he was quite upset at the Galilean cities where Jesus had performed some of his most powerful miracles, but they did not repent—Phoenician cities Tyre and Sidon, Sodom! (said Jesus and he could have mentioned Assyria), would have repented instead of carrying on in your Galilean pell-mell aggressive fashion (Matthew 11:20-24): "Come to me all you who are weary and burdened, and I shall give you rest. Lift my yoke upon you, learn from me, because I am gentle, and humble at heart, and then"—says Jesus, loosely quoting Isaiah 28:12—"you will find restfulness for yourselves" (Matthew 11:28-29).

So this is the gospel this morning from Isaiah 28: the Covenantal God is Rock and Jesus Christ is the cornerstone on which to build a sound, obedient daily life and culture, rather than set it up on sand (Matthew 17:24-27); the injunction is to do Jesus Christ's kind of justice in whatever your task at hand be (Micah 6:8, Matthew 5); and there is a sure promise of restful peace if you live by the Holy Spirit of outreaching gentleness (Galatians 5:22-6:2).

Let me still make perhaps a few provocative comments, in the vein of Isaiah:

God's Word of Isaiah 28 gives us direction for our life and our societal life in Canada today. That's what a Reformation church says. I'm afraid, however, we tend to privatize the Bible, reduce Isaiah's horizons of God's people embroiled in the struggles of principalities and powers of the day, reduce the God-message down to just 'me and my God,' me and **my** problems. That's very understandable given the problems some of us suffer under. But we are often such individualists, also in our faith. And such a privatization of the Bible makes it more like a devotional handbook rather than the sharp, two-edged sword which pierces to the very hidden thoughts and intentions of our hearts (cf. Hebrews 4:12-13) about how we live and think and talk in our Canadian society.

Do you mean we should identify the current Assyria and Egypt to be USA and Japan, and pretend Canada is Judah? No. Does Isaiah 28 offer advice pertinent to voting Liberal, Conservative, NDP, or Alliance in the coming election? What in God's world does God's Word have to do with playing hockey, McSorley, and the NHL mindset which we support by watching on TV? Does the Bible have something to do with buying a car, investing money, settling on a vegetarian diet or not?

For now I'll just touch on the three main verse points I have mentioned from Isaiah 28:

(1) Because the LORD is the jealous Rock and certain cornerstone of God's people, the biblical complaint that God couldn't distinguish God's people in Isaiah's day from the Canaanites—similar drive for violence, luxury, entertainment—that complaint faces us with the same large question: are we followers of the Christ distinguishable on the sidewalks of life today from the horde of practical atheists who mostly run our society? Have we, children of God, succumbed bit by bit to the powerful, beautiful four-colour advertising strategies that push you to covet swift Egyptian horses and be wistful about life in the fast lane? Or, are we perhaps "law-and-order" people in Canada who want to build…more prisons? Are we different in our dress (like the Amish)? No. Do we have a consecrated Sunday (as Conservative Jews have the Sabbath, and Muslims take Friday), or do we have "weekends" like every other secularized person?

I don't intend to answer the matters for you. I'm only trying to translate Isaiah 28's abiding question: If we/you together are followers of Jesus Christ, where does your buck stop? At the Rock of almighty jealous God, or is your certainty drifting a little bit in the wind? Does communion of the saints fade away for you after you walk out of the church building, so it's not a cooperative, communal mind during the week, but it's every man and woman for oneself, for example, in political and economic matters?

(2) Isaiah 28's directive on just-doing may be touchy, since we usually go to church to get away from politics, economics, and the news media. If God says **restorative** justice for the neighbour is the plumb line, what does that mean for becoming biblically wise on doing justice for Burnt Church native lobster fisherman, the Maritime Fisherman's Union, and Herb Dhaliwal's department which polices who makes what kind of a living and when, from the fruits of God's waters of the sea?

When "tax cuts" are highlighted in political platforms and championed to make the economy grow, do you wonder whether the idea that political government is called by God to do justice has not slipped a notch into appealing to our natural selfishness: if I make more money than the other fellow, why should I pay proportionately more for the good of the public commonweal; what I earn is mine—what do you mean "obligation to others"? Justice is that I get my "pound of flesh!" (Shakespeare, *The Merchant of Venice*, Iv,1)

Again, there should not be politics from the pulpit, but Bible reading and Bible study is not just for Bible reading and Bible study, period. Does the Scripture we read together shape our voting, buying and selling, deciding priorities? "Jesus saves"—that's right, but not in a vacuum. "Jesus saves from Tiglath-Pileser! (If I were an entrepreneur, I might try to market that as a "distinguishing" bumper sticker: In capital letters—'JESUS SAVES FROM TIGLATH-PILESER,' "Jesus saves from Me-First, Inc"....

We must not be fooled by the political party spin-doctors, says Isaiah 28: **restorative justice** that brings peace to the injured, unfortunate, poor, that focusses on **giving justice** rather than **getting your due**, is following Christ. Otherwise the land will suffer under God's curse. [When you get a $200 tax cut cheque in the mail, do I dare suggest as a pastoral aside, please do not invest it or go out for an expensive meal giving thanks to Mike Harris in your prayer for it; but without a second thought, sign it over to the CRWRC (now called World Renew), the Canadian Children's Poverty Relief Program, the Romanian Orphan Fund, a needy person in our own congregation, a redemptive societal program like NeighbourLink, and pray for grace to abound.]

(3) The restfulness Isaiah 28 offers, seconded by Jesus in the Gospel according to Matthew, is both utterly personal **and** fully societal, and terribly relevant. The harried pace of urban Canadian life we inhabit, increased by our technocratic "breakthroughs" which replace and hurry people with machines, seems to harbour a systemic, increasingly anxious restlessness along with their incredible advantages. How can we obey the call of the LORD to receive satisfying restfulness, peace, in our labours and troubles?

We need to build into our school system, for example, the time to give extra instructional rest to the slow-learner and provide openings for the inventive, gifted student to go beyond the curricular minimum, rather than force a factory time-clock yoke and work-to-rule upon a school. We need to honour the neglected in the church, the outcasts in the citizenry—prisons and asylums, the weak and destitute in the commercial world, the damaged in our families, the lonely ones in offices and at check-out counters. If we as Christ's body learn to practice doing justice and giving a rest to the weary—even by a simple encouraging word—the handicapped, in some kind of concerted fashion, who knows how our Canadian society could be given a taste of restfulness?

I know, our faith lives are full of holes, and we all have too much to do that immediately concerns us. But II Kings 17:34, the historical background to Isaiah 28, slips in a wonderful, hope-giving phrase about the LORD God's having given guidance to "the descendants of Jacob, whom God named Israel." The "Jacobs," the restless conniving deceivers, the LORD renamed "Israel," wrestler with God.

Despite our weakness, in spite of the enormous challenges, if you belong to the faithful misfits whom God lovingly calls "leftovers," as a warning to the successful rulers in the world (cf. I Corinthians 1:18-2:5) we don't have to solve the world's problems; we simply need to grow the vision and sensitivity of Isaiah 28 for the crying shames in the world, and then **wrestle with God together** (as a contemporary prophet of Isaiah, Micah, says) to "do justice, love being merciful, and walk humbly with our God" (Micah 6:8).

Anybody in my hearing who responds willingly to this call shall become more than conquerors—the remnant God saves become 'peace-makers'—because Christ blesses the young person or older person with stamina to not become weary and give up before evil, but shall preserve you to rise up with eagle wings, moved by the Holy Spirit to live in hope of the gentle Rule of the Lord acoming.

I READ **ISAIAH 30:15-18** as a final challenge and comfort for us with the Carter family, for any CLAC and CPJ workers within hearing, for all dedicated followers of the Christ who work in the government, banks, offices, landscaping, hospitals, schools and homes, for our fellow believers struggling in Sierra Leone, Palestine, Ambon, and especially for those all over God's world who wrestle with God in prayer:

Isaiah 30:15-18

THUS SAYS MY LORD, the LORD God, the Holy One of Israel:
In turning yourself around and in coming to rest, you could
    be saved;
in quieting down and feeling the reliableness of [the LORD] lies
    your conquering strength.
But you were not willing!
You said, "Oh, No! We shall take flight on horses!"
So there you went, running to save yourselves
(from the Assyrians, whoever the enemy is)
—"We shall take off on fast [horses]!"—
with the result that your pursuers showed themselves to be just
    as fast!
A thousand of you shall flee at the threat of one single person!
At the threat of five, you all shall run away...
    until you have become leftovers,
    like a signal flag on the top of a mountain,
    like a warning sign on a hill.

This is why the LORD God longs to be merciful to you
> (before, during, and after you become one of the faithful
> remnant)—

this is why the LORD God shall rise up to receive you most
> tenderly:

the LORD God is a God of [restorative] just-doing!
Blessed are all those who wait intently for the Lord
> [to come through].

22 October 2000
Willowdale Christian Reformed Church
Toronto, Ontario

3

On Doing Creatural Justice to Weeds in God's World[1]

TEXT: Isaiah 28:23-29

ISAIAH WAS A POET and teacher of philosophy (Isaiah 8:1) before he spent all his time prophesying to the misled people and corrupt leaders of Judah and Israel nearing their captivity.

I shall read just a double paragraph from Isaiah 28:23-29 to lead into the brief meditation this morning.

<u>Isaiah 28:23-29</u>

This is the Word of God:

PRICK UP YOUR EARS, and listen to my voice!
You all, pay close attention! Hear my speaking!

---

1 This breakfast meditation was given to a national convention of the Weed Scientists Society of America (WSSA) held at a Toronto hotel on February 8, 2000 AD. There was also a fascinating art show of photographs of beautiful weeds that were quite stunning.

Does a farmer keep on plowing and keep on plowing all the time
>   if he wants to sow seed?
Does he keep on opening up and turning over the ground
>   and continue discing his field?
Isn't it so, once he has made the earth level and smooth,
then he starts to strew around dill and scatter caraway seeds?
Then he plants rows of wheat, marked off squares of barley,
>   and rye around the edges?
The LORD God taught the fellow to do what is right (*mishpath*).
God his Maker educates the farmer.
Naturally you never thresh dill with a big threshing machine,
and you don't roll a wagon wheel over and over
>   on top of caraway plants:
No! Dill gets beaten out with a strong stick,
>   and the caraway seeds are harvested by hitting with a rod.
Bread grain is not supposed to be pulverized, is it?
>   Of course not!
You don't keep on threshing and thrashing the grain forever,
and drive the wagon wheel and horses over and over, on and on:
>   it is not supposed to be crushed to bits—
>   Do you get it?
>   Also such technical matters originate with Yahweh,
>   LORD God of the Angels,
God's deliberative way of putting things together is amazing!
Truly great is the wise way God figures and works things out!

ACCORDING TO THE BIBLE the LORD of the universe not only tucked a specially chosen people under God's eagle wing for protection (Psalm 91:1-6) and spelled out for God's people the Way they should live (Exodus 20:1-20) in order to be meaningful and avoid dead ends in history; but the LORD God of the heavens and earth deliberatively, in the amazing act of creation, ordered how every thing should go! even down to how you should plant and harvest dill and caraway seeds.

The matter of breathing, digesting, excreting, and growth got set up in us creatures, male and female, by the wise figuring out of the LORD God. The pressured formation under ground of limestone, pipestone and bedrock happens according to the creational ordinances structured by the "Let-there-be" mouth of the LORD. The network of an individual person's DNA and the limits to breeding between species are wonders fashioned by the inscrutable hand of God. The laws of becoming lonely away from home so you get stretched emotionally to make new friends, and the happiness of meeting old friends after years of not communicating with a person and being able to pick up precisely where you left off in a jovial communion is a setup spoken for and brought about creationally by the LORD God Yahweh.

The necessary order in mixing pigments of paints to get colours with a definite hue, brilliance and saturation; the basic, structured possibility for the formation and syntactical relation of words to make communicating speech a fact; the norm of delegated, limited responsibility without which neither a society of weed scientists or a band of thieves or a national government can operate: all these technical, caraway seed matters and fundamental, nuts-and-bolts structures buried in the reality of things and events, all these ordinances, laws, ways things are made to function, says Isaiah 28, originate with Yahweh, the LORD God of the angels.

This is a terribly important revelation that we live in a God-ordered world. That day and night, seedtime and harvest, rainbow and rain (Genesis 8:20-9:17), and the mechanics of becoming an angry person, the genetic side of intelligence, the time to leave father and mother behind, the how to make war, argue, and stir up a batter of banana-cranberry muffins: all these matters are bound to their respective ordering because it is the very covenanting, creational law-Word of the LORD providing for their existent glory.

This truth is what got the psalmists so excited in Psalm 1, 8, 19, 104, 119, the last five hallelujah psalms and many more: Good God! what a terrific law you spread out before us day and night, past, present and future, to discover, admire, harness and obey as men and women in your world, Lord! The blessing of your wisdom staggers the imagination with its intricacy, richness and playroom for joy!

The Older Testament never makes the mistake of supposing God's creational Word-order was "rational" in a logical sense. Proverbs 30:18-19 says it straight:

> Three things there be really, which are miraculous,
>   too wonderful for me to grasp—
> Four, you could think of, which I simply do not understand:
>   the way of the eagle in the heavens,
>   the way of a snake on the top of a rock,
>   the way of a ship in the middle of the ocean,
>   and the way of a strong young man **in** a maiden
>   able to bear a child—

Never let a human examining precision override and destroy the intriguing wonder of creational/creatural reality. God's ways in creation as well as in historical salvation are beyond the comprehension of our human theoretical analysis, says Proverbs, the Psalms, the prophets (Isaiah 1:18-20, 40:12-31), and the apostle Paul (Romans 9-11). The wonder of gravity, the ripening and decomposition of wheat, sorrow, an agreement or a promise between two people: these everyday wonders can take place and are to be experienced as creaturely opportunities manifesting the provident Word of the LORD for God's myriad creatures. And then you start to get the proper Older Testament dimensions which make the Newer Testament fully, biblically intelligible.

"IN JESUS CHRIST ARE hid all the treasures of knowledge and wisdom" (Colossians 2:3) does not mean Jesus will solve your differential equations or let you know a priori which genes will cross over chromosomes; Jesus would know immediately how to end the atrocities in Sierre Leone, Somalia, Kosovo; hold onto Jesus prayerfully tight and the medical break-through on cancer will be announced—No.

The Jesus Christ by whom and for whom all things were created, says Paul (Colossians 1:15-20), "in whom all the treasures of knowledge and wisdom are hid," is saying: I am the everlasting law-Word, the Logos, the Way, the Truth and the Life incarnate; whoever has seen and known me, knows my Father, Yahweh, whom to know, that is, obey, is shalom—impassioned contentment and fulness of corporeal existence world without end, albeit begun now in shadows and tears and mirror image script (I Corinthians 13:8-13), but anticipating through our forgiven sin and suffering, triumph (II Corinthians 3:12-118, Revelation 7:13-17)!

Indeed, because Jesus Christ is the personal Son of God, as Logos-Word of God become man like us two-legged creatures in every thing, says Hebrews, except sinning (Hebrews 4:14-16), the Word incarnate has an utterly unique cornerstone position in relating creation, and especially us humans, to the Almighty Creator. Much more can be said about that, but my point here now is this: Jesus Christ must not be reduced to a personal saviour who is your private mediator, because then your Jesus Christ is a different one than the Jesus Christ Suffering Servant prophetically heralded by the same Isaiah of this chapter 28 (cf. Isaiah 49-55) as a gift of God to rule the nations of the world, including weed scientists. As Paul puts it (Colossians 1:24-29): in Jesus Christ, finally, the mystery of God, the beginning, coming, cosmic, healing lordship of Yahweh, LORD God of the angels and all powers, was revealed to everybody in the flesh, as we say. If Jesus Christ is construed without this creation-wide, law-Word of the redemptive Creational God context, then human concerns tend to shrivel up into post-mortem, millennial vigils, and then God's children have lost a biblical sense of our vocational task as creatures afoot in God's world, called to be redeeming the time (Colossians 4:5-6).

HOW ARE WEED SCIENTISTS to redeem their professional time? Is your mandate from God to get rid of all weeds, since they are simply a result of Adam and Eve's fall into sin (Genesis 3:1-19)? Do we need weeds, like pain, to keep us humble and alert to evil? May humans experiment with plant stock, fish genes and human embryos without any restrictions? or is that making a Faustian pact with the devil in hopes of a Nobel prize?

Was physicist Robert Oppenheimer "right" to mastermind production of an atomic bomb (1943-45), which led to Hiroshima and Nagasaki and ending (?) an awful world war, but then decide in 1953, I cannot take part in developing a nuclear hydrogen bomb capable of such unimaginable destruction—was that the "right" decision? [The USA today has such nuclear missiles stockpiled in the thousands at home and abroad, with buttons in the hands of politicians who could "do it," even though they know it says "In God we trust" on the dollar bills].

My field is philosophical aesthetics; I am a teacher. I think after 40 years of teaching I can tell what Isaiah 28 means for pedagogy in transmitting a committed Christian vision to the younger generation in a field of study. You lead the horse to water, even give him or her a small cup of unpolluted, cool spring water; if he or she spits it out, you don't try to force it down their throats, if you want to be an Isaiah 28 educator, rather than a dictatorial indoctrinator. Given lecture and discussion time, because it is more complicated than weeds, perhaps, as a Christian aesthetician showing you slides of art, I think I could convince you that beauty can be wicked and that ugly paintings (e.g., of Christ's crucifixion) and tragic theatre where personae die horrible deaths, can be very normative art.[2]

---

2 The photograph on the following spread shows an empty field filled with glorious yellow dandelions to cheer up passers-by in Willowdale, Ontario."

But I don't know God's Isaiah 28 order for weeds and parasites, hybrid corn, genetically modified soybeans. That is your field of authority.

I can tell you, however, that Isaiah 28:26 says: Our versatile Creator LORD God of the angels, fully revealed in Jesus Christ, whose wisdom is displayed in creatural realities, despite the ravages of sin: God teaches the farmer, the pedagogue, art historian, and weed scientist "to do what is right," whether you do it or not. The word "*mishpath*" in verse 26 is a big biblical word: the LORD teaches those with Holy spirited, biblically ground eyeglasses—and sometimes those even ignorant of the LORD—to do justice (*mishpath*) to God's marvellous ways. That is, to "do what is (creationally) right", "good" as God originally made it to be, and to "do what is right" with worldwide, society-aware, for generations-to-come horizons: that is the injunction Isaiah 28 is proclaiming.

If weed scientists do not become seduced by the marvels you deal with, if you do not try yourselves to ape God, but humbly marvel at the LORD's ingenuity; if in your scientific experimental programs you are driven not by getting more and more money grants from government and pharmaceutical companies to relieve your university's overhead or bolster the company's balance sheet—to be implicated in competitive greed can blind people: but if you are driven by the Older Testament Isaiah 28 vision of the LORD's bounty and hear God's message of "doing justice" to the land (the environment), reinforced by a Newer Testament imperative "to bear your neighbours' burdens" (Galatians 6:2), so that you show weed-knowledge love to your neighbours, especially the poor in Africa, let's say, who cannot pay for any beneficial results of the complex technology: then, says Isaiah 28 and Romans 13:8-10, Galatians 5:16-6:2, you weed scientists will be doing what is "right," praising God and following the law...of Jesus Christ!

Closing Prayer

Dear God,

Please help these weed scientists to know what they are doing in your world.

Teach them to stay amazed at your creational marvels, and not try to act themselves like saviours. Lead them as your children into doing what is right in complex circumstances dominated by a tricky culture. Help them to clear blemishes from our grains, rather than plant genetic landmines in our food. We pray for all peoples, especially those who do not know how to pray in the Name of Jesus Christ, Amen.

8 February 2000
Weed Scientists Society of America
Westin Harbour Castle Hotel
Toronto, Ontario

4

God is impatiently waiting …for faithful restorative just-doing and hope-filled, politically aware prayer

Texts: Isaiah 30 & Philippians 4:4-7

The biblical book of Isaiah gives us a fairly detailed account of political history which God's people—our ancestors in the faith—went through once upon a time (doubling up the narrative of II Kings).

The modern North American attitude is normally: "Who cares what happened 3,000 years ago! What wars should we fight **today** to maintain our (national, or doctrinal) security?"

But that way of thinking about the history the Bible tells, I believe, is wrong. The apostle Paul says explicitly: Israelite history of the Older Testament happened to serve us as a recorded example, to shape our very consciousness (πρὸς νουθεσίαν ἡμῶν) so that we people of the faith might not desire evil as they did, and be destroyed (I Corinthians 10:1-13).

"You mean I have to hear and learn about Kings Ahaz and Hezekiah of Judah, ancient Assyria and Egypt, the superpowers of their day—dates!? Come on, tell us what we want to hear and sing, so we can become 'good little Christians'".

Would you be willing to live into the milieu and testimony of a few chapters of Isaiah, if it would help us know with biblical clarity how to pray for and against the governing policies of Prime Minister Harper, Premier McGuinty, and Mayor Rob Ford, as citizens who would follow Jesus because, says the Bible, "the prayer of a just-doing person is operational and has great power!"? (James 5:16).[1]

Historical setting of Isaiah's proclamation

THE BOOK OF ISAIAH is like a patchwork of warnings and promises, dealing with historical events in the lives of God's people (but not always reporting things in strict chronological order as do the book of the Kings and Chronicles). The highly poetic prophecies of Isaiah are also more indirect than the "Thou shalt" and "Thou shalt not" narrative of the books of Moses. Isaiah characteristically puts instruction this way: "Woe to you, if!—" and "Blessed are you, when!—" Think of Isaiah as being like the editorial pages of *The Globe and Mail, National Post,* or *Toronto Star,* but now the commentator

---

1 In 2019 one can substitute the relevant names of Justin Trudeau, Doug Ford, and John Tory, not to mention President Trump of the USA.

correspondent Isaiah is voicing what God self is declaring to all who can read and have ears to hear.

Isaiah is God's messenger particularly to Judah, whose ruling dynasty is in the line of King David. Early on (chapters 7-10), Isaiah treated the civil war between Judah and the ten northern tribes of Israel who solicited Syria's military help to subjugate Judah (c.733 BC). But Judah's King Ahaz, despite Isaiah's warning, appealed to Tiglath-Pileser of the Assyrian empire, paid tribute of silver and gold taken out of God's temple in Jerusalem! And then Tiglath-Pileser ruthlessly ravaged Damascus and laid Syria waste (II Chronicles 28, II Kings 16). When the subsequent kings of Israel tried to make a deal with the other superpower of the day, Egypt, to get out of paying tribute to Assyria (II Kings 16), Assyrian emperor Sargon II had enough, and in 722 BC finished off Israel, deported its people throughout the Assyrian empire, and populated Samaria with Assyrians (II Kings 17). The Ten tribes of Israel were destroyed as a people, says the Bible, because of their sin in trusting human military might instead of God's "Way" of doing what is right and providing restorative justice.

By the time we come to Isaiah chapters 28-32, Israel has been wiped out as a nation, and there is only little Judah left intact, under Ahaz' son, young King Hezekiah, whose advisers are faced with the two superpowers, threatening Assyria and mighty Egypt, both eager to dominate God's sinful chosen people for control and money.

Isaiah 30:1-3, 8-21, 31

WOE TO THE OBSTINATE unruly generation, says the
   LORD God
   [=Judah, looking for political allies],

who carry out a careful plan, but not one of mine!
who forge an alliance, but not one with my Spirit in it!
so that they add sin on top of sin—
(Woe to those) who get up to go down into Egyptland without
    asking what my mouth says,
to seek refuge in the security of Pharaoh
and get shelter in the comfortable shadow of Egypt.
But the security of Pharaoh will be for you all a shaming!
and taking shelter in the shadow of Egypt will be
    (your) humiliation....

Now, go write it down (Isaiah) for them on a stone tablet,
    engrave it in a book
so that it shall be there for days still to come,
    to be a witness forever and ever,
because this is a recalcitrant people, a deceitful generation,
sons and daughters who are unwilling to hear and obey the
    Guidance (תורה) of the LORD God,
who say to the visionaries (לראים), no more visions, please,
who say to the prophets (חזים), "Do not prophesy to us what
    is right!
Tell us what we like to hear, prophesy fantastic pipe dreams!
Distance yourselves from "the Way!"
Turn off from "the Path-of-life"—
Get "the Holy One of Israel" out of our faces!

That is why "the Holy One of Israel" says this:
Because you despise this Word,
and trust wholly in brute force and intrigues and rely on such
    clever might,
therefore, this bizarre wickedness (עון) shall be for you people
    like a crack in a high protective wall with a bulging out
    overhang about to collapse,
whose breaking to bits comes suddenly, instantaneously.

And its break-up will be like the smashing to bits of a
  potter's vessel,
  [That is what happened to Samaria and now threatens
  Jerusalem!]
smashed so mercilessly not a shard can be found in the
  smithereens
to carry a hot coal from the hearth fire, or to dip up water out of
  a cistern.
For this is what my Lord, the LORD God, "the Holy One of
  Israel" has said:

Only in turning yourself around and in coming to rest
shall you all experience having been freed;
only in quieting yourselves down
    and in calmly trusting (God)
shall you all find the brave strength you need.

But No, you would not consider it—
All of you said,
  "Certainly not! We will make our escape on horses!"
with the result that you indeed will have to flee—
and (you said),
  "We will ride racehorses!"
—with the result that those pursuing you shall be even faster.
A thousand (of you) shall run away before the threat of just one
  (Egyptian/Assyrian),
before the threat of five, you shall all run away until you are left
  alone by yourselves
like a lone post on the top of a mountain, like a signal pole on
  a hill.
And yet... that is why the LORD God is waiting impatiently to
  be gracious to all of you again;
that is why the LORD God has been getting ready to show
  mercy to all of you:

for the LORD God is a God of (מִשְׁפָּט) meting out what is restoratively just.
Happily blessed are all those who wait expectantly for the LORD
    God to come through....

Yes, O you people in Zion, you who dwell in Jerusalem:
you will not be weeping and weeping anymore!
God will assuredly be merciful to you;
at the sound of your crying out—
upon hearing it—God will be answering you...!

Although my Lord give you the bread of adversity and the water of affliction,
yet the One teaching you will no longer keep self hidden;
but your eyes shall be seeing your Teacher,
and your ears shall be hearing a word supporting you,
whether you want to go to the right or go to the left:
    "This is the Way! Walk on it!...."
But at the sounding voice of the LORD God, the Assyrians
    together will be terrified,
when God strikes them with God's shepherd club....

Isaiah 31:1-3 and 32:15-18

WOE TO THOSE WHO saunter over to Egypt to get help, those
    who rely on horses,
who fully trust in war chariots because they are so many,
and in warriors on war horses because they are very strong,
but do not consider "the Holy One of Israel" worth asking,
do not consult the LORD God!
However, "the Holy One of Israel" is wise, and so lets disaster
    happen.
God does not take back God's words,
but rises up against the household of those who are intent upon
    doing evil,
against the accomplices of those who see to it that really wicked
    deeds get done.

And Egyptians are only human, not God.
Egyptian horses are flesh and blood, not Spirit (force).
When the LORD God stretches out God's hand,
then the accomplices (in doing evil) will stagger,
and those being helped (to accomplish wicked deeds) will
   break down—
and all of them together shall be finished off.
   [God's people will suffer punishing troubles]
until the Spirit from on High will be poured out in a gush
   over us:
then the wasteland will become a garden for fruit,
and the fruitful field will become a veritable grove of fruit trees.
In those days ahead restorative justice will come to dwell in
   the wilderness,
and right-doing will come to settle down in the fruit garden.
Right-doing will work out into overflowing shalom,
and the fruit of right-doing will be a quiet composed certainty[2]
   and trustworthy safety for ever!
My people will settle into fields of overwhelming shalom,
in secure dwellings, near places of carefree peace.

This is the Word of the Lord!
Thanks be to God!

IF YOU READ ISAIAH chapters 28-32 this past week, you heard Isaiah tell the leaders of Judah: because you hard-drinking fellows and partying women (32:9-14) make gibberish of God's warning not to trust Egyptian power, soon you will be told in a foreign language (you will think sounds like

---

2   שָׁקֵט = a **political** restfulness; cf. I Chronicles 22:9, where the term is used to refer to the untroubled years of mature Solomon's reign before he went bad (as noted in I Kings 9-11).

gibberish—Assyrian) why you should not have trusted Egypt (28:7-22). God has apparently poured out upon you all a spirit of stupefying drowsiness, so you can't see, hear, read or understand what's going on politically (29:9-12). You worship God in the temple with automatic regularity like zombies, while you ache to make friends with cruel countries stockpiled with war horses and chariots (29:13-16; 30:16). Don't you realize: Egyptians are only human, not God! If you trust military might to bring you security, "the Holy One of Israel"—Isaiah's favourite way of referring to the LORD God—will let disaster happen to you: God does not take back God's words (31:1-3).

The Good News and Biblical Directive from Isaiah 30-32 and Philippians 4 for now

MIXED IN WITH GOD'S vigorous rejection of relying upon war machines and allies whose plans lack God's Holy Spirit, and warning that God's people will be smashed to smithereens like a potter's clay dish if they do not willingly follow the LORD's תורה, "Guidance" (30:9-14), is Isaiah's surprising revelation (30:18) that **God is impatiently waiting to show mercy and to restore shalom to those who do what is right, and who are waiting for the LORD God to come through**. When the Holy Spirit washes over you people and instills in you right-doing, then certainly God's people will come to live in neighbourhoods of lasting peace (32:15-18).

The Bible does not, in my judgment, tell us how and who to vote for in 2012/2020 AD. But Isaiah, sharpened up by the Newer Testament, does, I believe, provide counsel on how to judge and pray about political doings in the world—international relations as well as local policy decisions by our (elected) rulers. Otherwise, people who in communion would follow the lead of Jesus, will just do what seems right in their own eyes, like everybody else.

You can't just change names, however, and think you have God's Word for today: China is Egypt, America is world superpower Assyria, Ontario is Judah; so, before the tribes of Western Canada and its oil are absorbed by the USA and China, Canada should pull out of the unholy alliance of the United Nations, go piously pacifist, and wait for God to do God's thing with the millennium. That's not the way to read the Bible.

Since Pentecost and Romans 9-11, God's peoplehood are not a nation, one nationality…of Jews, Europeans, Westerners. And no nation is Older Testament Judah, no nation has a corner on being God's people. Not the secular Jewish state of Israel, not God-blessed America, and not even Canada. So how do we translate Isaiah's faith-charged, God-spired writings—"Write it down, Isaiah," said God (30:8-11), "so my Word will be a witness forever and ever, to every self-deceiving generation who are unwilling to hear and obey my 'Guidance,' and walk on "the Path-of-life" rather than tread the Way of the wicked, who perish" (cf. Psalm 1).

Isaiah 30:15 (repeating 7:4-9) and topped up by Philippians 4:4-7 incapsulates God's enduring directive for political leadership then **and now: <u>only</u> in stopping war** mongering, <u>only</u> in quieting yourselves down to forbear (τὸ ἐπιεικὲς) retaliation, <u>only</u> in coming to rest in God's injunction to do what is right rather than trust in armed power, military hardware and war horses, will <u>any</u> people find the brave strength you need to experience the genuine freedom of societal political peace which surpasses all common sense.

This sermon may not seem at first to address the personal needs you brought along with you to this worship service—your health and recurrent depression, your family problems, and joys, being in a work rut or unemployed, or wanting just the respite of a little sunny fellowship rather than talk about politics. But the biblical prophetic book of Isaiah is trying to give us a gritty vision that the faith to trust in God is much more than being saved from your problems to go to heaven, is much more than a matter of morality versus unethical sexual or financial corruption. **The book of Isaiah is telling us that our "bread of adversity and water of affliction" (30:20) happens in a real political setting that God wants ordered according to God's Word for restorative just-doing.** And those **political** matters (not "moral" affairs) like public health care in society at large, where your federal tax money is spent, the price of housing, and the library quality of neighbourhood life, are all intimately related to your daily personal living circumstances, and to the LORD God's concern for our obedience to God's "Guidance."

I can't treat everything before you need a cup of coffee, but let me make Isaiah's main point for the children taking notes:

1. Fighting never solves things, but merely harms the weaker;
2. The Christian life is not a hockey game; and
3. God is crying because so many winners will be losers, and many losers in life have not been told to have hope.

(1) Fighting never solves troubles. Fighting never solves things on the playground, nor in clashes between races, tribes, ethnic cultures, different faiths, corporate interests, or nations. Red-neck clans in the backwoods of Kentucky, USA, feuded and took revenge on each other for generations in the 1800's; Protestant and Roman Catholic factions regularly murdered one another in Northern Ireland for decades of the later 1900's); Palestinian Hamas and governing Israeli are locked into a 70 year rhythm of retaliation still today which **cannot**, says God through Isaiah, resolve in peace, but only increase hatred, misery, and exhaustion. Why can't political leaders, CEO's, rabbis and imams see it?! realize its devastating unending futility!? It is so exasperatingly sad.

If the pipeline debate in Canada—through BC or South to the Gulf—is a setup to make alliances, to tip the scales in economic warfare between a bankrupting USA and the bustling China dragon, and the Spirit of God is not integral to the planning and deciding on how to respect our natural resource treasures—only commercial benefits count—Canada may indeed expect long-term disaster predicted in Isaiah 31. "God does not take back God's words" (31:2), but is wise, and knows the hearts of greedy entrepreneurs, and shall punish wheeling and dealing for tactical advantage.

A first step to break the vicious circle of fighting and retaliation is for the circle of leaders and people to have a change of heart, be moved by God's Holy-making Spirit to trust that **the LORD God will act protectively** for the earth and human lives and make things whole. It takes a kind of resilient faith to believe God can still act on earth today. Insurance companies will credit God for a tsunami angel in Japan (March 2011) and an earthquake angel in Haiti (January 2010), so they don't have to pay compensation. Maybe we need to realize God's Spirit was at work in the act of Rosa Parks to stay on the bus (1955) and in the rhythmic preaching of Martin Luther King, Jr., which came to change civil rights legislation in the southern states of America; that God finally answered the diligent prayers of ordinary Christian believers in Eastern Germany to have the 1961 Berlin Wall broken down (November 1989); that God's hand orchestrated the non-retaliatory spirit of imprisoned Nelson Mandela and the change of policy taken by Afrikaner F.W. de Klerk (1990), so that apartheid policy in South Africa could be undone....

Do we have the faith to pray that **God** breaks down the Israeli wall cutting through Palestinian homesteads? Sometimes I think we have the global financial disaster pending—thank God!—because the financial world of brokers became an idol out of touch with economic work realities, an idol we who have bank accounts have been serving too, and that the rising influence of Islam in the world, with Muslims who want to live fundamentally according to their holy Qur'an book (whose banks have an alternative to charging interest on mortgages) has much to do with the fact that we Christians have not stood out as winsome disciples of Jesus Christ, but have been indistinguishable from the Enlightenment crowd of Western, winner-take-all political imperialism. With Oliver Cromwell we are sure to pray but also keep our powder dry since we want to fight too, rather than think defensively and prepare wisely to rest in faith that **God** will act.

(2) The biblically Christian life is not a hockey game. The biblically Christian life is not a hockey game, because following Jesus is not scoring points against opponents, body checking, and winning arguments, but is at heart just-doing, humbly giving-in! that is, **loving** the neighbour God created, including disreputable "Samaritans" (cf. Luke 10:25-37). And it is possible to discern whether political policies breathe "neighbour love" by judging whether they do what is right for the poor, give priority to what makes peace—no wonder Jesus declared, "Blessed are the peacemakers (εἰρηνοποιοί)!" (Matthew 5:3-12, v.9)—and at least moves in the direction of ruling **mercifully**.

For years I was proud of Canada whose armed forces were known to be "peacekeepers"; but I detect a shift in the wind, as if little Canada wants to mix it up with the Big Boys on the global hockey scene. God forbid we as a nation become compromised by the militarism of our "friends" who would police the world under cover of "human rights" while intent upon "protecting their own interests" **everywhere**. I know, especially political entanglements are complicated—there is never a simple, quick solution (Remember the trilemma King David was faced with by God when David proudly had General Joab count up his military potential; II Samuel 24:1-17)—but one can wonder whether God wants us to have a fleet of state-of-the-art **fighter** jets costing billions of dollars,[3] while other governmental services like rescue helicopters, need to be cut back to balance a deficit federal budget.

If you need to use a hospital in Ontario soon and only have minimal medical insurance, it costs about $250 a day for a semi-private bed, thousands of dollars for a surgical operation, and you get sent a bill for $45 to pay for the emergency ambulance (which needed new shocks). We can be thankful to God for the imperfect Canada Health Act because—Isaiah lets me say it (32:15-17)—a spirit of compassionate right-doing nestled within the political enactment of those laws, which bear the fruit of quieted composure for the sick in this province. So such care is available for those who pay less taxes than I do? Of course! **We are our neighbours' keeper**, if you can hear Isaiah's exhortation in chapter 1:16-17, which was spoken to God's special people who were fearfully scrabbling for their own welfare and security, and resounds throughout the whole book of Isaiah:

> Don't pray to me with folded hands!
> Your hands are full of blood!
> "Wash yourselves! Get yourselves clean!

---

[3] The current estimated price of one F-35 fighter jet manufactured in the USA is $89 to $105 million and costs $44,000 per hour to fly.

Get your dirty deeds out of my sight! Stop doing evil!
Learn to do things that are a joy!
Pursue restorative just doing!
Set straight the violent oppressor!
Protect and defend children without parents!
Argue in court for the widow!..."

It sounds like the book of James (1:9-27)!

If wisdom from the Holy Spirit is given to those who rule a city, they do not run it like a hockey game, but promote rapid transit so people can get to work on time, build community centres where youth can play and grown-ups exercise, and administer libraries like the one in North York where I watch seniors play chess and read magazines and newspapers too expensive for them to have a personal subscription. Our civic leaders develop the urban landscape so that the city becomes a mosaic of neighbourhoods where people walk the streets and are safe in their homes. Such shalom which Isaiah promises in 32:15-18, he probably believed would come to a repentant remnant of Judah's people after they returned from the disrupting, punishing exile pending; but **"restorative justice"—doing what is right to enable people to flourish**—is God's willed Way for bringing shalom on earth, as it is experienced in heaven. That's why, until Canada's government **somehow** adjudicates the injustice formerly done to native peoples with their land treaties, unrest will persist. And if the Israeli state, even though legally instituted in 1948 by well-meaning, guilt-stricken mighty Western nations, has misappropriated Palestinian Naboth vineyards as its territory: unless that be **somehow** recognized and set right, there will never be the carefree peace there that Isaiah envisions.

I am not a "liberal" ranting about my pet injustices, but we are wrestling to hear God's text booked by Isaiah and the moving revelation of 30:18—last point—that **(3) God is crying!** holding back blessing, impatiently waiting to show mercy to all of us struggling, woebegone, petulant sinful human creatures. "The Holy One of Israel" who rent the heavens and came down in the flesh of the Messiah Jesus Christ is aching to bring restorative just doing to the earth and us earthlings, says the Bible.

Well, why don't you do it, God? What's the catch?

The LORD God is waiting for the peoples of the earth to expect—and that means, to actively hope—that the Lord is coming in glory.

We can show that certain living hope by not making alliances with successful evil doings, but resolutely together, maybe painfully, patiently enact signposts of obedience to God's "Guidance," like the Christian School next door, NeighbourLink, The Lighthouse, *Christian Courier*, Citizens for Public Justice—you can name your own—institutions of sinful saints communally busy at restoring God's just order to important facets of human societal life. Such efforts take the stamina of hope, and are uninteresting to the sensationalist mass media because the efforts are calmly trusting God to bless the outcomes, even if we fail—that's the courage 30:15 talks about.

Yet God procrastinates coming—? Would it take a whole city, like Nineveh, to repent in sackcloth and ashes— would that encourage the Lord to show up in person?

Isaiah brings to the fore the political good news that justice, just-doing, is not just making sure you or the other gets your due, your "pound of flesh," but Holy Spirited just-doings are deeds which restore a congenial fulness of well-being to those participating in the matters at hand, even if they are not followers of Jesus Christ—those are tokens of the shalom acoming. Pastor Joel called our attention in November to Isaiah chapters 2, 19, 49, 61,[4] about God's punishing **and** blessing those who are **not** God's people too, even the Egyptians and Assyrians! God has his elect in every nation, says Psalm 87. God is not parochial, concerned for the good of just believers. God had Paul write young Timothy (I Timothy 4:10): we struggle and get hurt in following the Lord's "Way," because "we have set our hope in the living God who is the saviour (=restorer) of **all** people, **especially the believers.**" What a text!

God is crying because so few people are listening to God's Word, and because God's people are lax in speaking God's Word by embodying God's restorative just doing **on the earth.** We often think God is so slow in setting things straight, but that is because God is still waiting, weeping, to give us whom the Lord especially loves, time to be turned around, to **live by hope** as well as by faith and love, and to act like obedient children at large, not in private, but **in public affairs.** The Newer Testament

---

4   Isaiah 2:1-5; 19; 49:6 & Acts 13:47; 61:1-4.

centres God's "restorative just-doing" in the death, resurrection and ascension of Jesus Christ, and calls it "God's reconciling all things on earth or in heaven back to be at peace with God "(Colossians 1:19-20). So, anybody today who is **in Christ**, that is, touched and being led by the Holy Spirit, has been given this "ministry of reconciliation" (II Corinthians 5:17-20).

A good place to begin and maybe to learn how to effect reconciliation of **all** things with God is in our prayers. I wish I knew how to plead in prayer with God for Toronto, Canada, Europe, tribal turmoil in Africa, the USA elections, China, the world, as Abraham did for Sodom and Gomorrah: don't let disaster happen! Lord, for the sake of the few righteous, right-doing persons who live here and there, often under duress. Or, if we could pray more womanly, like Samuel's Mother, Hannah (I Samuel 2:1-10), and the expectant Mary (Luke 1:47-55): LORD God, frustrate the proud and mighty, humble the power-mongers, end warring and the trafficking in weapons, and lift up the lowly, so that **all** people will come to know that only you, O Lord, are the one true God. We need to cheer up God by being well informed of the crooked state of our worldly affairs, and then, instead of becoming judgmental, rigorously pursue right-doing, expressing with certain hope! our deep trust in God's gracious mercy to act...soon!

So, the message this morning is: do not allow the TV news and the depressing newspapers you read shape your consciousness on politics, but get your mentality from the prophet Isaiah, the mind of Christ. That means: (1) Stop fighting and threatening, fellows, ruling persons, and learn forbearance, with faith that God can bring peace on earth (Philippians 4:4-7); (2) Not competitive hockey, but the love act of restorative just-doing, especially for the weak, is the biblical Path-of-life (Isaiah 1:16-17); and (3) Not an easy prosperity but, aware of God's sorrowful impatience to act, as the apostle John exiled on Patmos put it (Revelation 1:9), we commit ourselves to share in Jesus' followers' persecution worldwide, the Kingdom of right-doing, with the happy patient endurance which is the joyful core of God-given hope!

Philippians 4:4-7

REJOICE IN THE LORD at all times! I'll say it again: keep on rejoicing! Let your forbearance be known to all kinds of people— the LORD is nearby! Do not be overanxious about anything, but in every kind of thing let your requests be known firsthand to God in prayer, in pleading, couched in thanksgiving. Then the shalom of God which surpasses all understanding will surely protect your hearts and your intentions in Christ Jesus.

Closing Prayer

THANK YOU, LORD, FOR the writings You gave us through Isaiah. Pour out on us your Holy Spirit, so we will wrap our little lives in the confidence of your gracious mercy, and become fervent ambassadors for the healing reconciliation Christ offers to all peoples. We are sorry you are crying for your world, LORD, impatiently waiting for us to respond to your love. Give us the faith, the compassion, and especially the sure hope that You shall indeed come through. Hear us, please, in the name of Jesus Christ, Amen.

    20 August 2017
    Willowdale Christian Reformed Church
    Toronto, Ontario

5

The Nature of Prayer to Which God Says "Yes": check out Hezekiah in Isaiah 36-39

TEXTS: Isaiah 38:1-6, 9-20; 39:1-2, 5-8; 36:11-15; 37:7, 14-20, 37-38, Mark 11:20-26

THIS MORNING THE BIBLE story and Older Testament Scripture-telling and singing, which lies behind the Newer Testament passage on prayer from Mark (listed above), is as long as the short sermon which follows. So please don't be nervous about the time; I'd like you live, childlike, into the vivid colour of the circumstances. This will be a Bible story for grown-ups about Hezekiah and historical events the prophet Isaiah recorded for us to hear as God's revelation to teach us, among other things, the nature and power of good prayer.

ONCE UPON A TIME a man named Hezekiah, when he was 25 years old, became King of Judah (c.728 BC) [Judah is very small on the world map]. The Bible gives Hezekiah's mother's name as Abi, Abijah (which means, "The LORD is my father"). Hezekiah's earthly father Ahaz had not been a good king. Now it was Prince Hezekiah, the son's turn, and Hezekiah did what was right in the eyes of the LORD God, says the Bible. He cleaned and repaired God's temple in Jerusalem which had become run-down and filthy, and got the Levites and priests back into shape, and had their wages paid again from tithes and first fruits income, to upgrade their musical services and reform their sacrifice routines.

Hezekiah removed "the Ashera and high places," which means, he put the sex shops out of business and broke up porn networks. Hezekiah cut to pieces the bronze serpent God once had Moses put up on a pole in the wilderness to save people from a plague of poisonous vipers (Numbers 21:4-9), because people now burned incense in front of that pole as a holy relic with healing powers (II Kings 18:4).

Hezekiah had his educated advisors, says Proverbs 25:1, collect and edit many of Solomon's good proverbs into manuals, to help his provincial officials learn how to administer justice in the outlying districts of Judah. (We call them Proverbs 25-29.) Hezekiah also fortified many Judean cities to give the people safe homes and good cisterns of water.

As reformational King Hezekiah tried to interest other Israelite tribes in celebrating the Passover in Jerusalem. They scorned him, but a few tribes came, and they had a grand old Solomon-like dedication time for seven days feasting on 1,000 bulls and 10,000 sheep—that's a lot of meat to eat! You can read all about it and more in II Kings 18-20 and II Chronicles 29-32.

IN THE FOURTH YEAR of Hezekiah's reign (c. 725, aged 29) the mighty superpower of the day, Assyria with General Shalmaneser laid siege to Samaria, the capital of the Ten Northern tribes of Israel, and after 3 terrible years, finally took it. Then in 722 BC the next Assyrian, General Sargon, mopped up Israel, deported the Jewish men, women and children who were dispersed throughout the Assyrian empire because, says the Bible, they had not obeyed the voice of the LORD God. So, no more Israel—wiped off the map.

Around 714 BC, in the fourteenth year of Hezekiah's rule (about age 39), Assyrian General King Sennacherib now comes to attack **Judah**. And Hezekiah got deadly sick.

Just listen now as we read and sing to you chapters 38 and 39 of Isaiah—the paraphrase of Hezekiah's prayer which John DeCloe will sing is printed in the order of worship.

Isaiah 38:1-6

AROUND THE TIME that Sennacherib of Assyria was preparing to invade Judah, King Hezekiah became ill, deadly ill. Isaiah the prophet, son of Amos, came to Hezekiah and said to him, "Thus says the LORD: put your house in order, for you are going to die; you shall not live any longer."

Then King Hezekiah rolled over with his face to the wall and prayed to the LORD God, "Listen, LORD God! Don't you remember that I walked faithfully, wholeheartedly, before you, that I did what was good in your eyes?"

And King Hezekiah cried and cried and cried.

Then the Word of the LORD came to Isaiah: Go tell Hezekiah, thus says the God of your father David, I have heard your praying; I have seen your tears. You know what? I shall add 15 years to your life, and I shall save you and Jerusalem from the might of Assyria. I shall cover your city (with my wings).

Hezekiah's Lifetime Extended

Nature and Death Undone by a Prayer

A graphic emblem conceived by Johannes Vollenhove, engraved by Nicolaus Visscher (printed by Philippe Losel in Rotterdam, 1734) depicts the roused Hezekiah with his startled courtiers, and holds the usual title, Scripture verse, and proverb. The Dutch, however, put it in the language spoken by the people, not in Latin. The Lord makes Hezekiah's lying sick abed to be healthy, and adds 15 years to the days of his life (II Kings 20:1-11)

Isaiah 38:9-20

THIS IS THE written prayer-song of Hezekiah, King of Judah, who lived after practically dying:

I said, am I to disappear through the door of the grave while the blood runs warm [in my body]? Do the rest of my years disappear? I said, I shall not see the LORD God in the land of the living! I shall not see people anymore, men and women who stand on the earth!

My time is torn up and taken away from me like the tent of a shepherd. I wove my life together like a weaver, but You have cut the threads from the loom. From daytime till deep into the night, You troubled me [with death]; like a lion You crushed all my strength: like a helpless swallow I cheeped, I moaned like a dove; my closed eyes [wanted] to open—to wee hours of the morning I wept.

My Lord! fear got hold of me! Stand up for me? What shall I say to God, for God is doing this? No sleep came because of my wretchedness. My Lord! Men and women live for these things—let me live! Make me well! Let me live!

O see! The bitter was bitter to me for my own good: all my sins You **threw behind your back and kept me safe from destruction. Those in the grave do not praise you; the dead cannot sing for you.** Those in the grave cannot enjoy your faithfulness: **the living, only the living glorify you as I do today**—a **father telling his sons and daughters of the LORD's faithfulness. Therefore, save us! LORD God, and let us play our songs all the days of our life near the house of the LORD.**

ISAIAH CONTINUES:

Isaiah 39:1-2

AT THAT TIME MERODACH-BÁLADAN Baladanson [an important Babylonian prince (began serving c.721 BC) itching to be free from Assyrian domination] [Babylon at that time was only a tiny part of the Assyrian empire]: this Babylonian prince sent letters and a present to Hezekiah, for he had heard that Hezekiah had been sick but had recovered his strength. And Hezekiah was buoyed up by the Babylonian envoys, and let them see his treasure house, the silver and the gold, the perfuming spices, the precious oil, the whole armory of weapons—the whole of what was in his store houses—there was not a thing in his household and in all his realm which Hezekiah did not show off to them.

ISAIAH HEARD ABOUT IT.

Isaiah 39:5-8

ISAIAH SAID TO Hezekiah: Hear the Word of the LORD God, God of the army of angels, "Take note! Days are coming when all that is in your household, and all that your fathers have stored up to this day, shall be taken away to Babylon—not a thing shall be left over!" says the LORD God. "And some of your own sons, your grandchildren whom you nurtured, shall be deported; and they will become castrated eunuchs serving in the royal palace of the Babylonian king."

Then Hezekiah said to Isaiah, "The Word of the LORD God you have spoken is good," because Hezekiah said (to himself), "[At least] there will be peace and reliable security while I am alive...."

Hezekiah song in Isaiah 38

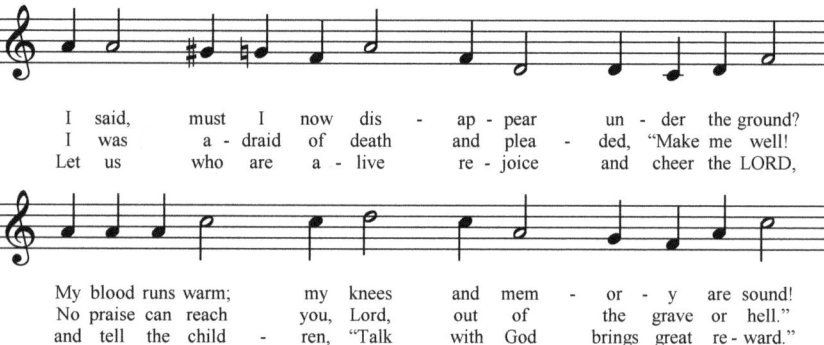

THE NATURE OF PRAYER TO WHICH GOD SAYS "YES"

Why rip the fab - ric of my life in ti - ny piec - es?
O, let me live! We were cre - a - ted to be tell - ing
So save us from des - pair; pro - tect us from those bring - ing

A mid - life death? O Lord, my bit - ter - ness in - creas - es!
your faith - ful - ness, for - giv - ing mer - cy so com - pell - ing —
de - struc - tive e - vil deeds which in - ter - rupt our sing - ing.

As mourn - ing dove I moaned, de - pressed, through nights of pain,
and then! You threw be - hind your back my sins and strife,
Life - long we thank you, God; please hear our mu - sic, cries,

and won - dered, could such suf - fering turn to joy a - gain?
and gave me — mir - a - cle — fif - teen more years of life!
and shouts of grate - ful praise, with prayer You make us wise.

TEXT: Isaiah 38:10-20 Calvin G. Seerveld, 2011© 21213131212
TUNE: Calvin Seerveld, 2011© Hezekiah

Now we go back to chapters 36-37 of Isaiah, which happened **after** the flashback of chapters 38-39 which we just sang and heard: that's why the book of Isaiah can be confusing.

So Hezekiah has miraculously survived, but has just acted politically foolishly; and Israel has been wiped off the map. I'll paraphrase what happened until we get close to Hezekiah's second prayer, which is printed in the order of worship.

Around 714 BC, in the fourteenth year of Hezekiah's rule (aged about 39/40), superpower Assyrian General King Sennacherib invaded Judah, captured all the fortified cities of Judah, and then demanded protection money to save Jerusalem. Hezekiah stripped his palace **and** the temple of the LORD of its treasures he had showed off to the Babylonians, and paid 3,000 pounds of gold and 12 and a half tons of silver (worth today about Cdn $88,500,000). Sennacherib pocketed the treasure, but then double-crossed Hezekiah (cf. Isaiah 33:1-2,7-9) and said he was going to destroy Jerusalem anyhow. So Sennacherib sent a large army with his emissary Rábshakeh to dicker with three of Hezekiah's cabinet advisors, Elíakim, Secretary of Commerce, Shebnah, Secretary of State, and Joah Asaphson, Minister of Culture.

Outside Jerusalem's wall Rábshakeh shouted in Hebrew: Tell Hezekiah, the great King of Assyria will wipe your tiny Jerusalem off the map! Why, I'll give you 2,000 war horses, if you have that many cavalry men to ride them! Don't rely on your LORD God—in fact, God told me to destroy Judah (36:5-10)

Isaiah 36:11-15

THEN HEZEKIAH'S AMBASSADORS up on the wall around Jerusalem said, "Look, speak to us in Aramaic (the learned diplomatic language) so the people all around cannot understand you."

Then Rábshakeh said, "Has my master sent me to speak these words just to your master and you, and not to the fellows sitting on the wall who are doomed with you to eat their own faeces and drink their own urine!?"

So in a still louder voice Rábshakeh hollered out in Hebrew: Hear the words of the great king, King of Assyria! Thus says the King, "Don't let Hezekiah deceive you, for Hezekiah cannot deliver you. Don't let Hezekiah have you trust the LORD God by saying, 'The LORD God will certainly deliver us; the city will never be given into the hand of the King of Assyria.'"

...WE ASSYRIANS HAVE CONQUERED everybody; their gods couldn't save them!

Hezekiah's diplomats didn't answer, but reported everything to King Hezekiah who sent them to tell Isaiah.

God answers Sennacherib's boast, said Isaiah, by saying,

Isaiah 37:7

"LOOK! I WILL BE putting a spirit in Sennacherib so he hears a rumour, and will go back to his own land, and I will have him struck down by the sword in his own land."

BUT A SECOND TIME Rábshakeh is sent to Hezekiah, and Rábshakeh brought a demeaning, intimidating letter.

Isaiah 37:14-20

HEZEKIAH TOOK IN HIS hands the documents from the hand of the messengers, read it out loud, got up and went to the house of the LORD God; and Hezekiah spread it out before the face of the LORD God.

And Hezekiah prayed pleading with the LORD God:
"O LORD God of the army of angels, God of Israel, seated
    above the cherubim,
You are the God, only You, of all the rulers of the earth,
You who made the heavens and the earth,
    bend down your ear, O LORD God, and listen!
    open your eyes, O Lord God, and see!
Hear all the words of Sennacherib which he has sent
    to mock the living God.
It's true, LORD God, the rulers of Assyria have laid waste
    all the nations and their lands,

> and have thrown those nations' gods into fire,
> for they were not really gods, but only things made by human hands, wood and stone—
> so they could destroy them.
> **But now, O LORD God, our God, rescue us from Sennacherib's hand**
> so that all the nation rulers of the earth may come to know intimately
> that You, yes! You alone, are the LORD God!"

SOON AFTERWARDS AN EPIDEMIC angel of the LORD God killed 185,000 Assyrian soldiers in one night.

Isaiah 37:37-38

THEN SENNACHERIB, KING OF Assyria, left and went home, and settled down in Nineveh. And as he was worshipping in the house of his god, Nisroch, Adrámmelech and Sharézer, his sons, bludgeoned him with the sword and, yes, they were able to escape to the land of Ararat. So Esarháddon, another son, became king instead of Sennacherib.

This is the Word of the LORD!
Thanks be to God!

MANY OF US ARE too well off to pray with the passionate intensity 40 year old Hezekiah did twice upon a time (cf. Hebrews 12:4).

You heard Hezekiah's first prayer John sang: "LORD, let me live! Make me well! Let me live! I can't praise you in the grave!" (38:16,18) Psalm 30 has the same wonderful argument with God: "Be my helpmate (עזר), LORD! since I'm no good to you in the grave!—" (Psalm 30:8-11)

And "the good" which Hezekiah was personally pleading to stay alive for is (38:19-20): to tell his children of God's faithfulness, and to sing psalms and make music in God's house. Don't you remember, God, how we got the Levite musicians to sing the psalms of David and Asaph again, like old times (cf. II Chronicles 29:30,35)!? And I don't doubt that when Hezekiah got his 15 extra years from God he instructed his not yet born son Manasseh in the covenant the LORD God had made with the line of David, even though Hezekiah's son Manasseh went on to become one of Judah's worst Davidian kings, doing exactly the opposite of his father, promoting the sex goddesses Ashtoroth even in God's temple! so popular as Ishtar with the dominating warlike Assyrian-Babylonian world culture of the time (II Kings 21:1-18).

NOT LONG AFTER GOD'S astounding merciful answer to Hezekiah's prayer in Isaiah 38 happened, Hezekiah wobbled in his political statesmanship by trying to impress the Babylonian envoys what a good ally he could prove to be against Assyria (Isaiah 39)—his heart was proud, says II Chronicles 32:25. Yet when Hezekiah faced the conquering Assyrian Great King Sennacherib, his prayer in Isaiah 37 has the ring again of desperate devout supplication for God to come through, the LORD **God of the army of angels** (that's what God "of hosts" means). Rescue your helpless people, LORD, from the global military might of Assyria (37:20) so that all the nation rulers of the earth will come to know experientially that only You are the truly almighty LORD God in the world!

It sounds like an Older Testament version of the Lord's prayer Jesus later taught his disciples: Hallowed be **Your Name; Your kingdom** come; **Your will be done on earth** as it is in heaven (Matthew 6:9-10).

And then God responds with a terrible, miraculous act by just one epidemic angel killing a whole army of veteran Assyrian soldiers, staving off the foreign exile of on-again-off-again sinful Judah.

WHAT CAN WE YOUNGER and older Canadian Christians in 2012 AD learn from this biblical revelation of Hezekiah's two prayers and their historical outcomes? We who have the James 5 update that "The earnest request of a just-doing person has a lot of operating power" (James 5:16b).

(1) **Prayer itself is more complicated than just you talking to God.** You may be as dedicated a sinful saint as Hezekiah was, but when you open your mouth to ask the holy God to listen to you, thank God! we have the Holy Spirit and Jesus Christ mixed up in this impossible activity—**I am really interacting with God!?** Unless the Holy Spirit is translating my stumbling thoughts and words and sighs into a **pure** petition, and unless Jesus Christ, like a defense lawyer at God's right hand (Hebrews 7:23-25, I John 2:1-6), tells God, "You should hear this case by Seerveld, Veenstra, Eygenraam": otherwise, our prayer is simply sincere empty verbiage, no matter how proper and pious and fluent the words may be (cf. Romans 8:12-17). Praying is a serious, amazing, difficult, even dangerous activity, just waiting to be done sinfully (cf. Luke 18:9-14).

This complicated nature of genuine prayer is why the outcomes are mysterious. We humans cannot "compel" the Almighty LORD God to be subject to **our** will, as if God be a great parental jovial Santa Claus in the heavens. It's true, Hezekiah got 15 extra years of life **after** God told him your earthly time is up, you are going to die. God saved the city of Jerusalem from the rape and destruction neighbouring Samaria had undergone, although Jerusalem was just as sinful…because there was found at least one righteous person in Jerusalem, Hezekiah, asking the LORD God for deliverance?

But when the great leader Moses, after 80 years of mediating tough service, **begged** God to graciously let him lead the Israelites into the promised land, God said, "That's enough now, Moses, don't talk to me about it anymore. You can have a mountain-top look at Canaan but strengthen younger Joshua to take over the task" (Deuteronomy 3:23-28). And when the apostle Paul implored God to take away his "thorn in the flesh"?—maybe epilepsy—which Satan gave me so I wouldn't be too sure of myself, writes Paul to the proud Corinthian congregation: I devoutly asked God **three** times, and God said, "No, my grace is sufficient for you; my power reaches its fullness in human weakness" (II Corinthians 12:7-9).

So, learning to pray as a fool-proof way to get what you want from God is not the nature or purpose of learning to pray more biblically (?).

(2) **Good prayer <u>focusses</u> on getting the LORD God's merciful just-doing to show up on earth among all people.**

Hezekiah didn't pray just to stay alive, but to stay alive so he could enjoy the promises of Psalm 128:6, and see his instructed grandchildren living faithfully before the LORD (Isaiah 37:19). [It took God an extra generation to come through: Hezekiah's **great**-grandchild Josiah, as boy King 8 years old, royally carried out a Reformation more thoroughly than did Hezekiah (cf. I Kings 22-23).]

Hezekiah didn't pray, "Save Jerusalem from the infidel!" period, but asked God to rescue us from evil so that all nations, especially superpowers trusting their military prowess and strategic ingenuity, would come to know that **only** the LORD God calls the shots politically.

In good prayer we, even in our needs, do not have priority: **prayer is not about us, but is about God! and us only as receptacles praising the Lord for the shalom to be received.** An earnest prayer request is proleptic thanksgiving (cf. תודה and εὐχή and Mark 11:22-24). That's a theologically careful way, in big words, to say: with prayer God does not give you a blank DUCA cheque to fill in and sign. Jesus Christ has signed the cheque. Now you fill it in (cf. John 15:7).

You can't rightly pray for peace on earth among warring nations if you yourself are not a peacemaker. You can't rightly pray, "Give us today our daily bread for tomorrow, Lord," unless you are somehow helping the hungry around you to be fed; otherwise you are demanding things selfishly for yourself to the exclusion of the LORD's Rule/kingdom coming to fruition among your neighbours. You can't rightly pray for forgiveness of your own sins, says the Bible, unless you **first** forgive those who have sinned against you (Matthew 6:14-15). Good prayer needs to be anchored in a lived, biblically informed faith that instinctively, at heart, knows what the evil is God wants us to be delivered from (Proverbs 8:13, 16:6). Prayer is not supposed to be a last resort but is a first step in a person's submission to be bodily in the action for the shalom the Lord will provide (cf. Ephesians 2:10).

(3) **The right quality and bearing for prayer is that of a trusting, "grown-up" helpless child.** Fortunately, God also mercifully blesses those who do not or will not pray. But the best prayer has a fresh naiveté to it that is blunt but respectful. "Don't be like a moth! Lord, eating away my most precious clothes! Let me become a little more cheerful before I am no longer here," prays Psalm 39. To pray at the drop of a hat is not childlike but childish and can trivialize prayer. When you are really afraid or whistlingly happy is the childlike time to pray. Especially intercessory prayer, for others, takes a considerable grown-up preparation, so you know what you are doing in God's presence; but it must not become sophisticated, routine, like reciting a prescription. Prayer is right when it has an innocent, open-ended personal vow character—"I'm ready, Lord, to give away my life for what is needed."

Elijah, whom the book of James features (5:17-18): Elijah's prayer for rain was prefaced by contesting and killing hundreds of Baal prophets, and then being scared to death of Queen Jezebel's threat to kill him: let it rain! so help me God! Much earlier in history, while his servants prepared a good veal barbecue for his God visitors,

Abraham had the childlike temerity to push God from 50 down to 10! righteous persons, to save Lot in Sodom and Gomorrah (Genesis 18). When the Canaanite woman in the Sidonian city of Tyre persisted with Jesus to give her crumbs of healing under the table for her daughter (Matthew 15:21-28), she like Hezekiah near death was not just **wishing** for something good,[1] but with oath-like tenacity was **promising** to sing to the Lord! when God granted her the ordinary, marvellous shalom of health.

Abraham, Elijah, Hezekiah, and the Syro-Phonecian woman's prayers were not bargaining with God—"I'll do this, if You do that "(*do ut des*): their prayers were not a Pascalian wager—cover all the bases to see if maybe it works—but were acts of swearing allegiance and thanks to the Lord for providing what God stands for—merciful just-doing!—even if God gives a Moses and an apostle Paul answer. It takes the simple faith of an utterly dependent, artless and uncalculating child for a grown-up to pray as God asks us to do: "Daddy (Αββα), please show us your overpowering love, and the satisfying peace given by the Holy Spirit in the hard times I/we are going through right now…" (Matthew 7:7-11, Galatians 4:1-7).

HEZEKIAH'S TWO PRAYERS RECORDED by Isaiah 38 and 37, which God approved, give us with ears to hear hope and

---

1   Heinrich Greeven, "Das Nomen εὐχή kommt, in der Bdtg Wunsch weder in LXX noch NT noch bei den AposVätern vor." (*Theologisches Wörterbuch zum Neuen Testament*, Stuttgart, Verlag von W. Kohlhammer, 1935, 2:776.

direction for how to pray for ourselves, our fellow believers and our neighbours with chronic illness, recurrent depression, minor and major addictions, guilt from sinning: we want to sing! Lord, about your munificent, compassionate forgiving and enabling gracious, even miraculous goodness! And we will get down on our knees, O God, to plead that You save your beleaguered people, the meek, and also the weak around the world, the poor and hungry little ones violated by the ruthless with their terrifying power of guns, cartels, tanks and bombs: **You** destroy the destroyers! LORD God of the angels, since we are not sinless enough to know how to stop the evil redemptively, so that **everybody**—we too—will recognize that only You are the merciful-judging LORD of the universe!

I'LL END BY CAPPING Isaiah with the passage from the gospel of Mark, starting us off on "prayer": how do you know what for and how to pray faithfully?

Mark 11:20-26

AND VERY EARLY IN the morning as they were passing by, they saw the fig tree dried out from down to its roots. Peter, remembering (the earlier occasion, Mark 11:12-14), said to Jesus, "Rabbi, look at that! the fig tree on which you put a curse has withered away!"

Then Jesus answering, said to his disciples, "Have trusting faith in God. Yes, I tell you truly, that whoever would say to this (or that) mountain, 'Be lifted up, and be hurled into the sea!' if he or she really does not doubt in his or her heart but believes that what they say will happen, it will be done for you.

That's why I say to you, 'All of whatever you pray for and passionately request, believe that you have received it, and it will be yours.'

"Whenever you all stand firmly praying, be forgiving if you have anything against somebody, so that your Father who is in heaven may also forgive you your failings (παραπτώματα). But if you do not forgive (other persons), then neither will your heavenly Father forgive you your hurtful missteps (παραπτώματα).²

THE EXHORTATION THIS MORNING was fermented in February 2012 when God kept me alive after a heart attack in January. But that experience of possibly dying reminded me of an earlier Hezekiah moment in my youth when I prayed as if my life depended on it.

As an American, just graduated from Calvin College and the University of Michigan graduate school in 1953, I was set up to be drafted into the U.S. Army to go fight in the Korean conflict (1950-1953). At that same time I was awarded a U.S. government Fulbright Scholarship to go study Christian philosophy in the Netherlands.

I went before my local draft board in Suffolk County, New York, to plead my case to be deferred, so I could continue my studies. They voted 3 to 1 to draft me. Because I got one dissenting vote, I could appeal to the New York State draft board, where I argued that the federal government wanted me to go do advanced study with this scholarship. The State Board voted 3 to 1 to draft me. Because I received one dissenting vote, I could make a last written appeal to the President of the Unit-

---

2   Cf. Matthew 6:14-15

ed States draft board. That's when I prayed—even though I wasn't a king of Judah—with a vow to God, that if You let me study, Lord, instead of the disrupting army service, I promise to give my years of study to You in a deep-going way.

The final U.S. President draft board voted 2 to 1, to let me go study with my Fulbright Scholarship.

I tell this today as a testimony to our Lord's action, not as a witness of my piety: God's answer to my vowed prayer has graced me like an invisible halo all my life. I did not have to go learn how to kill other people but could be trained on how to bring a contour of wisdom to the young.

Good prayer needs the persistent intensity of a vow, suggests the Scripture (Mark 9:14-29 and Matthew 17:14-20;[3] cf. Mark 12:41-44, Luke 18:1-8), where **you put your <u>self</u> sacrificially on the line to follow through.**

What someone is to pray for is more complicated, since we are not God (Matthew 6:8) but are sinful saints needing to be cleansed…of hypocrisy.[4]

Jesus was not saying in the Mark 11 passage, "When winter comes, fellows, some Sunday get a car full and drive out early to Blue Mountain in Collingwood. Instead of going skiing, stand in a line somewhere, and each try out the

---

3   N.B. Mark 9:29, καὶ νηστείᾳ! and Matthew 9:21! τοῦτο δὲ τὸ γένος οὐκ ἐκπορεύεται εἰ μὴ ἐν προσευχῇ καὶ νηστείᾳ.

4   Jesus' cleansing of the temple is suggestively woven into the context of both Mark and Matthew's account of Christ's teaching on the power of prayer, Mark 11:15-19, Matthew 21:12-16. Cf. also the vivid parable in Luke 18:9-14.

quality of your faith, and say to that Mound of Earth, 'Okay, mountain! Move over!'" Even if Blue Mountain earthquaked, and it got published as news in the *National Observer*, even such "faith to move mountains," the apostle Paul told the Corinthians and the Romans doesn't count with God, if you don't love...your enemy! (I Corinthians 12:2, Romans 12:14-21).

If there is somebody in your life or in this room you can't stand because of what they did to you once, or keep on doing, **your need to forgive** that brother or sister is the kind of **real biblical "mountain"** Jesus was talking about: it takes a miracle—it takes **God-faith** (ἔχετε πίστιν θεοῦ, Mark 11:22)—to forgive somebody who has deeply hurt you, or acts like a thorn in your flesh; but unless you forgive such a person, God shall not! declares the Scriptures sadly, forgive you your misdeeds (Mark 11:25[-26], Matthew 6:14-15).

Good intercessory prayer is clothed in action and is not just talk. What one prays for requires you to embody your request. It occurs to me, if I really pray for Harry Huyer in his lonely troubles with Parkinson disease, I should go walk around the block with him in the sunshine or rain. If I really pray for shut-ins in our congregation or those disappointed in their lives, I should bring them flowers, write a card, or share a joyful cup of coffee with them in person. If I really pray for a disbelieving friend or family member, I should openly practise the steady, inviting care of Christ for them in their vicissitudes and fears, no strings attached. Prayer is counting on God in the mix to bring surprises that attest to what is beyond human ability.

The Newer Testament book of James does not give followers of Jesus insurance that their prayers guarantee results, but like Isaiah promises with certainty that "the earnest prayer requests of a just-doing person has a lot of operational power" ("availeth much"). Let us rest in that sure, open-ended comfort, and ask the Lord to keep teaching us to pray by doing what is restoratively just, in love with mercy, and walking humbly with our God (Micah 6:8).

Closing Prayer

Dear Lord Jesus Christ, thank you for bringing our deepest prayers to God for attention and action. Please have your Holy Spirit make us pure enough, brave enough, and patient enough to cleave to You and voice your promises, and wait expectantly for your wise, often surprising and wonder-filled answers. Thank you for telling us about Abraham, Moses, Hannah, Elijah, Hezekiah, Psalm 6, 16, 30, John 17, and even Jesus' Gethsemane prayers, so like your adopted children we may follow in their trusting, suffering footsteps. We pray in your Name for the sorrowing, groaning world.

19 August 2012
Willowdale Christian Reformed Church
Toronto, Ontario

6

In the Older and Newer Testament of the Bible comes the Good News: NOTHING Can Pry God's People Out of the Loving Grip of God's Hand

TEXT: Isaiah 42:18-43:21

READING THE BOOK OF Isaiah around chapters 40-55 and 56-66 is not so easy for a couple of reasons:

(1) You have to see close-up and the distant horizon at the same time because different historical horizons are superimposed. So you need to figure out whether God's people in the split civil-war kingdoms of Israel and Judah are still facing captivity, or are the dispersed Jews already living enslaved under "World Conquerors" like Assyria (until Nineveh fell, c. 607 BC), Egypt (until the battle of Carchemish, 604 BC), Babylon (until captured by Cyrus, 538 BC)

and elsewhere (cf. Psalm 120); and how do God's people-of-faith today in our Newer Testament times relate to these old prophetic promises of liberation from the godless powers who aim to hold God's people captive?

(2) The truth of God's selecting Israel—the children of Abraham—as "my servant" (41:8-10, 42:19-20, 43:10, 44:1-5, 45:4) and then God's hand-picking the unbelieving Persian tyrant Cyrus as "my servant" (42:1-4, 43:14 [Cyrus is even called "the LORD's 'Anointed one' or 'Messiah,' and 'my shepherd' in certain chapters, 44:28-45:13]), and then our Christian awareness that 'Messiah' and 'servant of Yahweh' refer to Jesus Christ too (Matthew 12:15-21 quoting Isaiah 42:1-4!) can be confusing or difficult for quick or unschooled readers—which 'servant' is the text referring to, or is it all three?

(3) You wonder in a given paragraph, is it Isaiah himself talking? is God self being quoted? is there a commentator writing? and so much history knowledge is assumed all through one another it's hard to catch the allusions: it's all God's authoritative, highly poetic Word, but it's a little complicated to get the point, especially when the Isaiah passages constantly go back and forth between warning of punishment for sinners and giving promises of forgiveness and grace, as if the tough chapters teeter-tottered over to utterly joyful chapters—are the same people being referred to? Where does the emphasis fall?

I'LL READ TO you from Isaiah 42:18 to 43:21 in my careful translation, throwing in a few orienting names and details here and there to make it more clear. You can follow in your NIV, or just listen for now, but later I'd like you to look at certain verses—if you had your own Bible, you could underline phrases.

Reading the Bible is more important to me than the sermon. Sermons are just clumsy helps for you as younger or older persons to hear God's Scripture *speak*.

God's prophet begins in 42:18 by talking for God to the congregated people the way I am talking to you as God's people. So let's pretend you are God's special people facing exile in Babylon, and some of you live as near to the highrise Babel, Nebuchadnezzar's impressive urban development, as Brampton people do to Bay Street buildings and the CN Tower.

This is the Word of God for whoever present has ears to hear:

Isaiah 42:18-43:21

YOU PEOPLE WHO seem deaf, listen!
You people who have blindfolds on, take a look, so you get it!
Indeed, who is blind, if not 'my servant'?
Who is mute, if not 'my messenger' whom I am sending
    (out into the world)?
Nobody is "blind" like my consecrated one,
or as "blind" as 'the servant of the LORD God'!
You people have looked at things but have never really
    perceived what's going on.
Your ears have not been plugged, but you never really
    heard a thing!
The LORD God was pleased to show God's trustworthiness—
the LORD God gave the *Torah* importance,
    made it something glorious!
Yet...this misled folk lies plundered,

all of them stuck in holes in the ground breathing heavily from fear,
they are hiding themselves in caves like prisoners
> [referring perhaps to the terrible siege and fall of Jerusalem reported in II Kings 24-25];
they are like scavenged goods [carted off to Babylon] which
> nobody will reclaim,
like plunder that nobody is saying, "Give it back!"

Is anyone of you listening to this?
Are you paying attention so you can hear what's coming?
Who do you think gave Jacob into the hands of plunderers?
Who gave Israel away to the people who rob you blind?
Was it not the LORD God against whom we have sinned?
> —they were not willing to walk in God's way;
> > they did not listen to God's *Torah*—

So the LORD poured out the heat of God's anger upon that
> people,
> > the cursed violence of wartime fighting.

God set things on fire all around, but God's people didn't get it!
The fire singed the people, but they didn't take it to heart!

So now this is what the LORD God says,
the One who created you, O Jacob,
> the One who fashioned you, Israel
> > (into God's special recalcitrant people):

"Don't be afraid, because I have indeed set you free—bought you
> back out of hock!
I have called you by your name—you belong to me!
Yes, when you have to walk through the waters to the other side,
> I will be with you.
When you battle the undercurrents of the rivers,
> they will not pull you under.
That's right, when you even have to walk through fire,
> it will not burn you—
> > the flames will not give you burns!

for I the LORD God am **your** God!
I am the Holy One of Israel, **your** Messiah (Redeemer).
I will give up Egypt as your ransom;
I will give away [rich] Ethiopia and Seba in exchange for you
    [—the Persian conqueror Cyrus will conquer those countries,
    but let the Jews go back to Jerusalem!]
because you are precious in my eyes,
you are worth so very much—**I love you!**
I am willing to give up other peoples for you,
I will give up other nations to save your life!
So don't be afraid [my people], for I am surely
    right there with you.
I will bring your grandchildren and great-grandchildren
    back from the East,
And I will bring you all together from the West,
and I'll say to the North, 'Send them along!'
and to the South, 'Don't obstruct their coming home'—
I will bring my sons [home] from far away,
I'll fetch my daughters back from the ends of the earth,
everyone who is called by my name!
whom I created for my glory!
whom I fashioned and moulded [historically]...."
    [After this direct quote of love from God, the prophet now
    again first reports God's renewed, almost courtroom-like appeal.]
Bring on the blindfolded people who still have eyes,
the people who can't hear but have ears.
Let all the nations of the world gather as one together,
let all the peoples be brought together.
Who among them (and their gods) could announce what
    (God is going to say)?
Who among them can proclaim [God's great] primeval deeds?
Let them produce their eye-witnesses to show they
    (and their gods) are in the right!

Let them hear (what God has to say) and then confirm it, 'That's the truth.'

"You [Israel] are my witnesses," says the LORD God,
"You and my servant whom I have chosen,
so that you may know me intimately, come to trust me wholly,
and discern that I alone am God.
Before me no god was ever conceived,
and there shall never be any god after me.
I, only I, am the LORD God:
there is no other Messiah (Redeemer) except me.
I am the One who declared 'salvation is coming,'
made it happen, and let it be publicly heard
—there was no strange (god) with you then!
[That's referring to Israel when they were spending 40 years in the wilderness alone, "honeymooning" with the LORD, as Hosea and Jeremiah put it (Deuteronomy 32:10-12, Hosea 9:10, Jeremiah 2:2-3)]—
and you (Israel) are my witnesses," says the LORD God.
"I alone am God. And from now on [too], only I am God!
Nothing can pry (anything) out of my hand!
And who can undo what I (the LORD) carry out?"

So, this is what the LORD God says,
the One who bought you back out of hock
—redeemed you/is redeeming you!
The Holy One of Israel:
"For your sake I am sending (Cyrus) off to Babylon to tumble them all into becoming refugees,
and turn the high-jink festivals of those Babylon-people into funereal lamentations:
I am the LORD God, your Holy One,
the Creator of Israel, your kingly Ruler."

So speaks the LORD God, who made a pathway into the sea,

>   a little footpath through the violently troubled waters
>   —who brought out [Pharaoh's] war chariots and horses,
>   army and heroic warriors en masse…
>   and they lay down never to rise again!
>   They were finished off, like an extinguished wick—
>
> "But don't just remember the good old happenings;
> don't just focus attention on what's over and done with.
> Don't you see: I am doing something freshly new!
> Right now it is starting to germinate—can't you people see it?
> That's right, I am making a (new) road into the wilderness.
> I am originating streams of water through the deserted
>   wasteland—
> the wild beasts in the fields will honour me [for it],
>   jackals and wild ostriches,
> because I give fresh water in the wilderness,
>   streams of water in the desert,
> in order to giveaway plenteous drinking water to my
>   chosen people,
>   the folk I moulded [historically] for myself
> so they might show and tell my songs of praise…."

This is the Word of the LORD
Thanks be to God!

IT IS A PRIVILEGE to read and hear God speak in Isaiah. The tone of the text is so rich, like full wrap-around stereo-sound: the gnarled brass instruments with trombone sounds of God's being provoked and frustrated at Israel, whom God's prophet refers to sometimes as 'Jacob' (the deceiver), counterpointed by the exuberant strings full of promises and the cello intimacy of God's saying to this itty-bitty bunch of stupid people, 'I love you!' Then the clarinets, violins and trumpets, with full organ, take up the melody: I'll change the world's political events for you people, anoint a pagan Persian General Cyrus to pull you displaced, enslaved individuals dispersed among the nations back together as a people! So don't be afraid, my people, you belong to me; be comforted, have no fear, little flock of whom I, Almighty God, the only God! am the Shepherd, your Redeemer, Saviour....

FOR US TO HEAR God speak from this book to us today you've got to understand the historically embedded flashback/flash-forward way the prophet jostles God's people to **remember** the LORD's great deeds and their present predicament so they start to listen to what God's saying they may **expect**! If you look in your Bible how the verses jump around—

42:21 refers to Mount Sinai, God's giving them the *Torah*, around 1445 BC; and 42:22 refers to the fall of Jerusalem (586 BC), as bad a time as when Benhadad besieged Samaria and some Israelite parents in horrible desperation even ate their children to stay alive! (That's in the Bible, II Kings 5:24-31), and finally the men and women of Judah were deported to Babylon as slaves.

You don't see the connection, says Isaiah, between Mount Sinai long ago (v. 21) and your being captives in Babylon (v. 22), do you? Well, the connection is that even in Exodus 20 you didn't want to listen to me, says the LORD, and even during our 40 year honeymoon after leaving Egyptian snake and hawk gods behind, you people kept on quarrelling among yourselves, doubting my care, and lusting for Egyptian cucumbers, melons, leeks and meat (Exodus 17:1-

7, Numbers 11 and 16, Psalm 78). It's been the same old story among the indulgent Canaanite culture in the land of promise; so I finally had to punish you again by abandoning you to what you **want**, the attractive sex-gods and power-trips of Babylonian culture (42:24-25). But it's not much fun, is it?

Yet don't be afraid of me, says God (43:1,5; cf. 41:10,14). Although I briefly bring trouble into your history, I forgive up to the thousandth generation of my believing chosen people (Exodus 20:4-6; cf. Psalm 30:4-5). Remember, I brought you out of Egypt and gave you your own name and identity as a people called 'Israel' (43:1-2), and I am beginning to arrange things to free you from the present super-power Babylon (43:3-6)! **Nothing can separate you**, not even your communal sin of godlessness, **from the grip of my loving hand**, says the LORD (43:13).

43:14: I'll have the Persians subdue your oppressive Babylonian captors, just as—next verses 43:16-17—I finished off the pursuing Egyptian military machine for you once upon a time, to the amazement of the Amalekites (Exodus 17:8-15), Edomites, Moabites, Philistines, and other idol-worshipping Canaanite nations all around (Exodus 15:14-16). I, the LORD God, am the only living God in the world I myself created, and I want you to be glad in your lives, thankful, like the jackals and wild ostriches who have enough to eat and drink, so you will sing me good songs (43:20-21)!

HOW DOES THE BOOK of Isaiah fit into the whole Bible story?

The Newer Testament is like the concluding chapters of the one true story begun with the Older, earlier Testament.

The critical change that takes place after the Messiah was born on earth from the virgin Mary is that who **God's people** are is no longer determined simply by your having Abrahamic blood or being able to trace your lineage to the star of David (or by living on Palestinian real estate). According to the Newer Testament chapters of the one book we call the Bible, God's chosen people follow not in the blood-line of Jewish Aaron's priesthood but in the faith-line of non-Jewish Melchizedek (Hebrews 4:14-8:13, Psalm 110). So that's why an Italian centurion named Cornelius, a Turkish business-woman called Lydia, Antiochian pagans (Acts 10, 16:11-15, 11:19-26) who were filled with the Holy Spirit to follow the resurrected and ascended Jesus Christ: that's why they **all** could belong to God as God's adopted children, a peoplehood of the LORD God revealed in the anointed God-man Messiah Jesus.

Therefore, God's people have included Numidian Augustine, Frank Charlemagne, Saxon Alfred the Great, black African slaves brought to the USA South in the 1700's, as well as old Dutch burghers, Frisians, and even Canadians. Everybody here—children, young people, adults, old people—can actually belong to the LORD as God's people, you don't have to just pretend to be God's people. If you have God the Father, Son and Holy Spirit's name baptized on your head or body, you are called to be a member of God's peoplehood. Then the back-and-forth wrestling, loving speech of Isaiah holds for us too, since God's Word does not go out of date, and the Older Testament warnings and promises not yet fulfilled are still valid in a renewed post-resurrection way for those whose eyes and ears are opened by Holy Spirited faith to see and hear, even taste God's direction.

For example: Jesus says, in the famous chapters of Matthew 5, 6, 7, "Don't think I came to abolish the *Torah* and the prophets. I came to fulfill them.... You've heard it said, 'Do not murder.' Well, I tell you, anybody who is angry at his sister or brother is guilty of murder. And you've heard it said, 'Do not commit adultery.' Well, I tell you, any man who looks lustfully at a woman has already committed adultery with her in his heart."

So Jesus does not relax the earlier Exodus 20 *Torah* in the Later Testament Matthew 5-7, but intensifies it! Yet don't make the mistake of the Pharisees and Sadducees of Christ's day and whom the apostle Paul was acquainted with who read the *Torah* with blindfolds on (II Corinthians 3) and were still afraid of God as at Mount Sinai. God's *Torah*, law, is not repressive: 'Thou shalt not, thou shalt not, or you fail the exam to get into heaven'—No! That's the way pagan people, self-righteous people, secularized people mishear *Torah*, not God's people, who know a life of unfettered joy (cf. James 2:8-13).

You forgive the brother or sister who has hurt you so you don't walk around with the unbearable pack of anger on your back. You admire the attractive woman or man with a pure heart and sheltering look at what God has made so very good, but you are not cramped by an obsessive, short-circuiting drive to get it for yourself. If you steal or covet or worship the idol of Success or Fame or Big Money, says Isaiah 42-43, you brush away the LORD's intimate, guiding hug of faithful creaturely living, and ruin yourself, end up in exile—that's what has always happened to the children of Abraham, Isaac and Jacob, to the kingdoms of Israel and Judah, to the churches to whom John at Patmos wrote letters.

Yet God keeps on offering Guidance, Good News, the voice of Wisdom: let those who have ears hear and be my witnesses, says the LORD (43:10) and sing songs about my faithfulness (43:21).

BUT HOW DO WE Newer Testament Christians read and understand the political setting of Isaiah 42-43? Can we just transpose Babylon into Bay Street and the downtown Yonge Street strip or the egregious SALES—SALES—SALES of your local shopping mall? Did God use Gorbachev ten years ago like a latter-day Cyrus to break up the Soviet Union to answer the fervent prayers of thousands of Christians in Eastern Europe and Asia? Is Mike Harris' Conservative government cut on the model of Nebuchadnezzar's administration with respect to low-cost housing? If the United States of America is not 'God's people,' does its world domination of finance, heavy weapons manufacture, and ruthless benevolent Commercialism of human life and environment worldwide make it the reigning Evil Empire?

One has to listen to God carefully here so as not to make a mistake. Isaiah is not fingering Chrétien or Clinton as a new 'Messiah,' or localizing the Power of Mammon to 'Made in USA.' The Bible, Older and Newer Testament, is not a political almanac where we just fill in new names like a crossword puzzle. But our Isaiah passage of chapters 42-43 in the context of 40-48, with prophetic reach to Jeremiah and Daniel extending on to Paul's letters to believers in Ephesus, Corinth and Rome, and John's concluding book of Revelation which also signals the Fall of Babylon! (Revelation 18) and the final coming of heaven upon earth (Revelation 21), proclaims to believers living in Brampton that the LORD God is concretely, unmistakably busy historically in our day and is speaking directly to us, saying:

(1) **Nothing can pry you out of my hand, my people**—Isaiah 43:13 is repeated in Romans 8:31-39!—and when you walk into the Red Sea of saturation advertising and junk mail, the undertow of credit card debt will not pull you under, if you follow me and the Way I make through the tempting, treacherous waters to the other side (43:2,16,19).

The Bible does not reduce evil to ancient Egypt and Babylon, Nazi Germany or Megacorporate Business, but is exposing the principalities of Violence, Vanity and Waste—the names of evil are legion—which cruelly distract and blind God's people. Indeed, says Isaiah 42-43: plead with God to send a Moses to Ottawa, or a Daniel with a few wise friends like the CPJ, to ask the Authorities to let us go to educate children in the way of the Lord Jesus Christ without unjust penalties, and further, please God, somehow to honour treaties once made with aboriginal tribes in Canada generations ago about land, to show respect for keeping one's word even though it hurts (cf. Psalm 15:4).

(2) Just as I brought your ancestors out of Egyptland and their descendants out of Babylonian exile—Isaiah 43:3-6 is picked up historically and given a large cosmic setting in Ephesians 2 and 4:1-16—**my servant,** says the LORD God, **the ascended Christ Jesus, took captivity itself captive!** (Ephesians 4:8) **so you** ethnic Gentiles who have received my gracious gift of faith **are no longer strangers to Isaiah's message and refugee aliens exiled in the world, but are being brought together as "the [very] intimate household of God"** (Galatians 3:23-29)!

Isaiah 43 and Exodus 15 are not restricted to the Red Sea and Cyrus-decree events happening thousands of years ago, but are revealing God as the everlasting Redeemer of those whom the Lord loves (43:7)—"everyone who is called by my name! whom I created for my glory! whom I fashioned and moulded [historically]."

That is, if any of you Christ-believing parents have a daughter held captive in a godless Western university degree program, or a son virtually enslaved by management pressures in a business headquartered South of the border; if your grandchildren seem lost to the body of Christ and reading the Bible because they are addicted to the latest TV kids programs manufactured in the East; you may still claim the promise God makes in Isaiah 43: I will bring them back from far away, even from the ends of the earth, to be joined together in a holy communion of dancing laughter, witnessing to my saving them from hell-bent frazzlement and hopeless boredom.

And Isaiah 43 is not just about your blood-born children and grandchildren, but about all the baptized offspring you as congregation promise to receive in love, pray for, instruct, encourage and sustain in the fellowship of believers (CRC formulary for "Baptism of Children," *Psalter Hymnal*, p.961). Since there are more saints in the world than those at Immanuel Christian Reformed Church, you will be celebrating this joyous home-coming by singing new songs of "Hallelujah! Praise the LORD God!" with the returning younger generation straggling in from the West and East, the North and South, also with Brampton's Anglican, Roman Catholic, Baptist, United churches and others all together—this is the vision of Isaiah 43 as it resounds and reverberates up through the whole Newer Testament, anchored finally in Revelation 5:9.

In Revelation 5:9 the triumphant Lamb of God, it says, has paid the ransom for—redeemed back by his life-blood—those from every tribe and tongue and people and folk under the sun, and has fashioned them into a royal priestly community serving the only true God (cf. I Peter 2:9-10) who in Jesus Christ shall indeed rule over the whole earth.

THAT'S THE NOTE I'LL end on: the Redeemer of Isaiah 43 is the same Redeemer as the one revealed in Revelation 5. God the Redeemer truly speaks to us in the continuous Bible with historical sweep and imaginative prospects. And God doesn't get tired of always bringing God's stupid, infighting people back from their punishing exiles wherever they be, serving idols. We get tired of debating trivia in church-splitting arguments, and mourn the hate engendered by intransigent grown-up Orange Men wanting to parade themselves; and we despair at atrocities committed in Sierra Leone, Muslim Algeria, and the untouchable World Banks with their debit-sheets. So we are tempted to give up, become afraid, and succumb to household gods like a middle-class life juiced up temporarily by World Cup soccer fever, bouncy Spice Girl marketing, or a quick fix by upgrading to Windows '98. Maybe that's near where Isaiah 43 finds you this morning?

God cannot comfort you if you are comfortable. But "I do love you," says the LORD; "I created you for **my** glory. I am making a **new** road for you who are survivors through the wilderness of sin, a sound pathway through the troubled waters of a seductive, heartless culture." The 'new' way is the *Torah* which never gets 'old,' which is **not** an in-house parochial document on how to get saved, but is Good News for the public domain, and has freshly become '**the law of Christ**'—freely obey God and love your neighbour as a forgiven sinner! (Romans 13:8-10)—inscribed anew on your redeemed heart by the Holy Spirit (Jeremiah 31:31-34, Hebrews 8-10; cf. Proverbs 3:1-4) whose fruits of "love, joy, peace, patience, kindness, generosity, faithfulness, gentleness and self-control" (Ephesians 5:22-6:2) shall grace your impacted, strenuous and bruised lifetime.

If you young people, or older people, live day-in-day-out driven by **wanting things** rather than being content with how God satisfies your **needs** (cf. I Timothy 6:3-16; cf. Philippians 4:10-13), you will be a perennial refugee exiled in God's world. So don't keep the blinders of selfishness on, and open your ears to hear afresh the guiding *Torah* of the Lord: in marital disputes do not betray trust, in labour relations do not steal or covet, in life-death insurance be generous to the poor, in political decisions come through with restorative justice for the disenfranchised, in churchly matters do not bicker but wash your antagonists' feet, and since God took a break once upon a time and initiated the Sabbath to differentiate us humans from the fabulous animals who still have to put in seven days a week world without end, learn to enjoy regularly a day of rest. Then we who have been given a sturdy place-to-stand in God's love at the Holland Homes, TDCH, CLAC, ICS, or as saints-at-large in a congenial or abusive office situation: we may, without fear, sing in hope together to the Lord, "Let your Rule surely fill this earth!"

Closing Prayer

Dear Lord, our Redeemer,

Thank you for persisting in saving us leftovers from milling around afraid in the dark.

Thank you for the *Torah* as the living direction we may read and hear so as to follow in Christ's footsteps.

Please set things more 'right' in the world of nations whose gods are idols like bombs, luxury, knowhow without knowing why;

please pull us and our children and grandchildren onto walking the disciplined, forgiving, obedient footpath the Holy Spirit sets out, so that the vibrant songs of Moses and

Miriam, Isaiah and the Lamb, will be jubilant in our mouths to witness of your grace, strengthen us in our faith, and reach out to the loners, the cynics, the desperate and indecisive, and even hypocrites, with the overwhelming power and warmth of your jealous love.

We pray quietly confident in the name of Jesus Christ, Amen.

19 July 1998
Brampton Immanuel Christian Reformed Church
Brampton, Ontario

7

A Good Deed of Spilled Perfume, Despite the Poverty All Around Us

Texts: Isaiah 53:2-5, Malachi 1:10d-13, Mark 14:1-11

I will read first a brief section of Isaiah 53, then an angry retort the prophet Malachi reports of the LORD remonstrating with God's people who were faking their worship, short-changing God, and finally I will read the story in Mark 14 which is the text of this chapel meditation.

Isaiah 53:2-5
This is the Word of God:
Like a root out of waste land he grew up before
    the face of God.
He was without beauty. He had no dignity.
If we had looked at him, there was no comeliness
    to have attracted us.

He was despised, a reject of men, a man of sorrows
who knew grief so intimately
    you would aver your face from him;
he was so despicable he was not worth looking at.

    But did you know:
it was our griefs he bore. It was our sorrows he carried.
We thought he was hurt, wounded, oppressed by **God,**
but he was jabbed through because of **our** dirty deeds.
He was beaten down for the sake of **our** guilty wickednesses.
That the punishment lay on him gives us grace!
By the welts on his body are we made whole.

Malachi 1:10d-13

"...I DON'T REALLY WANT to receive a donation from your hands (says the LORD to God's people). Why, from the rising of the sun to its going down, my Name is great among the nations of the world. Everywhere incense is offered to my Name—a pure offering! Yes, my Name is greatly esteemed by the nations at large." This is what the LORD God of the Angels says.

    "But you people desecrate it all when you say to yourselves, 'Oh, the altar of my Lord is a little dirty; its food-offering is a bit stale.' 'Oh my,' you people say, 'It's all somewhat boring,' and you stick up your nose at me," says the LORD God of the Angels. "You bring me stolen goods as your offering, what is defective and sickly! Am I supposed to accept that gladly from your hand?!" says the LORD God.

Mark 14:1-11

IT WAS JUST TWO days before the Passover feast of unleavened bread. The chief priests and the learned teachers were looking for a tricky way to get a hold of Jesus to finish him off. But, they said, not during the feast days, lest there be a riot of the people.

Now Jesus happened to be in Bethany at the home of the leper Simon, and he was sitting at the meal table. A woman came in who had an alabaster flask of pure spikenard ointment, very costly; breaking open the flask she poured it over Jesus' head.

There were some present who were incensed. "Why this waste of anointing perfume!?" they said to one another. "That much spikenard could have been sold for more than $60,000 and given to the poor." And they kept on lambasting her until Jesus said, "Let her alone. Why do you keep on bothering her? She has done something beautiful to me. **You** will always have the poor with you (cf. Deuteronomy 15:1-11), and whenever you feel like it you can do them good, but you won't always have me around. She has done what she could, she's come ahead of time to anoint my body for laying it in the grave.

"You know, let me tell you: wherever in the whole world the good news is preached, what she has done shall also be mentioned, as a kind of tombstone for her."

Judas Iscariot, one of the Twelve, went off to the chief priests with the intent to deliver Jesus into their hands by some trickery. They were delighted to hear it and promised to give him money. From then on Judas kept looking for a way, without too much trouble, to betray Jesus.

This is the Word of the Lord!
Thanks be to God!

BOTH MATTHEW AND MARK introduce their final chapters, which report on Christ's ordeal and death, with this ceremonial act of extreme unction in Bethany at the home of the leper Simon.

Christ had told his close followers that he himself would be "sacrificed" at the time of the Passover (Matthew 26:2). The members of the Sanhedrin would have liked nothing better. They were convinced that Jesus was demon-possessed and a dangerous and popular heretic (John 8:30-59); and part of the oral law tradition by which they lived said (with reference to Deuteronomy 17:8-13), that trouble-making rabbis should indeed be executed on feast days so that the massed people would be impressed by the punishment of insolent, law-twisting leaders. But the ruling high priests and experts in canon law did not have things under control; so they justified underhanded means to achieve their end.

Christ's disciples and hangers-on, meanwhile, seem to us, who have so much hindsight, incredibly slow-witted. But it may help us to understand the fussy obtuseness and petty jealousies of Christ's followers then (and see how similar we are to them), if we realize how Jewish their orientation was. Christ's disciples, like the Pharisees, wanted to be good people, to do what Yahweh required of them by the law. The trouble is, they expected to be rewarded for their good behaviour, and the letter of selfish justice overpowered the spirit of obedience.

IN CONTRAST, THE POINT of the story before us in Mark 14:3-9, framed by an account of the secretive judges of Israel and the premeditated furtiveness of Judas in Jesus' very inner sanctum, is to reveal to us the open-hearted, non-self-seeking nature of what is truly "a good deed" (*kalon ergon*) that pleases the Lord.

The extravagance of the woman's act need not be overemphasized—the kibitzers probably inflated the price anyhow to fit their righteous indignation about how much the poor had just lost. But Christ's rebuke is important. He was throwing Deuteronomy 15:1-11 about "the poor"—the law they were citing for their criticism—back in their faces, and Christ was cutting the work-righteous heart out of their sinful insistence on good works.

Deuteronomy 15:4-6 says there will be no poor among Israel if the folk keep the Lord's commands. So the existence of poor people in the land became evidence of disobedience on the part of God's folk. Can you hear the cutting edge in Christ's voice? "When you feel like it, **you** can do good to the poor. Go ahead! But don't make the needs of the poor the cornerstone of your kill-joy policy—"

Christ, indeed, goes further, because he knew the incipient legalism that lay in every serious disciple he attracted. Pious Jews not only kept the Ten Commandments from their youth onwards (cf. Matthew 19:16-22), but also believed in performing the deeds of charity (*ma'asim thobim*) prescribed in Isaiah 58:6-7: liberating the oppressed, feeding the hungry, sheltering the homeless, clothing the naked, visiting the sick. You can ruin such "good works," however, either by becoming selective on who is set free (cf. Matthew 25:31-46), or by making certain you show up well in doing them (cf. Matthew 6:1-4).

"This woman has done a 'good work' and you didn't see it!" says Jesus. It was an open act of love, not for show and without false modesty. There was no thought of getting something out of it: it was done for a dying man. It does not fit any prescription! Completely unexpected, simply lovely, imaginative, gentle, and full of mercy. "She has done something beautiful to me."

Christ's remark about the woman's lovely deed (Mark 14:6), along with the LORD 's stern rebuke in the book of Malachi for those who brought God not their "first fruits" (cf. Nehemiah 10:34-39, Matthew 6:33-34) but their leftovers as an offering, should help us examine ourselves, how we give our studies to the LORD, and to reject the Pharisaic (Humanist) dogma that taught "prescribed good works give us credit with God." And Isaiah 53, which explicitly describes the Suffering Servant we shall be specially remembering in the coming Lenten season preparing for the Easter celebration, our Lord, as one who was "without beauty," needs to be heard by all of us who have ears, as a contrasting overtone to the sounding of the Psalms which extol the glory of God's creation.

Our miraculous world with its stunning creatural sights and amazing animals belongs to Almighty God. But history also belongs to our long-suffering Covenanting God, with all the vicious, mean, self-righteous obscenities we humans have "created." The biblical passages before us give good direction by bringing together the provoked LORD God, the sorrowing Christ, and the woman's act of love, to present a most appropriate prompt for keeping a biblical sense of what is crucial in our tasks at the university, and even give us wisdom on formulating a scripturally led policy for our generation's historical engagement in the arts.

When you study not to impress your professors or parents or peers or to get good marks and a job, but to bring your precious studying lifetime as an offering of incense to the LORD, then the hard work is hallowed by God's grace. Then the written paper completed, the oral examination finished, even the botched laboratory assignment you needed to do over, or the insightful idea you just floated past a friend, or spending time to think through a difficult problem with a muddled neighbour to clarify the issue: all smell as sweet in God's nostrils as Noah's sacrifice of thanksgiving for being saved from the punishing flood (Genesis 8:20-22). God is jealous of how we spend God's gifts in our hands, and the LORD wants the best we can give away to our neighbour (without expecting quid pro quo). When you know how to lead a child to the alphabet so that she or he becomes fascinated by the marvel of reading, or if you can tell by a practised glance whether the infection is viral or bacteriological and help the suffering patient, if you can make a Bible passage speak its message so you disappear and God's voice is heard, then God finds your offering has the fragment odour of flowers and spices.

When art is crafted for God and neighbour, without the idealistic fanfare, and is simply spilled like an offering of perfume as this woman did, reported in Mark 14, then you as musical artist have God's authoritative blessing. If you have been gifted by the Holy Spirit to write songs, or to draw the human face, to tell stories to children or to grownups so their mouths drop open, to paint colours that bring cheer to the sad, or film shapes that stop the self-assured with uneasy reflection, or if you can be trained to make choreographed gestures that bespeak righteous anger or redemptive tenderness, then you have Jesus Christ's explicit approval for such "good works" of love.

That is the gospel truth, even if influential people who may have guilt-stricken consciences, says Paul (I Timothy 4:1-5), should say, "Is a university higher education—where you only get a head full of theories, concepts and strange ideas—worth all that time and expense? And do we need all this sensuous art stuff? The cost of a painting or an anniversary sculpture or a mural in the public building is too high. Don't commission a poem for a birthday. All that money can be saved to mount an evangelism campaign or be given to the starving poor in sub-Saharan Africa!"

Such well-fed critics of costly study and the arts, says Christ sharply, will always have a ghetto outside their neighbourhood, which they can remedy anytime they put their mind to it. But do not hinder the solitary, struggling scholar who doesn't "produce" stuff you can sell or can be immediately packaged with "Jesus Saves"; do not hinder the lonely poet with budding insight, my gifted, solitary actor stymied by secularist settings, or the young Christian sculptor, all of whom are sinful to be sure but who cannot put bread on the table for their family with the analytic and aesthetic gifts the Holy Spirit gave them to give away: do not make it so hard, my friends, for them to spill their perfume over my body, says the Christ, over my often tired, beleaguered, recalcitrant yet expectant people, or even spill that perfume over the neighbours who maybe never had anything "beautiful" done to them either. Such little offerings of thoughts and artistic acts of love are worth remembering.

A GOOD DEED OF SPILLED PERFUME, DESPITE POVERTY NEAR US

PURE ACTS OF LOVE are quite rare among us who are neighbours, I think. Yet the Lord calls us to a life of "good works," deeds of genuine love which God has even prepared for us, in Christ, to walk in, says Paul (Ephesians 2:8-10).

It is just very hard for us who are so self-conscious of our Christian tasks and who know as well as the scribes how to exegete Scripture to special-plead all kinds of good things we have in mind: it is very difficult for any of us to whittle ourselves down to be just like a little child again, to unlearn, as it were, all that the Lord requires, and simply do acts full of mercy to our non-selected neighbour.

But that is where the biblical answer to legalism starts, and where the biblical wisdom on cultural priorities takes root. Not in restrictive money-righteous polemics which pits these "good works" against those. Not in risky "leaps of faith" nor in "sinning bravely." The mature Christian life simply enjoins us to exercise our diverse gifts in deeds of wise love that pay attention to our neighbours' concerns and plight (Psalm 15, Philippians 2:1-11, Romans 12), and surprise God with their cheerful generosity (cf. 2 Corinthians 9:6-8).

Such good works are indeed worth mentioning, as the Lord put it, wherever in the whole world you want to preach the good news that Jesus Christ laid down his life for men and women while they were still sinners. Why, if you can point to such good works on earth, redemptive acts of philosophical thoughts and artistically spiled perfume among them, all kinds of people might even come to believe the gospel of Jesus Christ they hear so piously talked about.

If you personally act the way this woman did with her treasure of perfume in the account of Mark 14, then you, as student, as scholar, as secretary, as artist too, are at home with the Almighty Holy One, despite your trials, and you shall never—not on your life!—be shaken to pieces, says Psalm 15, but will be remembered by the Lord who is returning, whenever the good news of salvation is quietly revealed in deed (cf. Matthew 25:31-46).

Closing Prayer

O LORD GOD, YOU who know us inside out, how we both hide our sins from You, and show off our faith in public, please teach us how to do works that are truly good, deeds of sheer thankfulness, wisdom, mercy, and imaginative love, so that people all around will be moved by the Holy Spirit to believe in the Rule of your Son, our Lord Jesus Christ, Amen.

>27 February 2000
>Institute for Christian Studies chapel service
>Toronto, Ontario

8

God's Calling Us to Become Melchizedek Mature in our Faith

TEXTS: Isaiah 54:1-3 and Hebrews 5:4-6:12

WE WILL JUST READ a few paragraphs from Isaiah 54 and Hebrews 5-6. Let me give you the setting.

During the first 39 chapters of Isaiah's prophecies booked for us there was civil war between the ten tribes of Israel and "David's line" in Judah. God's people were fighting among themselves as usual, each enlisting different godless allies. An end result was that Judah's ally, Assyria, eventually wiped Israel off the map in 722 B.C.

Married man Isaiah with his wife and two children lived long enough to experience Assyria's invasion of Judah itself under Sennacherib, which God thwarted, during the rule of good King Hezekiah (701 B.C.). But Isaiah had to tell Hezekiah (because Hezekiah made the mistake of sidling up to the rising superpower Babylon) God would someday also send God's people of Judah into Babylonian exile (Isaiah 39).

Chapters 40-55 in this book comfort's God's people, speaks tenderly to the children of Abraham, Isaac and Jacob (Isaiah 41:14-16, 51:1-3), promising that the almighty covenantal LORD God of heaven and earth, throughout the rise and fall of superpower nations, is going to bring a generation of exiled believers back home, back to the city of God—the Persian Cyrus will humble great Babylon (Isaiah 44:24-45:17)—so that even the unbelieving nations will say, "My! the LORD has done great things for God's people" (Psalm 126:2).

I will read my own careful translation of Isaiah 54:1-3;

Isaiah 54:1-3
This is the Word of God:

BE JUBILANT! YOU WHO were unfruitful
    and never gave birth—
Break out into songs and shout aloud!
    you who never knew labour pains.
For the children of the one who was left lonely alone shall be
    many more than the progeny of the one who is married:
    (this is what the LORD God says!)

So, people, make the place your tent covers larger!
Let the tent tarpaulins where you have settled down be
    stretched out farther—don't hold back!
Lengthen the tent ropes you have
    and hammer the tent stakes in more firmly!
That's right! You will be spreading out both
    to the right and to the left,
and your children's children will come to rule over nations;
they shall come to dwell in the cities people have deserted.

AND NOW WE READ a section from God's book "To the Hebrews." The original audience were probably Christian Jews struggling to grow up out of their legalistic upbringing, where you had to sacrifice again and again as priests in the line of Aaron did, to make good for sins. These Hebrews who had agreed to follow Jesus Christ were trying to grow up to be priests in the order of a mysterious Melchizedek, and to realize that one sacrifice once upon a time on the cross left you free simply to mature in thankful deeds.

Again, a few key verses of my translation are printed out for you to check, but you could just listen: the Bible is meant to be heard, Hebrews 5:4-6:12. This too is the Word of God:

Hebrews 5:4-6:12

(THE KEY POINT ABOUT becoming a high priest is this:) a person does not take the honour upon oneself, but is called (to the office) by God, as Aaron was (Leviticus 8, Numbers 16-17). The Christ too did not push himself forward to be made a high priest, but God called out to him:

You are my Son. Today I have begotten you. (Psalm 2:7)

And in another place God says:

You are a priest forever, according to
the order of Melchizedek. (Psalm 110:4)

During the days of his incarnation Jesus offered prayers and fervent requests with loud cries and tears to the One who was able to save him from death, and Jesus was heard, thanks to his circumspect awe before God. Although Christ was (from the start God's) son, he learned obedience through what he suffered, and having been brought to a final and full maturity (of obedience), Christ became the one responsible for the everlasting salvation of all those who obey him, the one designated by God to be "high priest after the order of Melchizedek."

There is a lot we could say about this (Christ as Melchizedekian high priest), which is difficult to make intelligible, since you people have become lazy in your listening. Although by this time you people ought to be teachers, you still need someone to teach you again the ABC's of what God has said. In fact, you have become adults who still need milk and can't stomach solid food!

Everyone who lives on milk (like a baby) is not able to handle the matter of talk and thought that does what's right. Such an adult is infantile. Mature people thrive on solid food. Mature people are those who have habitually exercised their sensitivities to discern what is honest-to-God and what is evil-minded.

Therefore, people, let's get past the basic doctrines of the Christ and move on to mature business. Don't keep on laying down the [same old] foundation of "repent from doing dead works" and "believe in God." I mean, don't keep on again and again about "the teaching of baptismal washings" and "ordination," about "resurrection of the dead and everlasting judgment": let's get past all that elementary stuff! And we will grow up (into the mature significance of Christ's high priesthood), God willing—

It is impossible, you know, for those who once and for all were brought into the light (of God's grace), who once tasted both the gift from heaven and had come to be sharing in the Holy Spirit, that is, who experienced the live (preached) Word of God and the moving powers of the Coming Age, but then stopped short, stepped backwards: it is impossible to stir them again to a radical change of heart if they deliberately turned away from maturing, because then they are busy crucifying the Son of God again in their own lives, actually holding up (the claims of Christ's high priesthood) to ridicule.

You know what I mean: the earth that drinks up the rain falling down upon the ground again and again, giving birth to plant life suitable for food to those by whom the soil is cultivated, that earthy ground shares in the blessing from God. But earth that bears thorns and thistles is good for nothing and is in danger of being accursed (by God), fit for burning.

Even though we're talking tough this way to you whom we love, we are confident that you are on the track of the better things, things which lead to restoration. After all, God is not unfair. God will not forget the work you did and the selfless love you have showed for God when you served your fellow believers, which you continue to do now.

But—and that's the point!—what we passionately desire is that each one of you may come to show the same earnest eagerness you have for brotherly and sisterly love, show that same zeal to reach the full maturity of the (Christian) hope, on and on till the end come, so that you don't settle down lazily, become sluggish, callously hardened [unmoved by the imperative to become mature]. Instead, start acting like (grown-up) people who through a trusting faith and long-suffering patience do come to inherit the (riches of) what God has promised.

This is the Word of the Lord!
Thanks be to God!

LET'S LISTEN TO THE admonishing Newer Testament passage first, and then end with the exciting, outstanding promises of the Older Testament passage on this odd Sunday out between a Christmas celebration and the church's recognition of what is called Epiphany next Sunday.

THE BOOK "TO THE Hebrews" is practically a sermon with the whole Older Testament as text, referring to Genesis, Leviticus, Judges, Proverbs, the prophets, and especially Psalms 2, 110, and 95. The main thrust of this complicated, educated book is that the mediator Jesus Christ is lord above and over all the powerful angels (Hebrews 1-2), and is a saviour who surpasses the leadership of figures like Moses, Joshua (Hebrews 3-4) and Abraham (Hebrews 6:13-7:28), so revered by the believing Jews. Because the Messiah Jesus suffered by being born to grow up and sacrifice himself like a mysterious Melchizedek high priest— who turns up out of nowhere in Genesis 14 to bless "Father Abraham"—Jesus Christ's singular atonement on the cross ends our needing to keep on visiting Aaron-type priests and working off the debt of our sins on the weekly installment plan.

Therefore, says God's book "To the Hebrews," since you Christ-believing Older Testament-oriented believers know this important change, and the complete, satisfying rest Jesus Christ's birth on earth provides you faithful ones, don't slough off! Don't be satisfied with the minimum of salvation! Don't rehash in baby language and just repeat the same old basic doctrines all the time. Don't settle down and relax, pull back from growing up in the faith, from putting down stronger roots in God's Word and becoming seasoned plants which flower and produce fruit....

If you don't respond to God's spoken word and the indwelling of the Holy Spirit by growing up, maturing to deeds worthy of repentance (Matthew 3:8), you are stuck in damnable trouble, says "Hebrews," fit for God's cursing. Because you are scorning what Christ's birth and suffering life among Pharisee and Sadducee leaders and bungling disciples meant, you are ridiculing what Christ's death, resurrection and ascension to the LORD's right hand is all about: bring the blessing of doing what is right into God's world again.

That's what the name "Melchizedek" means priestly king of setting things right, doing justice on the earth before God's face, reconciling the world of human cultivation back to God. And if you deliberately stop growing up in faith, says "Hebrews" 5-6, you are rejecting faith-induction into the order of Melchizedek; you are hardening your heart and sinning against the Holy Spirit! as your forefathers and mothers did who therefore were never allowed to enter the promised land (Psalm 95:7c-11, Hebrews 3:7-4:11)!

THIS IS ONE OF the most serious passages of the Bible, and it is utterly clear: if like a patch of good ground the Holy Spirit plants a seed of faith in you—as child, younger or older person—and you regularly receive the sunshine of good biblical preaching and showers of blessings from God through fellow believers, but don't take root as a plant that grows above ground, you are faith-dead. If, as a plant above ground, you grow a good cover of fig leaves but bear no fruit, no edible figs, what good is that for a fig tree (cf. Luke 13:6-9, Matthew 21:18-22)? If you do grow up and become a spindly thorn of bitterly sharp critique, a thistle of perpetual discontent, you are also fit for burning, says our text.

This book "To the Hebrews" is addressing especially congregations of believers, "denominations" too, you could say, who never get past the milk of the gospel, who spend precious historical time rehearsing, repeating orthodox tenets to themselves, like mantras, as if that be a saving obedience to the Lord, or who argue endlessly about "Who can be baptized?" "Who can be ordained!?" —I'm not making this up. It's right there in Hebrews 6:2— "What kind of body will we have after death?" (cf. I Corinthians 15:35-50), etcetera.

Look, says our "To the Hebrews" text: to get the biblical basics straight is important. To reject "self-righteous works" and to affirm "faith in God revealed in Jesus Christ" as the only way to be saved is a cornerstone of the Christ's message (Ephesians 2:8-10). That those who die in Christ will be "resurrected to everlasting life" and that those who say Jesus Christ was only a good man masquerading as god will experience "death for keeps" at the final judgment coming (cf. John 5:19-29) is also fundamental to membership in Christ's body—certainly! But turn those basics into Melchizedek service, or those basics condemn you! says God's Word.

When grown-up men and women engage in arm-chair theologizing while the world cultures go to hell; when adult people who claim to be "Christian" deal in speculative trivia, ecclesiastical minutiae, or harangue one another even about important faith matters so much the Church keeps splitting off splinters, and they displace the central matter of our growing up to serve neighbours wholesome bread and cups of unpolluted water: such adults are infantile! says the Bible. Shame on them! Who would want to belong to such an immature mess?

RIGHT HERE TWO THINGS need to be said from our text, so there be no misunderstanding. First, about "perseverance of the saints" (Canons of Dordt, point 5), and second, what constitutes "faith-maturity."

(1) The Church of the historic Reformation led by Martin Luther (1483-1546) and John Calvin (1509-64) highlighted the fact that faith is a gift of God's grace (CD 2:7) mysteriously worked in human hearts by the Holy Spirit through the Word of God (Belgic Confession art. 7 and 22; CD 3/4:6-8,10-14). God says, "I want to adopt you as my kid" (Galatians 4:3-7, 1 John 3:1-3), and you are moved to respond, "Thank you, Lord" (cf. Colossians 2:6-7). Once you actually are thankfully made an adopted sister or brother of Jesus Christ, you may be certain, says Scripture, that God shall preserve your life for ever! through physical sickness, mental imbalance, temptations, grave sin, even death (Heidelberg Catechism, Q/A 1), because you corporeally belong completely now, forgiven once and for all by Melchizedek Christ's sacrifice—your brother!— you belong permanently to God (cf. John 10:22-30; BC art 23; CD 5:8-10).

"To the Hebrews" 6:4-6 reminds us that God's instilling faith in us human creatures takes time. There is a process in which Christian parents, for example, or a Christian teacher, are used by God quietly to instill that openness in a child to be primed for adoption. Or, a daughter who truly prays, or a son who "met Christ," as one says, at summer camp, can be used by God to "get" to a sceptical father, or to a mother in the doldrums, with new life!

Christ's parable about the soils (Matthew 13:1-23) makes the same point of historical preparation, testing, wait-and-see what happens: will the person's heart pounded hard by the feet walking over it let the birds pick off the seeds God's Spirit throws there before they germinate? Will the gravel in the soil of a person's life stop one from having the simple childhood prayers once learned from growing roots in reading the Psalms? Will the thorny bush of domineering/rebellious family relations choke out any faith seedlings? Or will soil conditions allow the Holy Spirit's implantation of faith to grow up into a responsive Psalm 1 tree?

"To the Hebrews" chapters 5-6 are describing people who have been touched by God's Word somehow—family, synagogue, church, media—and been fed from the updated gospel of Melchizedek Jesus, leaving Aaronic rituals behind. But these Christian "Hebrews," these people have decided they don't like the new taste of Christ discipleship. They are irritated by the Holy Spirit's promptings to become personally active as saints—who, me? "I'm saved. Leave me alone. I don't want to grow up. Just give me my weekly milk shake so I don't have to chew any undigested roughage—that would take effort."

But the saving faith God gives is not like a stone—plop!—dropped into a night deposit bank vault box. Faith worked in humans by the Holy Spirit is not a life insurance policy you cash in on the other side of the Jordan. The faith that makes Jesus Christ your holy brother for good is something alive that grows, deepens, gets stronger, or it dies, smothered, snuffed out. Those persons who decide not to grow up faithfully have spurned the Holy Spirit, have missed the priestly king Melchizedek service boat that counts, even though you may "talk" a good game in baby language and follow Aaron's rules and regulations to the crossed t's.

"To the Hebrews" has its sights on more than individual persons too. The context of God's booking this Word is the historical rejection of Jesus Christ as Messiah by the Jewish nation. Jesus wept at his so-called "triumphal" entry into Jerusalem because "the Hebrews" then did not know they were rejecting the peace he offered, it says in Luke 19:41-44. "The Hebrews" were expecting Jesus to expel the Romans and take over the power politics of High Priest Caiphas' job in the line of Aaron. They were not expecting the Messiah to sacrifice himself in the order of that "other," practically unknown high priest, Melchizedek (Luke 19:11; cf. also Luke 24:21). "Melchizedek rule" has the ruling shepherd lay down his or her own life for the sheep (John 9:40-10:18).

Saint Paul also takes three chapters (9-11) in the long letter to the Roman church to point out carefully, very sensitively, that certain of "the Hebrews" elected by God! as a people failed the LORD God by corrupting God's compassionate law into a legalistic network of "do-it-yourself religion." So those "Hebrew" branches were cut out of the tree, and non-Hebrews were grafted into the tree of God's people. God has me say this, says Paul, in order to make the dead wood, both Jewish and Gentile! jealous of being alive, and thus maybe save some of them, (Romans 11:13-24).

Christian parents have sometimes been afraid that "To the Hebrews" 6:4-6 means that their children who have left the church are reprobate and can never be saved. That's wrong. The Bible shows again and again how God's grace reaches out to recover the lost sheep and to reclaim even the prodigal son or daughter (Luke 15). This paragraph "To the Hebrews" is more about parents or singles who go to church regularly, mind their P's and Q's, but live in a rut of sluggish, self-satisfied ungratefulness.

This Scripture is about congregations of believers which do not "grow up." Their unforgiveable sin are sins of omission and loss of Melchizedek vision (cf. II Corinthians 5:17-19). It's scary when one realizes how much orthodox, confessing denominations tend to resemble the picture painted here of "the Hebrews," because there is not much hope given by the Bible for professional hypocrites (cf. Matthew 23). Hypocrites don't know they are hypocrites: they are good guys, with a stunted introverted routine, a kind of arm-chair faith; they just never grew up in their faith, never had their easy chatter translate into difficult deeds; they didn't become mature in God's world. And they end up not far from but outside of the kingdom of God, says the Bible (Mark 12:28-34, Matthew 8:5-13).

(2) What constitutes "faith-maturity?"

A theological degree from Ontario Bible College (now known as Tyndale University) or a Ph.D. in philosophy is no guarantee of faith-maturity. Also anybody who shows off his or her faith is immature. It is significant that when Saint Paul criticizes "speaking in tongues" at public worship services (although he speaks in tongues privately himself), and cautions against singing mindless songs (I Corinthians 14), God has Paul say, "Don't be babies in your abilities to think things through. You can be inexperienced babies, if you want to, in doing evil! But become mature in your abilities to perceive what's going on, making judgments" (I Corinthians 14:12-20).

Faith-maturity is knowing and acting out what pleases God (cf. Romans 12:1-2). To be full grown in faith means you have the wisdom of the Holy Spirit to discern what is really good for your brother and sister, yourself and the neighbour, rather than what is only apparently good, or evil. To grow up in the faith-bonding with the Lord is to become fully trusting, sure of God's love and direction, seasoned and savvy, with stamina for actually building, in any given generation, what God wants done on the earth.

A few examples? A young woman recently visited our home who had spent 13 years teaching tribesmen and especially women inland in Sierra Leone to read words and numbers and to write down the stories of their oral history as she told them about Jesus, to protect them from the encroaching secularist Western culture. When political rebels came through Alikalia looting and raping, burning the house to the ground she had built after living there ten years, she escaped for her life. But she soon went back—the Kuranko converts to Christ had to stay there; why should Westerners flee before their mission of love is done? That's a foolish grown-up faith kind of insight.

Suzanne Christie, who directs our multi-church NeighbourLink outreach in North York had a director come into a meeting fuming, "I hate Christians! I hate Christians! They're so cantankerous, deceitful, stubborn, ungrateful—" Suzanne quietly smiles and says, "I'm a Christian," and then she teaches her fellow workers to begin their day of finding volunteers to help the helpless (and those who take advantage of you), begin their day by all praying together, also for kindly, more gentle Christians. That's mature faith at work under fire, in my judgment.

Gerald Vandezande of the CPJ (Committee for Public Justice) was asked a week ago to speak to the assembled Metro Council of Toronto on whether to raise taxes for social assistance programs. "You began this day's meeting by singing, 'O, Canada!'" he said. "What does it mean for you municipal political leaders to 'stand on guard for Thee,' O Canada? Ten cents more from every Metro taxpayer would keep the shelters for the many homeless derelicts in Toronto open during the months of bitter winter cold. 'Stand on guard' for the weak...." I believe that's childlike grown-up Christian faith counsel.

But maturity of faith doesn't need to be dramatic or dangerous in a public forum. It seems to me that any grown man here who would read Psalm 51, 32, or David's final words in II Samuel 23:2-7, until his heart was seared and he broke down and cried, praying, "Lord, be merciful to me, a sinner": that would be a mature faith-act. It would certainly affect the way one plays hockey or rides the subway. Sometimes the most mature act of faith is childlike in trust, with the grown-up grit of complete dependency on the Lord of life, forgiveness, and death.

Or, if I may mention a personal item: on assignment from the Lighthouse, my wife, Inès, has visited for an afternoon regularly every week for four years now a bed-ridden fellow named Nick and a few senile women at the Barton Place nursing home downtown, show-and-telling this or that, sewing on buttons, bringing little gifts that soon get stolen, just listening faithfully, becoming an unobtrusive partner of sorts over time. To me that tells of a patience I lack, an edifying love that invisibly breathes a grown-up faith of Melchizedek service. According to Scripture, it's really like spending an afternoon with Jesus himself—imagine!—every week for four years, an afternoon tête-à-tête with Jesus (Matthew 25:31-46).

You probably have a dozen examples yourselves of what it means to grow up in faith, trust, an understanding faithfulness before God's face.

Because of the "Melchizedek" emphasis here, faith-maturity means for us: be certain you exercise your growing obedience to God **outside** the church door too, **outside** your family, **outside** your circle of Christian "Hebrews." Maybe you noticed that in the last paragraph of the Newer Testament text I read (Hebrews 6:9): God's writer, after quite forceful, direct admonishing language, says, "beloved"—I'm talking tough because I love you. I know you believers sincerely help one another; you are on the right track; don't wallow in recriminatory false guilt (That's what elder Dan Carter, from his background, correctly keeps on saying); but show that same zeal you have for loving one another to loving your neighbours! by steadfastly living out fully, maturely, the visionary hope peculiar to God's adopted (elected) people: ALL creatures shall come to magnify the LORD (Hebrews 6:10-11).

That's precisely the Old promissory, prophetic note of Isaiah, Micah and others which God started to cash in for us with the birth of Jesus Christ in Bethlehem, something all the savory and unsavory characters mentioned later in "To the Hebrews" chapter 11 were waiting for (cf. especially Hebrews 11:32-40). All kinds of people came under the spell of Christ's Melchizedek Rule: low-paid uneducated shepherds (Luke 2:1-20), wealthy wiseman intellectuals (Matthew 2:1-15), Ethiopian eunuch civil servants (Acts 8:26-40), Roman military centurions in Capernaum (Matthew 8:5-13), even "Hebrew" Pharisees! like Nicodemus and Joseph of Arimathea (John 3:1-21, 19:38-42; Luke 23:50-53).

MENTION OF THIS GROWN-UP hope that all creatures shall come to magnify the LORD (cf. Isaiah 56:8) brings us back, in conclusion, to the exciting passage from Isaiah 54, about later generations of God's people ruling over nations.

The Newer Testament always needs the Older Testament of God's Word sounding through it to keep the cosmic, societal, cultural scope of the obedience required of us by the LORD in place, so that we historically anemic people not reduce "the world" God loved so much to be less than **the whole world**—the environment, cities, the nations and their treasures (cf. Revelation 21:22-27). That's what our passage "To the Hebrews" itself says: don't be satisfied with a mini-gospel, with a Readers Digest version of the Bible story made simple. Go for the grown-up version of God's revealed will, which includes Isaiah, and the backdrop of political superpowers, principalities! knocking God's people around, taking them captive.

"LENGTHEN THE TENT ROPES you have, and hammer the tent stakes in more firmly," says our text, for you are going to be hosts to more than your little band of believing "Hebrews." Cities, goyim nations, strangers, will be coming to live under your sanctifying rule! unbelievable as that may sound to you exiled in Babylon.

Metaphors are tricky, because they are ambiguous. "Make your tent bigger" refers to real estate appropriation, believes an orthodox Jewish Zionist today, and is a divine injunction to misappropriate Palestinians from more of Palestine. "Expand your tent flaps and grow!" I can hear a TV evangelist or American "church growth" advocate read into it a projection of target goals to be met by the year 2000, and the command for a "bigger buildings and larger barns" construction program.

But we who are the new Israel (cf. Hebrews 8:1-10:18), the Christian Hebrews today, the grafted-in branches of

God's people, the historical body of Christ with a Reformation faith-tradition, should not make the mistake of reading this promissory vision of an expansive rainbow of cultures submissive to the God revealed in Jesus Christ, misread it down into terms of numerical growth or renovating our buildings. God's true prophets are talking a certain large vision of orientation, task and openness with training, to bring bread, grain, literacy to the world at large in the name of the Messiah, concrete Good News for all races—Blackfoot Indians in Saskatchewan, orphans in Romania, Mexican peasants, African traders, Western white male bankers, cruelly subjected Muslim women in Asia.... What a tent full it is and will be! if we respond with faith-maturity to the LORD's calling to populate cities with saints and come to a holy rule over nations.

Remember: it is a Melchizedek rule over peoples, priestly sacrificial ruling, diaconal leadership in the governing, in ordering commerce, in arranging a public transport industry. "Christian" ruling never would throw its weight around if it had a majority government because Christ eschews blustering infantile manipulation—cutting 20% civil sustenance to the impoverished and giving 20% "Christmas" bonuses to the efficient wealthy—that's evil! Melchizedek governance channels richer service, gives Daniel-like counsel to the current Nebuchadnezzar, whether it be Bob Rae or Mike Harris. Melchizedek Christian ruling over the nations is to be truly a ministering civil servant, doing justice, loving, keeping good promises, and walking humbly with the LORD (cf. Micah 6:8).

IF WE LIVE IN the hope, the actual expectation under God's promise, that our children's children, a coming generation, in spite of our relative cultural barrenness, shall indeed be blessed by God to set policies for family justice, design neighbourhood-city jurisdictions, construct environment-friendly legislation, apportion out health care equitably, promote labour intensive employment: such a program is so at odds with what is current, we had better start preparing our children to take on such matters. Scripture seems to say you need to be faithful stewards in small matters before the Lord makes you a manager responsible over more serious operations (Matthew 25:14-46).

If we people in this room cannot hear Isaiah 54 as an urgent bona fide directive for us to encourage our children to become Christian lawyers and judges, Good Samaritan business men and women, architects of housing for the poor, holy certified educators, then that might be symptomatic of the fact that the Western Christian church has indeed fallen under the judgment of Hebrews 6:4-8; and our complicity with colonialist, imperialist sins of the past centuries which left mostly thorns and thistles behind means we Westernized power brokers are unable to repent of our compromising ways which preached otherworldly holiness while our ancestors exploited others' resources for our earthy success. If we can hear the metaphoric call this morning, however, to open our eyes and hands to the world, beginning in North York NeighbourLink, Toronto, on to the uttermost reaches of CBC radio, then we need to hammer in our tent stakes more firmly too.

That's an Isaiah 54 way of saying the "To the Hebrews" point of becoming faith-mature, grown-up, as a congregated body of God's people. The LORD wants more than unskilled labourers in the vineyards.

God wants, for example, faith-mature songs: melodies and texts true to the reach of God and human sorrow and joy afoot in history that ring true to actual life. Listen once more to Genevan Psalm 25, stanza 3, so you can remember how a faith-mature song sounds. [JOANNE SINGS] That sinuous Dorian melodic line from our Reformation tradition has a steady comfort that can forthrightly weep with those weeping and be glad with those who are happy at the same time: it could be sung before a single mother living in a shabby one-room basement apartment next to the furnace pipes in downtown Toronto and bring chastened hope to us comfortable suburban dwellers, "On your people, LORD, have mercy." As we sing recently minted songs of praise, let us not forget our rich treasury of older tent post songs, new songs that don't go out of date.

The LORD wants faith-mature wise women and men who know the heart of God, that is, know intimately the Holy Scriptures. Grown-up believers who profess biblical faith in the Reformed communion should have knowledge of the Heidelberg Catechism, Belgic Confession, Canons of Dordt, The Contemporary Testimony, not just have them lying flat on the ground, but as tent posts fixed in your memory. The crux of reaching Christian manhood and womanhood maturity as a Spirit-filled congregation, however, is to have the Bible percolating through your thought and talk, funding your imagination, convicting you of God's all-sustaining covenantal faithfulness, so you can hear the full counsel of God, comparing Scripture with Scripture in your consciousness, having the Bible honed to an active vocabulary at work in your daily life.

It's okay to be a novice in Bible reading and young in Jesus Christ, but it's not okay to say, "I'm too busy to grow up in knowing what Almighty God booked specially for us to understand; I'm content with the headlines—God created, Jesus saves, the Holy Spirit, uh—" Maybe, if you've never read this Book of God's salvation of the world in history through from cover to cover, the communal Bible-reading program beginning in January would be a way for some of us to grow up in hearing God speak at length, rather than our being content with snippets. Translate your Christian baptismal mark into a deed of maturing, growing in stature, spending quality time with the Lord rather than just with the TV set. If it takes an effort, well, hammering the tent stakes in more firmly as you lengthen the tarpaulin ropes of our Isaiah/Hebrews vision is not for lazy, layabout believers.

If you need to be primed for this visionary Operation Shalom Tent-coverage, and you could have but neglected to hear the Pastor's October evening series on the Psalms, I feel sorry for you. To make amends—

young people or older ones—you could start by getting a tape of the 6 October evening service on Psalms 1-2, and grow up with the scintillating vision of hearing the cries of a multitude of peoples (Revelation 19:1-10) magnifying the LORD. Those sermons on the Psalms are worth inviting unbelievers to our worship services, and might even stir any Christian "Hebrews" present this morning into the circumspect awe of God which would reverse the judgment of "To the Hebrews" 6:4-8.

> So, people, make the place your tent covers larger!
> Let the tent tarpaulins where you have settled down be
>   stretched out farther—don't hold back!
> Lengthen the tent ropes you have and hammer the tent
>   stakes in more firmly!
> That's right! You will be spreading out both to the right and
>   to the left,
> and your children's children will come to rule over nations;
> they shall come to dwell in the cities people have deserted.

Closing Prayer

DEAR LORD GOD REVEALED in the baby Jesus Christ who grew up, who grew in the stature of wisdom, who learned obedience by suffering for us sinners as a Melchizedek high priest, please give us immature believing creatures, and anybody present who has difficulty trusting You, give us the biblical vision of a Welcome tent covering all the nations of the world with safety and shalom, with the tent stakes of mature faith anchored deep in the ground of your saving love, so we and our children can give sure direction to those who may have lost the Way. Help us to be responsive ground, Lord, that brings forth good mature fruit in its season, worthy of repentance. Teach us at Willowdale to be a royal priesthood that washes the feet of others than ourselves, as our Friendship Community Church affiliate in the Jane-Finch area is trying to do. Use our priestly service in such a way that all kinds of people will come to magnify You, O LORD!

We pray in the name of the Messiah, our Lord Jesus Christ, Amen.

OUR FIRST RESPONSE WILL be to sing Mary's song, "Magnify the LORD!" The half of the congregation on my right, sing with the piano. The half on my left, sing with the organ which will begin at (1) when the piano reaches (2). Let's do it without books—the words and tune of this Taizé song of mature faith are not complicated: "Magnify the Lord...."

If you are comfortable enough with your body to let your arms accompany the song, please do so. EXAMPLE A few persons are prepared to do this walking around the church in the aisles singing. If you think it would make God happy, please join them. They are not drunk—it's only 11:30 a.m.

This is not a test of your faith-maturity or Pentecostal leanings. It's not to be done for other people to watch so much as to magnify the Lord in your corporeality. It's something children, youth, 20s-30s and Seniors could all do happily together in a jumble of sounds.

Don't feel bad either if you just want to sing. Sometimes when I'm sad in church, I don't feel like being forced to clap off the beat either. God accepts our laments and praise done with integrity as we are.

Magnify the LORD

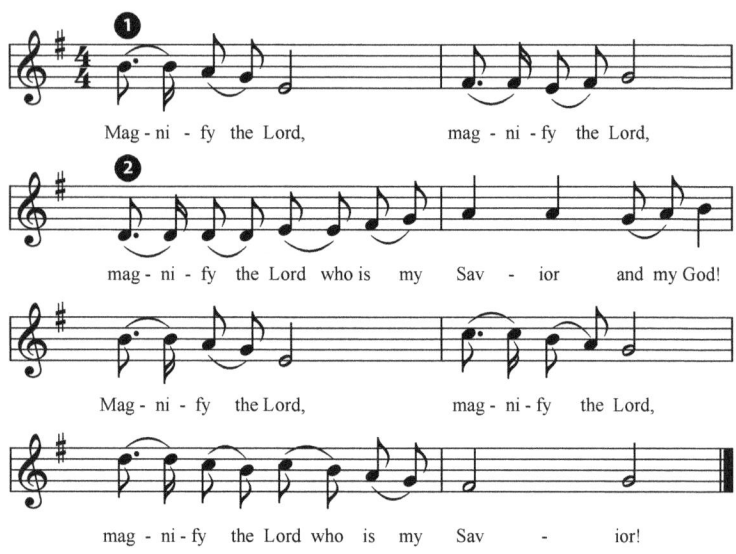

TEXT: Luke 1:47, vers. Bert Polman, 1985
TUNE: Jacques Berthier

PM
Magnificat

29 December 1996
Willowdale Christian Reformed Church
Toronto, Ontario

9

Biblical Reformation among God's people: Confession of our sin and being clothed in Christ's redemptive deeds

Texts: Isaiah 59-60, Psalm 33:12, 18-22

To any unbelievers who are present, as well as to you who profess to be the people of God: we shall read from both chapters 59 and 60 because together they catch what you often find in Isaiah side by side—the terrible depiction of current sin that is breaking God's people to pieces and the promise of blessing, an apocalyptic picture of how the LORD shall come through to redeem all those, especially the churched dropouts, who repent and accept forgiveness. Isaiah 59 and 60 reveal the misery of us people who need reformation and the glory of the LORD who can and shall use followers of Jesus Christ in the city of Toronto to bring light into the darkness hereabouts that will never grow dim again, and to serve water for the faint who then shall never be thirsty again.

It may help us to hear Isaiah 59-60 now, if you imagine these words as being spoken for the children of Israel while captive in the city of Babylon. Listen to the passage I read now as coming to God's people who have been displaced from their own land and are living, not so badly, in a city about the size of Calgary, foreign to the LORD. And they sometimes wonder, why in the world doesn't God set things straight! and free God's own people from this Babylonian mess and bring us to the new Jerusalem, as the LORD promised?

Please follow in the RSV/NIV translation you have. I'll make a few translating precisions here and there, especially on the key texts, to make the meaning plain.

The Older Testament is like a three-way lamp bulb. It gives light first on the historical situation in which the account or prophecy was given and reveals how God did things for God's people once upon a time. Then it switches on, in the context of the whole Bible story, what the LORD is after in the world God created, how from beginning to end, God in Jesus Christ with the Holy Spirit is working out God's merciful judgment and compassionate grace for all creatures. And finally, because this writing is our Father in heaven talking to us, if you're on your knees and listening carefully, the final arc of light goes on and you hear the LORD speak direction to you on what we are supposed to do together today, joining ourselves into the body of Christ for bringing the liberating Rule of the LORD upon the earth.

So we should keep those three horizons of lighting on as we listen to God's Older Testament Word this evening of Isaiah 59-60 section by section.

If you have cone to hear the Word of the Lord, as spoken by Isaiah, then now is the time to listen intently. Since the Word of God is being spoken in your hearing, half-way through these chapters when you hear the words, "Get up! you people of God!" I'd like to ask you to stand up liturgically, to show how you are listening. Don't pop up like a jack-in-the-box, and don't get up slowly as if you're leisurely stretching between hockey periods. When you read the Bible, that's our Father in heaven talking to us, and it is very appropriate to be sitting alert and responsive, able to get up respectfully, to meet God's voice, as it were, halfway.

<u>Isaiah 59:1-8 Recitation of sin [woman's voice]</u>

YOU SEE, THE HAND of the LORD is not at all too weakened
    to be setting (us) free,
the ear of the LORD is never stopped up
    from hearing (our needs):
it is your dirty deeds that have acted as a blank wall
    between you and your God,
your shameful sins have caused God to go hide God's head
    so God can't hear you!

That's right, the insides of your hands betray blood stains,
your fingertips are even bent with the double cross;
your pursed lips gossip twisted truth,
your tongue sidles along with what's crooked....

There is not a plaintiff who is innocent,
and nobody practises law with utter honesty;
people snuggle up to what's bland, and talk tripe,
they are pregnant with difficult labours
    but give birth to only an evil smell.
They sit brooding on snake eggs and spin out spiderwebs:
whoever eats their snake eggs is a dead person
    —crack one and a poisonous viper leaps away;
and the fibres they spin are never good for clothing,
nobody can cover his shame with what they weave:
all their industry adds up to is stinking hot air!

Great deeds become gross deeds in their hands!
Their feet run toward evil and are in a hurry
    to spill the blood of anyone who is innocent;
what they think up is simply trumped up nonsensical vanity;
    their highway is paved with violence and destruction
—the way of shalom is simply not known to them experientially—
there is absolutely no justice on the path they take:
they tie their own walk up in knots for themselves!
everyone who goes their way never knows what it means
    to be at peace.

Isaiah 59:9-15a Confession of our sin

[first person plural—chorus of voices]

THAT'S WHY THE MERCIFUL justice (of God) is held off
    from us!
That's why getting things done the way they were meant
    to be done never materializes!
We wait for joyful light, and what do we have? Gloomy darkness.
We hope for bright daylight, but we walk around in a kind of
    obscuring twilight.
We tap-tap-tap like blind men tap along a wall,
We feel our way as if we have no eyes,

We stumble around in full daylight as if night had come;
among sturdy, healthy people
    we look like dead men and women!
We complain, all of us, like growling bears,
We zannik and coo like a cote of doves.
So we expect justice!? but it shall not happen.
We are keen for (the Lord's) final redemption!?
    but it's a long way away from us—
because the number of times we have broken faith with you,
    (O Lord,) are too many to count,
our sins are firm evidence against us.
That's right, we can remember all the times we have fallen away
    from doing what You want—
we know very well our guilty crookednesses:
    the denial of attachment to Yahweh and hypocritical deceit,
    pulling back from following our God,
    talk that ruins people, bitchy malicious talk,
That's why the merciful justice (of God) is pushed back,
    kept away,
That's why having things done right,
    the way they are supposed to be done,
    remains in the distant future.
Yes, truth you could trust has been crippled in the city centre,
    straightforwardness can't even get into the place—
So that's how it has come to be that trustworthy truth is absent,
    and whoever abstains from evil gets plundered.

59:15b-20 Assurance of Pardon

[woman's voice again]

Now the LORD GOD saw this mess and it bothered God
    that no justice was being done,
God saw there was nobody!—and it flabbergasted God—
that there was nobody consecratedly concerned

to set things straight.
So (God decided to let) God's own outstretched arm bring
 deliverance for God,
God's own healing righteousness—that would be God's
 certain support.
So the LORD God got dressed up!
Doing-what's-right became God's (snug) spear-proof vest;
Delivering-things-victoriously served as helmet for God's head;
God pulled on the close-knit mesh of Equitable retribution for
 outer armour,
and stormed out (to meet the enemy)
 cloaked in jealous love (for God's people).

The LORD God shall match and complete whatever deeds
 were done:
  righteous anger for the persecutors,
  comeuppance for God's enemies.

God shall match and complete the deeds done in the most
 distant coastlands.
And (peoples) from where the sun sets in the West shall stand
 in awe at the Name of Yahweh,
and (peoples) from where the sun rises in the East
 shall bewonder God's stunning glory,
for the LORD God shall come
 like a damned up river (broken loose,)
  which the (Holy) Spirit of Yahweh forcefully drives forward!
The Redeemer will have come to liberate Zion!
And God will have also come to take back those dropouts
 in the people of Jacob
  who (nevertheless) somehow got turned around
—this is what the LORD God Yahweh says!

I am the One, says the LORD God Yahweh—
This is **my** Covenanting with them,

It is **my** Spirit which rests upon you,
It is **my** Words which I have put in your mouth,
And my words shall never fade away and be faint in your mouth
    or in the mouth of your children
    or in the mouth of your grandchildren
—says the LORD God Yahweh from right now on forever and
    ever and evermore.

Isaiah 60:1-22 Apocalyptic Psalm of Glory Promised

[man's voice]

(GET UP! YOU PEOPLE of God!)
Get up! and let (your joy) shine (through!)
For your Light has indeed come!
The glory of Yahweh is flashing down upon you!
    Yes, take a look!
Darkness still covers the earth, a depressing darkness hangs over
    nations of the world,
but the LORD God Yahweh lights you up, as it were,
    with lightning!
God's brilliant gloriousness is starting to flame light upon you!
Peoples of the world are beginning to crowd their way to your
    shining brightness—
even kingly rulers are starting to come to your shining
    which flashes bright like shook foil.
Turn your eyes around and take a look!
All of them together are gathering and coming towards you:
    your sons come from far away,
    and your daughters are being tenderly carried on the hip—
when you see that, you will smile broadly,
though your heart still be shocked atremble,
    it will slowly expand (and rejoice)!
Yes, the very richness of the sea will turn itself over to you,
Resources of the world peoples will stream in for you to tend!

a heaving mass of camels will cover you from sight,
young dromedaries from Midian and Ephah in Arabia;
all those that come from Sheba bear gold and precious perfume,
    announcing with fanfare the praise of Yahweh!
All the sheep and goats of Kedar flock together near you,
the (fat) rams of Nabojoth kneel to be of service to you,
they climb up to my altar as a pleasing sacrifice—
I intend to deck out my temple with splendour!

What's that coming up like a cloud of flying things,
like doves winging to the openings of their dovecotes?
Those are sailing ships massing for me, (the Lord,)
    the commerce ships of Tarshish in the fore,
bringing your children back home from distant lands,
carrying their silver and gold with them,
    to (honour) the Name of Yahweh your God!
    The Holy One of Israel!
for God has indeed made you a stunning glory!

The children of strange peoples shall build up the walls
    of your city;
foreign kings shall be your willing servants—**don't you see?**
I hurt you, (my people,) when I got so angrily worked up
    (at your sin,)
but in my (everlasting) Grace I love you compassionately!
The gates of your city will be open all the time
    —day and night they won't be closed—
to let men and women bring in the resources of the peoples of
    the world for you to tend,
their kingly rulers being led in too ....
Yes, the people and governing rulers of the world
    who will not be of service to you, (my people,)
    shall go to pieces,
those world peoples shall be laid waste,

become a deserted wasteland.
The glorious look of Lebanon shall become yours—
Phoenician juniper trees, sycamore-fig trees, cypresses,
> all together—
in order to embellish the place of my holiness,
so that I can decorate artistically the place where I rest my feet.
The sons of those who pressed you down to the ground
> shall now walk toward you themselves hunched down,
all those who made fun of you before
> shall now kowtow to the soles of your feet.
and they shall exclaim,
> "Yours is a city of the Lord!
> This is the holy city of the Holy One of Israel!"

Instead of your being an abandoned city, a hated place where no one ever passed through,
I (the Lord) intend to make you into something worthwhile forever,
something that will be a joy for one generation after another generation.
You will have the cream of the world's nations to drink,
You will suckle on the overflowing abundance of the earth's kings.
You will come to know experientially that I am your saviour,
> the Strong One of Jacob,
> the One who makes good for you!
Instead of bronze I will bring gold,
> instead of iron there will come silver;
instead of wooden things it will be copper,
> instead of stones, (strong) iron.
I shall establish HEALING PEACE as your administration
and MERCIFUL JUSTICE as your government!
Never again will wrongdoing be heard of in your land!
There will be no devastating violence, no confusing fragmentation
> anymore within your territory!

Call the walls of your city (and land MIGHTY) REFUGE!
Name the entrance gates PRAISE PORTALS (OF GOD)!
The sun shall be no more your light by day
nor the moon shine for you to brighten (the night),
but the LORD God Yahweh self shall be light for you forevermore,

Your God will be there (openly) to brighten you to glory.
Your sunlight will never go out anymore,
and your moonlight will now never disappear
—that's right! Yahweh will be Light for you forever and evermore!
the days you spent (darkly) weeping shall have been completed!
Your whole folk will all be just-doing citizens;
They shall cultivate and subdue the earth forever and ever,
Like young shoot(s) I personally planted, one(s) I hand-made,
In order to let Me (the Lord) be glorified!
The most insignificant person (among you) will become a
    thousandfold meaningful, and
The weakest (of you, my people,) shall become a nation of
    mighty stalwarts.
I, the LORD God Yahweh, when it is time, shall get it done quick!

Psalm 33:12, 18-22

BLESSED IS THE PEOPLE whose God is the LORD Yahweh,
The folk God has chosen for God's own heritage.
The eye of the LORD is upon those that listen to the LORD,
on those who hope in God's mercy
    to deliver them from death, and to keep them alive in famine.
We wait for the LORD: God is our help and shield.
Our hearts rejoice in the LORD
    because we trust God's holy name.
O LORD, let your steadfast mercy be upon us
    for we hope in You.

This is the Word of the Lord!
Thanks be to God!

You can appreciate the problem of the Jews in exile. They had problems keeping their identity as God's people in that pagan city. There was no temple worship. That's like telling you and me the church institution has stopped existing; there's no place or community to go to anymore on Sunday to worship. Still worse, the first exiles thought they might be going back soon—they hadn't listened so well to some of Jeremiah's early sermons where he had prophesied that two generations would die in captivity (24:1-14). But when Jerusalem finally got burned to the ground in 587 BC, Zion the holy city was turned into a dump, a wasteland abandoned by every living thing except jackals: when the exiles began to realize they might die in Babylon and their children probably would die there too, and there was no city of God to go back to! they had problems. Again, that's like telling you and me heaven is gone; there's no place for you to go to when you die. So what do you do now?

First of all, God's people in the distant city of Babylon kept up the Jewish language, made certain the boys got circumcised, advocated keeping the sabbath as best you could and certain fast days—when you pray, face West, where Jerusalem used to be—kept track of what's clean and unclean meat, kosher and unkosher entertainment. These are the days when the Jews started to multiply precept upon precept. Otherwise, after a while, you could hardly tell the difference between a Jew and a Babylonian on the streets of Babylon. Somewhat like today, you can hardly tell the difference between a Christian and an unchristian person on the streets of Toronto, in the subway, on the job—especially if there is no Bible-teaching church to go to or no real heaven to talk about! God's people in captivity didn't have the vision, were too fragmentized, lacked the cultural power to act concertedly as God's people. So they boxed themselves in as best they could, put up makeshift boundaries, and made the most of a bad situation in a city that didn't belong to God, they felt.

MAYBE DANIEL WAS MAKING waves at the supreme court of Nebuchadnezzar, Belshazzar, and even the new administration of Darius, but according to Isaiah 59, let's say, for the second-generation exiled Jew it was pretty much business and sin as usual. Scripture details it graphically in 59:3-8: God's people were as crooked as the respectable go-getters of Proverbs 1:10-19. And Isaiah's point is that whenever God's people happened to wish they had fewer troubles and said, "God, you know, you should do something about that," the LORD couldn't take their request seriously.

When God's people are sinning—you wouldn't believe this unless you read it in the Bible, Isaiah 59:2—God goes and hides! God can't stand to see the people sin; so when they do, God hides God's face! When children of God, who bear the name of Jesus Christ, start their bitchy, malicious talk that ruins other people, God stops up God's ears, it says. So no wonder, if out of our same mouths come cursings and blessings (James 3:1-12), false witness and true confessions, soul-searching hopes and petty, self-serving bickering—no wonder our prayers that the LORD come quickly don't get through. It takes a holy, right-doing, persevering person of utter integrity, says James 5:13-18 (cf. also Luke 11:5-13, 18:1-8), before prayer has much power and gets God doing things like healing and rescuing and restoring the glories of a new Jerusalem.

So it's not that the LORD's hand is too short or too weak to set us free from our captivities, and it's not that the LORD is hard of hearing: it's just that our own sin blocks the way between almighty God and us, rears up a blank wall so that all we get are the hollow echoes of our own self-righteous, duplicit voices. That is our misery.

Next, Isaiah 59 portrays a moving confession of sin, vv. 9-15a, in the first-person plural:

Let me paraphrase again the thrust of that biblical paragraph which we read earlier:

> We grope for the wall like blind people
>   because we don't know the way to go!
> We know how to find fault and growl, but we've lost the
>   art of how to praise you with the timbrel and dance
>   —our harps are hung up on the willow trees....
> We believers look anemic on the face of the earth,
>   making do with the tatters of Babylonian culture
>   that only cripple us the more.
> We think we are strangers in a foreign land and have
>   forgotten that we are called
> to be servants of the living God redeeming whatever our
>   hands touch!

OUR TRANSGRESSIONS, V.12, OUR sins, our iniquities, our double-crosses, denial, rebellion, oppression, revolt, deceit, curses, back-biting, injustice, falsehood, underhanded crookedness—only Psalm 51 matches the profusely rich vocabulary of these verses on the devious variants of sin—our sins testify against us! It's as if the prophet wants to exemplify how believers can make a clean breast of what separates them from God, confess fully how faithless, gutless, stupid, mean and godlessly we children of God can act—get it all out! because when there is no weaseling, no excuses, no blaming somebody else, just simply repentance that has you waiting limp, completely subject to the covenanting will of God: to such confession of sin the LORD God responds like the passionate, jealous lover God is!

59:15B THE LORD TOOK it all in—the captivity of God's people, the wickedness that prevailed, the contrite and humble admission of God's people's sin and helplessness; and it displeased the LORD that there was no justice. It bothered God that nobody was setting things straight. So God decided to set things straight all by God self! The LORD wasn't going to let the sin of God's people hold God back forever from instituting righteousness, the freedom of shalom, upon the earth. It had hurt God to see God's own special city burned to the ground, and it vexed the LORD that God's people in Babylon were developing a captive mentality—it simply shouldn't be that way among the sons and daughters of the living God who is the Ruler of the heavens and the whole earth! So, the way the prophet Isaiah tells it, 59:17, God got dressed up!

That's important, because Jeremiah 13 says God wanted to wear God's people into battle like a loin cloth, but God's people wouldn't stick to God's hips that close, didn't want to fight; so God had to discard them. Even earlier than these chapters (cf. Isaiah 20), when Judah still had time to change its ways and to forestall being raped by foreign soldiers, God had commanded the prophet Isaiah to walk around Jerusalem for three years without sandals or clothes on! in order to demonstrate to the comfortable citizens of the city of God what was coming to them if they didn't repent. That would be like God's telling the most important preacher you know to appear on TV in his underpants for a dozen television spectaculars in order to dramatize to God's people in North America how they will be stripped and mocked soon if we don't change our way of life—God feels rather naked, it seems, without God's people helping God set things straight; so God punishes in kind and strips us naked, leaves us to be barren fruit trees.

But the LORD got dressed up, it says, 59:17. God put on a vest of genuine trustworthiness, a helmet of liberating victory, the clothes of punishing retribution, and threw on a cloak of jealous love for God's people. And then, all dressed up, the LORD God stormed out of heaven to set things straight like a damned up river broken loose, in order to requite the enemies of God's children for their brutalities and to appear to Zion, to Jacob (59:20). You know what "Jacob" means? "Deceiver," the second-born, weak-kneed grandson of believing Abraham, a tricky-dick whom the LORD nevertheless picked to be God's chosen child. God got dressed up to be Redeemer of Jacobs, covenantal drop-outs! who nevertheless somehow were turned around from their prodigal waywardness to be bought back out of hock, freed from their sin as well as their captivity, given the Holy

Spirit and Word of the LORD in their hearts and mouths and hands, and restored to a full glory by the Holy One...of Jacob, to glory that starts to explode like a fireworks finale in chapters 60, 61 and 62.

THINGS REALLY START HAPPENING—a biblical reformation gets going—when God's people stop sinning. But the point we have landed on here to remember is that God all dressed up brought and brings justice, redemption, and shalom into the world when it's time, with or without God's people helping.

That's the way it's always been. When there were no saints to lead God's people in the paths of right-doing because the son of Hezekiah was a Manasseh, or when the reformation Josiah later began in Judah was set back and undermined by the wickedness of kings Jehoiakim and Zedekiah, God used, all by God self, Nebuchadnezzar! to set God's people straight. And it is so that later on when potentate Nebuchadnezzar was up on his CN Tower one night enjoying the skyline of Babylon, "the great city I myself have built," "—That's not right," said the Lord, and the next morning great King Nebuchadnezzar was on all fours eating grass like an ox, his naked body wet with the dew of heaven, his fingernails and toenails getting as long as a bird's claws, until he came to his senses and knew that the LORD God rules the rulers of people and gives power to whomever God will (Daniel 4:28-37)!

A generation later Prince Belshazzar threw a state banquet for a thousand people, tied in with a little worship service for the moon god Sin and thought he'd use some of the gold dishes that had been consecrated for offerings to the LORD —That's not right, said the LORD, and since there were no young writers or journalists among God's people able to set the ruler straight, God all-dressed-up-by-God self telegraphed the message on the wall—Daniel was called out to translate—and scared Belshazzar silly: "Tonight, O show-off king, I will require of you your life;" and the next morning great Prince Belshazzar was dead (Daniel 5).

And Isaiah revealed in earlier prophecies (44:24-45:7) that the LORD anointed! the pagan Persian Cyrus as "my servant" to set God's people free from the Babylonians, and even to start rebuilding the holy city and a new temple for the LORD!

The point is that God prefers to use men like Moses and Joshua and David or women like Deborah and Esther to carry out God's will on earth; but the LORD is willing to do it with the likes of Jacob and Rahab, Jephthah, Cyrus!, the eunuch Nehemiah, the persecuting felon Saul turned into Paul. The LORD is even prepared to set things straight all by God self, so to speak, as God did when God sent God's only begotten son into the world to be born of a virgin betrothed to a carpenter, who then suffered himself, died himself, was raised from the dead only by God self (cf. Romans 8:11); and it was all done to set God's passionately loved people permanently free from sin so they could live truly like the redeemed, free!—chapter 60 of Isaiah—saints on the earth surrounded by the halo of exciting light and holiness that spells victory! fulfillment, reunion, praising cultivation of the earth (60:21) yielding good fruit that shall go on forever and ever and ever with feasting and singing!

When you turn up the New Testament light switch on Isaiah 59-60 you see and understand from our passage that God's taking on flesh in Jesus Christ is God getting dressed up (or "dressed down," if you will); at least, God is putting on the clothes of redemption. Jesus Christ is the genuinely trustworthy, covenanting, triumphantly saving, judging and passionately sacrificing LORD in fully clothed action (cf. Colossians 2:9) intent upon setting straight the groaning of all creatures waiting for the redemption of the bodily life of us humans (Romans 8:19-23, cf. John 3;14-18). Jesus Christ as God in human dress, appearing as Redeemer for God's people, even though Jacob didn't expect God in that lowly suit of clothes or particularly want what the Messiah, the Anointed One of God-in-the-flesh, Immanuel, had to offer.

I'M NOT MAKING THIS up. Isaiah 61:1-2 was quoted by Jesus when he preached in his hometown of Nazareth (Luke 4:18-19), filled with the Holy Spirit, it says (Luke 4:14). The prophecy of Isaiah is fulfilled in me today, said Jesus (Luke 4:21, cf. Matthew 5:17-20), because I bring good news for the misfits! for broken-down, broken-hearted people, for those who are captives of their evil desires—redemption and healing and jubilee! for the blind and the lame who hang around the temple, and for the foreigners who haven't kept the commands of Moses from their youth up but who seek only the Rule of God's right-doing first (cf. Luke 18:15-30, Matthew 6:33-34)!

And that hometown congregation got so mad they tried to kill the Redeemer (Luke 4:28-30). They didn't want God's house to be a house of prayer for all kinds of handicapped people; they wanted only normal, orderly, straitlaced people with a good Abrahamic blooded pedigree (cf. Matthew 21:12-16). Already early in his earthly ministry Jesus alluded to Isaiah 59:19 when he commended the liberating faith of the Roman centurion from the far West, high above what he had found anywhere in Israel, which was busy forfeiting its birthright (Matthew 8:5-13).

All the poetry in 60:1-3 about light piercing the darkness, fascinating the nations, kings, and later on the description of camel caravans (60:6) laden with gold, frankincense and myrrh, can't help but remind you of Isaiah 9:1-7 about light piercing the darkness and the people going wild with joy because the war is over! a child has been born to us! whose name is "Miraculous counsellor, Almighty God, Everlasting Father, Prince of Shalom," and whose government shall never end! We Newer Testament believers who follow Christ know that the angel Gabriel quoted this very Isaiah passage when the angel announced to Mary that she would give birth to a boy to be called Jesus, because he would save his people from their sins and would rule over the house of Jacob forever and ever (Luke 1:30-33, cf. Matthew 1:18-22).

So we Christian readers know that Isaiah 59-60 has the revelatory dimension of God's sovereign appearance in history as the Redeemer-born Jesus Christ. Isaiah 59-60 is picked up in Luke 1-2. But we need to see that Isaiah gives that gospel body! The birth of Jesus Christ is the beginning of the end for evil doers in history (59:18). The birth of Jesus Christ is the light of the world for Orientals and Westerners (59:19), the light of the world for Romans, Greeks, Samaritans, odd balls, outcasts, middle-class—all nations, all kinds of people (60:1-3, cf. 56:1-8). The birth of Jesus Christ—never forget it, the next time you "celebrate Christmas"—was a humiliation of sorts for God: God had to get all dressed up by God self (59:16-17) because nobody could set straight what we human creatures had done! There was God all dressed up alone, and hardly anybody had a place for God to stay, as a baby (Luke 2:7) or as a grownup—I don't even have a foxhole or a bird nest, said Jesus (Matthew 8:18-22). The birth of Jesus Christ was a lonely business for God. You see, God doesn't want to be dressed up all by God self. God the LORD wants to wear God's people, and to live inside and be at home in the lives of God's children, the sons and daughters of light (Ephesians 5:3-14).

THAT'S WHERE WE NON-JEW "ethnics" can pick up Isaiah 60 now, because the birth of Jesus Christ was the crucial, historical occasion of Isaiah 59:20, and the sons and daughters of Jacob by and large boggled it (as we know from Matthew 23, Acts 13:44-52, 18:1-6, 22 and 26, Romans 9-11), with the amazing result that we who have been touched by

God's grace and moved to become children of believing Abraham by faith—whoever can pick up this book and read believingly, understanding what you read (cf. Acts 8:30-31), is given the blessing to live under its promise (Romans 4:13-25).

That's the punch line for this evening, pointed toward biblical reformation. Isaiah 60 is a live, earlier testamented promise of God whose final three-way bulb dimension has not yet been fulfilled and which holds right now for all those who take God at God's Word. You don't have to be a Jew. You don't have to be Dutch. You don't have to have been born with Christian parents, be smart or over 25. If your ears hear the Scripture for this evening, you may live as the redeemed of the LORD! It's not just me talking about the Bible for a while. Isaiah 59-60 is God talking to you.

Sure, there's a lot going on in Isaiah 56-66; chapter 56 has the astounding news that the blessings of the sabbath and worship in God's house will be open to foreigners, heathen! who join themselves to the LORD, even sexual misfits like eunuchs who join themselves to the LORD. "I want my house to be called a house of prayer," reports 56:7, "for all kinds of people." Chapters 57-58 describe basically how God's chosen folk, with leaders like dogs who have so much dog food in their bellies they can't even bark—God's folk do wicked things, because God seems so far away. The believers don't know, it says in those chapters, that the kind of "fasting" the LORD wants is to share bread with the hungry, give housing to the homeless, clothes to the naked (58:6-7 is what Matthew 25:31-46 picks up); that is, true piety, people, is not minding your P's and Q's so much as doing what liberates your neighbour from evil.

There's a lot going on in the rich chapters of 59-60 too; but it's not confusing. (1) Isaiah 59-60 held out hope for the Israelites in Babylonian captivity. (2) Jesus Christ on earth said, Isaiah is talking about me and my ministry. (3)—using all the wattage—Isaiah's prophecy speaks to us who live "in the last days," as the Newer Testament calls it (II Timothy 3:1): Isaiah 59-60 speaks to us about what's going on in history—Alberta politics and electoral reform, world-depressing economic life, secular educational policies that kidnap the minds of kids, infighting churches with left and right factions: Isaiah 59-60 speaks to us about how God does things and expects us to respond in the time since the resurrection of Jesus Christ, after his ascension and his sending the Holy Spirit publicly, so to speak, into the world at Pentecost, yet before the second and final, glorious coming of the LORD when the LORD shall restore all by himself with God's angels the creation completely, and "the redeemed shall obtain permanent gladness and joy while sorrow and mourning flee away" (Isaiah 51:11).

TO LIVE AS THE redeemed of the LORD under the promise of Isaiah 59-60 means this:

First (A), if you confess your sin and are become new men, women, youth and children, rest in the certainty that God's promises and calling to you, your believing children and grandchildren, are for keeps (Isaiah 59:21, cf. Romans 11:25-32!?). Be at peace with the gift of God's covenanting Word and Holy Spirit as the only source of comfort, wisdom, and truth=light (Isaiah 60:19, John 14:15-26)! And count on it, expect surely, that the untold wealth of the nations of the world will be refined by fire and brought to you to be offered in praise to our holy Redeemer—Isaiah 60 resonates with the triumphant, apocalyptic tones of Revelation 21:23-27.

Also, because of the confidence in your redemption offered by Jesus Christ and the restoration already beginning, which your eye of faith discerns, second (B), you girls and boys, fathers and mothers, youth, grandparents, unmarried ones: let us get dressed up… in God's clothes—that's what biblical reformation is all about! Wear the shirt of real integrity, says Ephesians 6; put on the head covering of rescuing others— let taking vengeance be God's act, the LORD's close by—wield the sword…of the Spirit! the Word of God that exposes the Lie, and pray tenaciously, because we don't fight people so much as Sin, the devil, principalities and powers wrecking things in their losing battle (Ephesians 6:10-18, Philippians 4:4-7). In anticipation of fruitful, unending cultivation of the new earth (60:21), run the race, you redeemed, in sneakers of good tidings of great joy—forgiveness, refuge, and cups brimming over shalom (Isaiah 60:18, Ephesians 6:15, Psalm 23): do not run the race in the ungodly rags of provoking recriminations (Galatians 5:13-26), hypocritical, self-righteous judgments (Matthew 7:1-5, Romans 12:3-21), and waspish stinginess (Isaiah 56:1-8, II Corinthians 9:6-9).

Biblical reformation is characterized by Martin Luther's planting a tree today even if you are certain Christ is coming back to judge the world tomorrow—so certain you are of God's faithfulness and glory and our humble task, in spite of the terrible weakness and misery we let show.

Biblical reformation is characterized by John Calvin's startling thesis that the highest calling on earth is in politics (*Institutes of the Christian Religion* 4:20), because as believing magistrate you have the office to tender God's merciful, glorious justice to disbelievers too, lightening the weight of their incredible misery.

Biblical reformation is characterized by Abraham Kuyper's institutional deed—not just talk—of inaugurating a university on a biblical, reforming basis, free under God from domination by church or state yet serving them both with academic studies dedicated solely to the glory of God, despite the miserably sinful learning that plagued it.

Biblical reformation will be characterized by you Christians in Toronto/Calgary pulling together— even if you don't like one another so much—as leaders and followers, because the LORD Jesus Christ has made you Jacobs one body to bring a concerted witness of insight and healing and sound direction in deed to this hustler of a city, which the LORD loves even more than God did Nineveh (cf. Jonah 4).

Sure, our miserable reformations come and go—Luther, Calvin, Kuyper, even our own. But the good news from Isaiah tonight for modern man and woman is this: the Christian does not have the defeatist mentality of a captive. A living Christian has utter sureness in the office of sharing in Christ's Rule of the LORD's wedding garments (cf. Matthew 22:1-14), and we go up in winsome, Reformational smoke as a living sacrifice of thanks to our risen LORD seated in heaven and waiting to come make all things permanently new.

Isaiah 60:1-2, 20b-22

Can you people in Toronto hear me? asks God.
Get up (people of God)! Let (your joy) shine (through)!
for your Light has indeed come!
The glory of the LORD God is flashing down upon you!

It's true, Darkness still covers the earth.
A depressing Darkness hangs thick over the nations of the world.
But the LORD God shall be light for you forever and ever,
    and your days of mourning shall be finished.
All your folk shall be tried-and-true citizens of right-doing;
they shall inherit and cultivate the earth forever!
—like a young shoot I planted, (says the LORD,)
    one I hand-made in order to show my stunning glory:
the most insignificant of you will become a thousandfold
    meaningful,
and the weakest of you, (my people,) shall become
    a folk of great strength!
When it's the right time,
    I the LORD God will get it done quickly!

THIS EXHORTATION OF ISAIAH 59-60 culminated a three day "Reformation Festival" organized by Bert Polman in 1976, when he was professor at Ontario Bible College (now Tyndale University).
Friday opening event:
Devotions by, John Franklin, Ontario Bible College,
Keynote address, "Art, Worship, and the City," Nicholas Wolterstorff, Calvin College (now Calvin University)

Saturday 10:00 a.m. to 4:30 p.m.
Workshops on liturgy and the arts
1. Music for children
   Urban art
   Liturgy for baptism
2. Contemporary music
   writings of Margaret Atwood
   Liturgy for Lord's Supper
3. Film on worship, "Many Different Gifts"
4. Principles for liturgical change
   Church music—organ and choral literature

Sunday evening,
Festive worship in Convocation Hall, University of Toronto, "Isaiah 59-60," 1976. Calvin Seerveld, Institute for Christian Studies.

> Meditation modified was also
> presented at the Christian Reformed Churches
> of Calgary, Alberta, on Reformation Day,
> 31 October 1982

10

The Incredible Generosity of God for us Ungrateful Pixilated People: Becoming a Listening, Faithful tzaddiq

Texts: Ezekiel 18, Matthew 20:1-16, Romans 4:4-8

["pixilated"—NO; "tzaddiq"—YES]

God's people surviving around Jerusalem in 600 BC had been Godless enough, off and on, for 15 generations since Kings Saul, David, and Solomon, so that God finally had most of them deported to the faraway land of Babylon, superpower of the day. Son of a priest, the visionary prophet Ezekiel, and his wife, who lived around that time of Jeremiah, was deported to Babylon too in 597 BC, when young wiseman Daniel was sent to Nebuchadnezzar's court as a counsellor. Ezekiel lived in Babylon, not at the palace but uncomfortably with God's exiled people—no temple, no sacrifices—who were grumbling, "We're stuck here in this God-forsaken foreign land because our parents sinned! The older generation disobeyed God, so **we** get cavities in our teeth; **we suffer because our parents were wicked!**"

Ezekiel 18: 1-5, 9, 19b-20, 26-32

AND THE WORD OF the LORD God came to me again saying: What is it with all of you from the land of Israel mouthing this proverb:

"The fathers (and mothers) have eaten sour unripe grapes, so their children's teeth are pixilatedly frayed."[1]

As I live, says my Lord,[2] the LORD God, this proverb should certainly not be spoken any longer by you people of Israel! Do you know why?

---

1 To translate the proverb of Ezekiel 18:2 I couldn't help but use the wonderful word "pixilated," which means "unbalanced," "daffy." קהיוּהת means "whimsically ground-down," "peculiarly sensitive." Martin Buber translates it," Söhnen werden Zähne stumpf!" The good King James translation of the Ezekiel 18:2 proverb has "the children's teeth are set on edge," meaning "The next generation's bite is toothy awry, teeth are mismatched, a bit nervous, anxious. So, with a little license, I translate תקהינה as "bluntly sloughed off"; the teeth are "set-on-edge scratchy," like grinding fingernails on a blackboard—"pixilatedly frayed." Eugene Peterson's paraphrase radically changes the biblical metaphor, but makes the proverb's point: "The parents ate green apples, The children got stomachache?"

2 אדני יהוה (Adonai Yahweh): "Adonai" is a more intimate and gentle designation for God, as "my Lord," while "Yahweh" specifies the Covenantal LORD God who has officially taken Israel/Judah under God's almighty wing for keeps.

All living persons belong directly to me. Do you people get it? The parent person as well as the child person belongs directly to me. That's right! So **only the living person who sins, that person courts death.**

(vv. 5, 9) **A man or woman who is a tzaddiq** (צדיק)[3] **does what is mercifully just and truly reliable** (משפט וצדקה)—**the tzaddiq walks in my creational ordinances** (בחקותי), **and keeps my promising judgments** (משפטי), **in order to do what is truly reliable** (אמת): **that person is a tzaddiq, and shall surely live, says my Lord, the LORD God** (נאם אדני יהוה)

(vv. 19b-20)…If the child has engaged in what is mercifully just and really trustworthy, carefully kept all my creational ordinances (והבן משפט וצדקה עשה את כל־חקותי שמר ויעשה אתם היח יהיח) then that child shall surely live. The living person who sins shall die. **The child shall not have to bear the guilty sin** (עון) **of the parent, just as the parent does not have to bear the guilty sin of the child. The trustworthy reliability of the tzaddiq is owned by the** (עליו) צדיק), **and the godless wickedness** (רשע) **of the wicked person is owned by the wicked self** (עליו).

(vv. 26-29) When a צדיק turns away from right-doing integrity and commits strange wrong-doing (עול) and strangles in their evil (בעולו), for the wrong-doing committed, that person shall have to die. Nevertheless when a wicked person turns away from his or her evil doing which they have been doing, and then does what is mercifully just and full of trustworthy integrity (משפט וצדקה), those persons shall certainly save their life. Because that wicked person carefully looked at and reflected on (what he or she was doing), and **turned away from all the strange wrong-doing** (פשעיו)

---

3   *Tzaddiq* (a "righteous" person") = One who has genuine integrity, a *Bewährter*, one who withstands and comes through for God while and when being tested by temptations and troubles.

which was being done, he or she shall surely live, they shall not have to die.

Yet the house of Israel says, "The Way of my Lord is not right (יתכן)."

Is it not **your** ways, O house of Israel, that are not right?

(vv. 30-32) Therefore, says my Lord, the LORD God, "O house of Israel, I will judge you (אשפט), every human person, on his or her own way of life. So repent and turn away from all your misdeeds (פשעיכם) lest they be the stumbling block stupidity (למכשול עון) that trips you up. Throw away from yourselves all your unfaithful misdeeds with which you people made yourselves disobedient. And **strive to ready for yourselves a new heart and a new spirit. Why would you want to die, O house of Israel, for I have no pleasure in the death of those who must die,"** says my Lord, the LORD God. "So turn yourselves around and stay alive!" (והשיבו וחיו)

This is the Word of the Lord!
Thanks be to God

It is important to realize when you read the finished Bible we have in our hands, that God's Word spoken truly at different times in history **develops** the revelation of God's will for us to understand.

The proverb the disgruntled Babylonian captive Jews were repeating, to blame their parents, came from their distorted remembering the Mosaic catechism they had learned (Exodus 20:5): "The jealous LORD God will punish children for the idolatrous iniquity of their parents to the third and fourth generation"—

Ezekiel 18 does not contradict Exodus 20:5, but subtly fills in, you need to remember the next verse of Exodus 20:6

too: "but the jealous LORD God will show abiding covenantal love **to the thousandth! generation** of those who love Me," says God, "and keep my commandments."

OF COURSE, ONE GENERATION benefits or is handicapped by what it inherits from the previous generation's cultural acts. When my brother and I came home from school in the late 1940s, there would be a Mother-homemade double-sized (12"x20") chocolate cake with rich chocolate icing and a quart of milk waiting for us. So my childhood was filled with unpleasant dental appointments, because in those days you got a dulling needle only for pulling teeth, not for the painful drilling to fix cavities. But my parents also read us kids the Bible in such a normal way you came to believe, yes, it was **God's words!**

Ezekiel 18:19-20 says clearly what God had already told Moses in Deuteronomy 24:16: Parents shall not be punished for their children's wrong-doing, nor shall children be punished for their parent's wrong-doing; only for their own sin shall a person be punished.

So don't try to pass the buck, and absolve your complicity, you exiled people in Babylon (or in Toronto, blaming your parents for your hang-ups). The LORD God will judge each of you on your very own Way-of-life (Ezekiel 18:30). So own up on where you stand now as a community. Is what you trust unwaveringly solid? Is your communal witness first of all one of tears and praise **to God**?

EZEKIEL 18 HAS A further fascinating revelation, beyond straightening out the limited responsibility of generations.

God opens up the matter of your personal past related to your personal present. Anybody who has a history of doing bad things, big or small, and turns over a new leaf, and starts to be merciful to others and trustworthy, that person shall be blessed with life, forever! But any person who has done good things all his or her life, and begins to commit strange evil deeds, big or little, will trip over their stupidity,and die out—

"That's not fair, God," said the exiled Jewish believers. "You forget the misdeeds a person did, wipe the slate clean, but don't remember the good deeds a person did, to their credit!"

"Look," says my Lord, the LORD God—this is the most gentle expression in the whole rough and tumble book of Ezekiel—"I don't want to punish anybody, and have people die; so, regardless of wanting credit for being a sometime do-gooding fellow--you exiles have not been so pure-minded and perfect as you think[4]—repent, stop bitching, turn around, and become a *tzaddiq*, one who **gratefully** walks in my creational ordinances of caring love, keeps my promising directive of listening to Me, and just do what is truly long-sufferingly reliable in your circumstances."

NOW WE READ THE Newer Testament follow-up in the gospel according to Matthew 20:1-16:

Matthew 20:1-16

IN THE KINGDOM OF Heaven-Rule it goes something like this: A superintendent went out very early in the morning to hire workers for his vineyard. Upon agreeing with the workers for a denarius a day (the usual wage), he sent them to work in the vineyard.

---

4   Cf. II Kings 17:5-23, especially vv. 19-20.

Going out around nine o'clock he saw others just standing around in the marketplace. The Super said to them, "You go work in the vineyard too, and I'll pay you whatever is right. So they went.

When the Super went out again around noon and at three P.M., he did the same thing. And then around five o'clock when he went out, he found still others just standing around; so the Super said to them, "Why are you just standing idle all day here?" And they said to the Super, "Because nobody hired us (to work)." He said to them, "You go (work) in the vineyard too."

When it was around evening sunset time, the Owner of the vineyard said to his Super, "Call the workers and give them their pay, beginning with the last and then going on to the first."

When those hired around five o'clock came, the Super gave them a denarius (the usual daily wage). Now when those hired first (early in the morning) came, they supposed that they would receive more; but each of them too received the one denarius. So when they received it, they started grumbling against the Land-Owner, "Those last guys only worked one hour, and you paid them equal to us who bore the burden of the (whole) day and the burning heat!"

But the Owner answered one of the protesters, "My good fellow, I am doing you no wrong. Didn't you agree with me to work for a denarius (the usual daily wage)? Take away what belongs to you, and go. I willingly choose to give to the last fellow the same as I gave you. Is it not permissible for me to do what I choose with what belongs to me? Or is your eye envious, because I am kinder than necessary (ἀγαθός, gütig, generous)?"

That's the way it will be (in the Kingdom-Rule of God): the last (or "least") shall be first, and the first ("those apparently most deserving") shall come last.

This, too, is the Word of the Lord!
Thanks be to God!

Jesus told this parable-story to his closest disciples who had just expressed astonishment that Jesus said a rich man or woman would have great trouble getting into the Kingdom of heaven, and then Peter chortled, "Well, **we** left everything to follow you!"—to which Jesus agreed, but then told this parable to try to help teach his disciples, including us, how unlike us humans God figures things and acts.

Why did the labourers who worked the whole day for a regular day's wage get so upset—"That's not fair!"—rather than be glad that the fellows who worked only part of the day also got enough money that day to buy food for their families? Those "full-time" workers in the Lord's vineyard are like the Babylonian exiled Jews who couldn't stand it that God **forgave** the past evil deeds of persons who "turned around," because they got something for nothing. It's like the elder son in another Jesus parable (Luke 15:11-322) who gruffly, bitterly told the Father, "I've slaved all my years for You, and You never gave me even a goat for a birthday party, but when this young black sheep of the family voluntarily comes back to the fold, you slay the fattened calf in his honour for a banquet!"

What the disgruntled exiled Jews in Babylon, the long hot-day labourers, and the dutiful elder son did not get is that the **God of the holy Scriptures not only forgives <u>sinners</u>, but is <u>generous</u> with blessings.**

We humans look out first of all for yourself; it's also right, we believe, to get what you work for, and don't jump the line. But God sees things differently, according to the Bible, upside-down, least first and first last. **God has no pleasure in**

punishing people. God's justice is not getting an eye for an eye and a tooth for a tooth (Matthew 5:38[5]), a full day's work slaved at for a full day's pay. **God turns the other cheek and gives people more than what is deserved or earned.**

The Biblical word for this action of the Covenanting God is "Grace," χάρις, **undeserved** mercy, surprising surplus, happy-making, joyful spoken fulfillment of needs. "That's somewhat like the way my Olympic hockey experience felt," Danelle said quietly. "Out of the blue, I got called to play glorious, prestigious Olympic hockey."

We people are naturally selfish, covetous, often stingy, don't want to lose face. The "forgiveness" we practice is more like bargaining and arranging bail: our antagonist gets temporary release, with forfeiture of the security if you hurt me again. God's offered forgiveness is a permanent amnesty. God simply **forgets** (Jeremiah 31:34) our peevish vanity and respectable put-downs of neighbours and any godless dirty deeds, because God self in Jesus Christ **erases** what **we** did wrong, blames it on Jesus! (II Corinthians 5:21[6]) who says, "Yes, I did it!" and therefore **justifies us** frivolous or mean or self-serving humans.

EZEKIEL AND MATTHEW'S MESSAGE about God's ready forgiveness and bountiful grace is so hard for us humans to accept and believe, because of our ingrown penchant for

---

5   Cf. Exodus 21:23-25, Leviticus 24:19-20, Deuteronomy 19:21.

6   "God made Jesus, who did not know sin firsthand, to be sinfulness on our behalf, so that we might in Jesus Christ own the justified righteousness God requires." Cf. also Hebrews 2:9.

work righteousness and our abiding Reformed awareness of our being sinful. The apostle Paul wrestled with the dispersed Jews in Asia Minor throughout his missionary ministry to disabuse their serious conviction of do-it-yourself-salvation. You are not saved from sinfulness by your deeds (Romans 9:16[7]), no matter how hard you try, although you will be judged by the Way you live, the spirit in which you do things daily (Psalm 62:12; II Corinthians 5:10; Revelation 2:23c).

Take Father Abraham, writes Paul: Abraham was declared righteous by God, not because he had done something special to earn it, been circumcised, but because God called him to lead a special (stubborn) people which God had chosen to be an unlikely light for the whole world (Genesis 12:1-3), and Abraham believed God's out-of-the-blue call, and decided to do it (Genesis 12:4, 15:6; Romans 4:1-3,22).

And then Scripture declares Romans 4:4-8:

Romans 4:4-8

"To the person who works, wages are not counted as if they dropped out of heaven (κατὰ χάριν, a free gift, as if given by grace): wages are what you deserve to get (for working). But to the person who is not working to get something, yet trusts (πιστεύοντι) in **the One** (=God) **who makes good for** (justifies) **the ungodly person**, that trusting is reckoned (λογίζεται) toward that person's justification (δικαιοσύνην, being righteous, a tzaddiq)."

This matter is comparable to what David says about the happiness (μακαρισμόν, blessedness) of those people to whom God grants justified status (δικαιοσυνήν) without their working for it:

---

7   Cf. Romans 9:1-18; Galatians 2:15, 3:5; Ephesians 2:1-10.

"Happy are those whose law-breakings have been forgiven, and whose sinful wrong-doings have been covered over. Truly well-off is the man (or woman) to whom the Lord does not impute (λογίσηται, יחשׁב) sin at all!"[8]

This is amazing stuff in Romans 4: Paul, turned-around Saul, is quoting dirty David who became "a man after God's own heart"—believe it or not, the Bible (I Samuel 13:14, Acts 13:22)!

I PUT IN BOLDFACE what is practically unbelievable, the crux of the Bible's good news: **God in Jesus Christ makes good for the <u>ungodly</u>!**

That factual revelation tops up Ezekiel's notice of God's strange forgiveness for turned-around sinners, and Matthew's account of God's generous nature, by certifying that we women and men, even the most ungodly (any hardened hypocrites here?) can be made whole, become right with God, by God self, the Owner of the vineyard. You are not **saved** by your works—all you routinely do in Church, how sweetly helpful you are toward other people during the week. Strictly speaking, you are not saved by **your** faith either! Remember the key passage of Ephesians 2:8: "Yes, **by grace** you have been saved, *through* faith, and this (faith) is not your own doing: it is the **gift of God.**"

Most of us raised in the Church have heard that verse before, but I think I am just beginning to grasp the enor-

---

8 My hunch is that David wrote Psalm 32 a couple of years after he wrote Psalm 51, when the Bathsheba dust had settled a bit.

mity of the point. If **my** faith is not a work that saves me, if **my** faith does not merit salvation and is simply the conduit for how salvation happens and becomes "effective" (Romans 3:25): if only God's gift is what counts, how do I get it! without working for it?

How did childless Abraham busy doing "works" with Hagar, how did murderer-adulterer David, tax collector for the imperialist Romans Matthew, Paul who had been killer Saul: how did they get God's gift of total forgiveness and generous blessing reckoned to them (Romans 4:22) with a life of tumultuous shalom?

Simply by responding to the Super Holy Spirit's call to follow Jesus into the vineyard as God's adopted child.

You may not fully understand this, Nicodemus, but you need to be born again like a little child, get a new heart and a fresh grateful spirit. Don't stay grown-up intelligent and ponder tiresomely whether God chose you from eternity or not—am I an 'elect' or be I a 'reprobate.' No, if you have an open ear and can hear like a child this live wire of the Scriptures, maybe "out-of-the-blue," **you are being called by God right now!**

> "All you who are tired, worn out, carrying heavy burdens, come to me, and I will give you rest" (Matthew 11:28-30),"says Jesus.

> "If you rest in me, and my words abide alive in you, ask for whatever you wish, my child, and it shall be given to you" (John 15:7), says Jesus Christ.

And Jesus Christ is as historically real a person as Shakespeare or Abraham Lincoln, the Son of God born of the virgin Mary and crucified under Roman governor Pontius Pilate. This Bible too, trusted and disputed by grownups for more than 20 centuries, is as truly God's words and directive for us as God speaking to Moses on Mount Sinai in the desert and Jesus confiding to his 12 disciples in Galilee, Palestine.

All a person needs to do is heartfelt say as the startled young boy Samuel once did, "Speak, Lord, for your servant is listening…" (I Samuel 3). "Yes, Jesus loves me! this I know, for the Bible tells me so…in Ezekiel, the gospel according to Matthew, and the apostle Paul's letter to the Romans."

THE HEIDELBERG CATECHISM, the confession of our Reformational Catholic communion has it exactly right:

Lord's Day 23
Question & Answer 61

Q. Why do you say that by faith alone you are right with God?

A. It is not because of any value my faith has that God is pleased with me. Only Christ's satisfaction, righteousness, and holiness make me right with God. And I can receive this righteousness and make it mine in no other way than by faith alone.

Lord's Day 25
Question and Answer 65

Q. It is by faith alone that we share in Christ and all his blessings: where then does that faith come from?

A. The Holy Spirit produces it in our hearts by the preaching of the holy gospel, and confirms it through our use of the holy sacraments.

Those answers interpret Romans 5:1: "Therefore, since we are justified by faith (worked in us by the Holy Spirit) we have peace with God, thanks to our Lord Jesus Christ."

You don't need to stay a kid forever—God welcomes and provides for maturity—but "childlike simple" is the only way to enter the Kingdom of Heaven (Mark 10:13-16), **trusting what you hear from the Scriptures.**

So, whether you hear the Good News of forgiveness and the call to work in the vineyard early in the morning, or at five o'clock, maybe even later in your life time: trust the calling of the Lord, "Come on in, the water's fine; learn to swim in the Bible!" Come to revel in reading the Scriptures, truly hearing the LORD God speak to you in what is written down. Enjoy celebrating the eucharist with other adopted children, because celebrating liturgically the Lord's Supper is the place where you together practise saying, "Oh, Yes, I remember your death and resurrection for me, dear Jesus Christ." And then one receives more and more grace to develop what Proverbs 22:9 calls "a **generous** (thankful) eye" like that of the Owner and Super in Jesus' story Matthew 20 recorded, "so you share your bread with the poor."

EZEKIEL—UNDESERVED FORGIVENESS FOR turned-around sinners—the gospel according to Matthew—God's grace is overflowingly generous—and Romans (the whole Bible hangs together)—we respectable-looking ungodly people are justified who childlikely accept the Holy Spirit God's calling us to go out as a simple *tzaddiq* and thankfully pick ripened sweet grapes for the up-and-coming generation so their teeth will not be pixilatedly frayed.

Closing Prayer

THANK YOU, GOD, FOR calling each one here who heard Your incredible offer of forgiveness for our continual failures to love You wholly and our neighbours as we carefully treat ourselves.

Please get that good news through our noggins, so we can rejoice and be thankful, faithful, and excited harvesters of grapes you have planted in Willowdale, Toronto, and in countries around the world—

We pray in the Name of Jesus Christ, our Lord, Amen!

Psalm 115 (as benediction)

Leader: Not for us, LORD, not for us,
but do something glorious for Your name!
Make something solid and shining to show Your
covenanting Grace and utterly dependable faithfulness!
Why should the peoples all around say,
"And where now is their God"?

People: **Our God is in heaven!**
Everything that pleases God, God completes!

Leader: Their "gods" are solid gold and silver,
but made by a human hand.
Their fake gods have a mouth but cannot speak;
they have eyes but cannot see!
Ears they have but can not hear;
a nose is there, but they cannot smell
their hands cannot touch things.
Their feet cannot go for a walk.
No sound passes through their throat.

People: **Like them become those who made them!**
Like them become all those who feel secure with them.

Leader: Israel! get to feel secure with the LORD God:
People: **a relief and a protection is the LORD for such people.**
Leader: [Priestly] house of Aaron!
    bind yourselves only to the LORD God:
People: **a relief and a protection is the LORD for such people.**
Leader: You [newcomers] who fear Yahweh!
    trust—trust the Lord God:
People: **a relief and a protection is God for such people.**

Leader: The LORD God has kept us in mind: God shall bless—
People: **Bless the house of Israel!**
    Bless the [priestly] house of Aaron!
    Bless those who fear the LORD God!
Leader: —the unimportant ones together with the very important ones....
    May the LORD God prosper you, you and your children.
    May you all be blessed by the LORD God,
        who made heaven and earth.
    Heaven [you know] belongs specially to the LORD:
    the earth is what God gave for the sons and daughters
        of man [to tend].
    Dead men and women do not praise the LORD,
    not one of those who have gone down to where it is deathly still.
    But we people here, let us praise the LORD!
    from now on and forevermore:
People: **Thank God—hallelujah!**

        28 July 2019
        Willowdale Christian Reformed Church
        Toronto, Ontario

11

The LORD God is a Prodigal God who Gives Grace to Sinners Even Before they are Historically Ready to be Delivered from their Captivities

TEXTS: Ezekiel 33:1-20, 34:1-16, 20-31, with Luke 15

I CANNOT COUNT ON everybody's having prepared for the message by reading chapters 33-34 of Ezekiel during the past week; so I'll excerpt from those chapters in a careful idiomatic translation before we go to Luke 15. Maybe you could just listen, as if you are hearing a Bible story told to grown-ups. The key thing is to hear **the tone** of what is written for us, and to realize that Ezekiel and Luke are connected—the Bible is one amazing interconnected true story book—"shepherds"/"shepherd." God seems to repeat the message again and again, as if the people to whom Ezekiel and Jesus brought God's Word had a short attention span or were in a hurry to do something other than listen to God talking to them, so God wanted to try to make certain they could get the point—"shepherds"/"shepherd."

A FEW YEARS AFTER VIP intellectuals like Daniel and his educated friends were deported from Judah to Babylon (605 BC), Ezekiel and his wife—he was the son of an important priest in Judah—were taken away from home to Babylon in 597 BC. That's as if all of you were roughed up by foreign soldiers and had been shipped off to Cairo, let's say, Babylon—a bewildering, rich wicked city-state like London, Paris, Moscow, New York City and Tokyo all combined. You didn't know the language, but your kids were exposed to its pop songs, films and fast food. This was punishment by God—called "the sword" by Ezekiel—for having lived pious godless lives for a generation. Your believing relatives and friends in Toronto/Hamilton, Ottawa and Montreal had suffered a similar "sword" 125 years ago, and had been shipped off to Asia, scattered throughout Siberia, by superpower Assyria.

After a few years in Babylon, God called Ezekiel to be a prophet, a "lookout" watchman for God's people, a little late in the game. After 10 years in Babylon the Great, Ezekiel's wife dies (Ezekiel 24), just about the time, 587 BC, Jerusalem, Toronto/Hamilton, the City of David—like "heaven on earth" for the believing Jew—was burned to the ground by Nebuchadnezzar's Babylonian soldiers. No heaven anymore ever to go back to!? What now? said God's people exiled in Babylon.

Ezekiel 33:1-6, 10-20, 34:1-16, 20-31

(33:1-6) THE WORD OF THE LORD God came to me [says Ezekiel]:

"Son of Man (Adam), speak to the children of your people, tell them (God says), When I let a sword come upon a land, and people of the land appoint a certain person from among their leaders, make him or her to be "lookout person" for them; [if and when] "the lookout" sees the sword coming upon the land and blows on the *shofer* [long, booming alpine-sort horn] to warn the people; upon hearing the sound of the *shofer*, if anybody fails to take warning, and the sword comes and finishes off him or her, that person's blood shall be on his or her own head. Whoever has heard the sound of the *shofer* and does not take warning, that person is self responsible. If he or she had taken the warning, they would have saved their life.

"However, if 'the lookout' sees the sword coming and does not blow on the *shofer* so the people are not warned, and the sword comes and takes away the life of one of them, that person is indeed taken away in his or her guilty transgression but for the lifeblood of that person I hold 'the lookout' responsible...."

(33:10) "SO, YOU (EZEKIEL), YOU son of man (Adam), tell the house of Israel, this is what you people said [when you were undergoing the destruction of Jerusalem]: 'Our rebellious misdeeds and punishable sins are upon us! We are wasting away because of them—how can we go on living?'"

GOD TELLS EZEKIEL, My people have been scattered all over the map because their shepherds were not looking out for them; so it looks as if my sheep will die in their aimless, godless, guilt-punished exiled living.

(33:11-20) "Go tell them, (Ezekiel): As I live, says my Lord the LORD God, '**I take no pleasure in the death of guilty wrongdoers, but rather that the wicked turn around from their crooked way and live!** Turn around! turn around from your crooked evil ways! Why do you want to die, O household of Israel?!'

"So, you son of man (Adam), say to the children of your people: the integrity of the right-doing fellow will not save him or her on the day of their sinful disobedience; and the wickedness of the godless—he or she will not be stumbled by it on the day they turn away from wickedness. [The right-doing person will not be able to live by his or her righteousness on the day when they sin.] Though I say to the right-doing person, 'you shall surely live': if that person trusts in his or her integrity and commits what is wrong, all of his or her right-doing will not be remembered; that person shall die, because of the stupid wrong-doing committed."

It's true, says God, "righteous" observance of laws will not save you.

"Again, though I say to the godless, 'you shall surely die': yet if the underhanded crooked fellow turns away from his or her sinful offense and does what is just and right—gives back the pledge [taken for a loan], restores what was taken by robbery, keeps on **walking in the ordinances of [genuine] living**, [v.15 is important] without committing stupid wrong, that person shall surely live and not die. All the sins which he or she has committed will not at all be remembered against him or her. If he or she has done what is just and right, that person shall live.

"The children of your people keep on saying, 'It's not proper—this Way of my Lord—' But you know what? **Their** "way" is not 'proper'!

"When a trustworthy person turns away from actually doing what is right and commits what is truly foolish, it means death approaches that person by those stupid deeds. But when a wicked person turns away from doing what is wicked and starts doing what is just and right, because of those trustworthy deeds, they shall begin truly living.

"But you people keep on saying, 'The Way my Lord does things is not quite right'….

(Listen!) **"I will judge each one of you, O house of Israel, according to the Way you walk.…"**

(34:1-9) THE WORD OF THE LORD God came to me [says Ezekiel]:

"Son of Man (Adam), prophesy **against** the shepherds of Israel.

"Prophesy, tell them, yes, especially the shepherds [the lookout persons], thus says my Lord [Adonai] the LORD God, 'Woe to you busy shepherds of Israel who have been putting **yourselves** out to pasture: should not the shepherds take care of **the sheep**!?"

"You [shepherds] consume milk, you dress up with [the sheep] wool, you slaughter the fattened one for sacrifices; but you do not feed the flock [=give them good pasture]. Those suffering weakness you have not strengthened, the sick you have not helped get well, the broken-hearted/crippled ones you have not held and given aid, those who strayed away you did not bring back home, those who got completely lost you did not go looking for: you have brutally dominated the sheep with oppressive force. So the sheep were scattered (all over the place) because there was no [attending] shepherd; they became food for all the wild beasts of the field. They were scattered everywhere—my sheep [says God] were aimlessly wandering all over the mountains, on every high hill, my flock of sheep were scattered over the whole face of the earth—there was nobody searching (for them), nobody looking out (for them).…"

"Therefore, you 'shepherds,' hear the Word of the LORD God: As I live, says my Lord the LORD God, is it not so!: because my sheep have become prey, my sheep have become food for all the wild beasts because there is no [attending] shepherd, and my shepherds are not looking out for my sheepfold; but the 'shepherds' have given **themselves** [green] pastures and have not given good pasture to my sheep; therefore, you 'shepherds,' hear the Word of the LORD God."

THEN GOD HAS EZEKIEL remonstrate strongly against the delinquent shepherds of God's scattered/scatter-brained people:

(34:10-16) "THUS SAYS MY LORD the LORD God, Do you realize!? I stand **against** 'the shepherds.'?! I will demand my flock of sheep back from their hand. I will stop them from pasturing sheep. And no longer will the shepherds just take care of themselves. And I will grab my sheep safe out of their mouths so they will not become food for those 'shepherds.'

"For **thus says my Lord the LORD God, It is I, I myself will go find my sheep; I will see to it they are truly looked after.** Just as a shepherd looks out for his flock in a day when he is smack in the midst of his sheep spread all over the map, **so will I truly look after my flock of sheep.**

"I will snatch them away from all the places where they have been scattered on a day of obscuring clouds and thick darkness. I will lead them out [exodus!] from being among the peoples (of the world). I will gather them from all over the earth and bring them into their own land, and I will tender them food on the mountainsides of Israel nearby running waters in all the inhabited places of the land. I will shepherd them on good pasture. Their meadows will be on the mountainous best spot of Israel. There they shall lie down in good green grass; they shall graze in verdant pastures on the mountain sides of Israel.

"**I myself will be shepherd of my sheep. I will get them to lie down [for rest], says my Lord the LORD God.** I will look out for those who are completely lost, those who have strayed away I will bring back home, the wounded/handicapped I will hold close and give aid to them, and I will give strengthening resources to the weak. But I will ruin the fat cats and the strong-arm boys—I will treat <u>them</u> to justice!"

(34:20-24)…"THEREFORE, THUS SAYS MY Lord Yahweh God [to all **sheep**]: That's right! I, I myself will judge between fat sheep and thin sheep, because you [stronger ones] have pushed aside with flank and shoulder all the weak sickly ones and knocked them down with your horns until you have shattered/scattered them abroad. But I will liberate my sheep so they shall no longer be there as prey (for the powerful). I will judge what is right between sheep and sheep. And I will set up over them one single shepherd who shall lead them to good pasture—my servant "David." He shall lead and feed them, and shall be shepherd to them. And I, the LORD God, will be God for them; my servant David shall be prince among them—I the LORD God have said it!

(34:25, 28-31) "I WILL SET UP WITH them a covenant of shalom and shall banish wild beasts from the earth so that my sheep may dwell securely (even) in the wilderness and be able to sleep (safely) in the woods!…No more shall they be prey for the (godless) nations (*goiim*); animals of the earth shall no longer devour them: they shall dwell with security and nothing will terrorize them. I will provide fabulous gardens for them so that no more will they undergo suffering hunger on the earth and will never again have to bear the humiliation before the [godless] nations. Then **they shall know intimately I the LORD God Yahweh am their God, I am with them**, and the household of Israel are my folk—thus says my Lord the LORD God.

"O you, <u>my</u> sheep, the sheep of <u>my</u> pasture—you mortal creatures!—I am your God!" thus says my Lord the LORD God."

This is the Word of the Lord!
Thanks be to God!

With Ezekiel 33-34 fresh in our minds—first spoken to the dispersed sheep, the people of God in strange environs, and about **bad** shepherds, and God saying, "I'm going to take over directly as shepherd" —let's also hear the way Luke reports in chapter 15 on Jesus' fulfilling the "David task" as a prince shepherding God's people. Rabbi Jesus acted more like a storyteller in the tradition of "the wise" than as a "Thus says the LORD" prophet. But Jesus brought the Word of God to sheep and goats and even the 'shepherds' in Israel who, in Jesus' day too, instead of taking care of the harassed sheep wandering aimlessly around (Matthew 9:35-37), were taking care of **themselves** and their perks.

This is the gospel according to Luke 15.

Luke 15

Now there were all the corrupt collaborating tax collectors and outright sinners around there who kept coming to Jesus to be listening to him. Both the [very proper] Pharisees and [the legally trained theological] teachers grumbled disgruntledly: "This fellow hosts! outright sinners and is sitting down to eat meals with them!"

So Jesus told the [orthopractic] Pharisees and the theologically straight leaders this story:

Would not anyone of you who had responsibility for a hundred sheep and lost one of them not leave behind the 99 in the desert and go off to look for the lost one until he find it? And upon finding the lost one he puts it up on his shoulders, and is very glad. Coming back to the family home he calls together all his friends and the neighbours and says to them, "Be happy and congratulate me, because I found my sheep, the lost one!"

Let me tell you, [said Jesus]: Just like that there shall be joy in heaven over one sinner who is turned around [to obey God] rather than over 99 righteous ones who have no need of a turnaround.

Or, (take this story):

Suppose a certain woman who has ten drachma loses one drachma. Will she not light a lamp, sweep the house, and look (for it) carefully until she find it? And upon finding the lost coin, does she not call together her friends and neighbours and say, "Be happy and congratulate me, because I have found the drachma which I lost!"

Let me tell you, [said Jesus]: In just the same way, joy happens in the presence of God's angels over one sinner who [at heart] is turned around [to God].

Then Jesus told (them) another story:

A certain man had two sons. The younger of the two said to the father, "Father, give me (now) the part of the possessions that will fall my way (by inheritance)."

So the father divided up his livelihood between them.

After not many days the younger son, converting all the goods into cash, got away from home to some place faraway, and there he scattered his goods while living prodigally.

It happened, after he had squandered all he had, there came a powerful famine in that faraway place, and (especially) he began to suffer from want. So he went searching and attached himself to one of the citizens of that faraway country who sent him off to one of his estates to feed pigs. And he really wanted to stuff his belly from the leftover cobs of what the swine chomped on—nobody was giving him (anything).

Coming to himself he said, "How many of my father's hired workers do not enjoy more than enough food to eat, while here I am starving to death from hunger. I'll get up, go to my father, and say to him, 'Father, I sinned against Heaven right in front of you. I am no longer worthy to be called your son. Make me to be one of your hirelings.'"

So the younger son got up and went off to his own father.

While the younger son was still a long way off, his father saw him and was deeply moved with tenderness. Running! the father fell on his son's neck and kissed him profusely ("prodigally").

The son said to him, "Father, I sinned against Heaven right in front of you. I am no longer worthy to be called your son—"

But the father said to his slaves, "Quick! Get the finest robe out of storage and clothe him! Put a ring on his hand and shoes on his feet! Bring out the fattened calf, slaughter it, and digging into the festive meal let's make merry! For this fellow, my son, was dead, but has come to life again! This fellow, my son, was lost, but has been found!"

So they began to party and feast.

Now the father's older son was, of course, out working in the field. As he came near to the house, he heard good music and much dancing. Summoning one of the young boys the older son kept on asking, "What in the world could all this goings-on be about!?"

And the boy told the older brother, "Your brother has come, and your father has slaughtered the fattened calf, because your father has received your brother back safe and sound."

The older son became angry, and he refused to join in.

Then his father came out and entreated him (to join the party).

But he answered the father by saying, "Look, for so many years I slaved away for you, and never did I go against your command; but never did you for me give so much as a (little) goat so I could party with **my** friends. But when this (other) son of yours, who gluttonously devoured your life's possessions with prostitutes! comes back, for **him** you slaughter the fattened calf!?"

But the father said to the older angry son, "My child, you are indeed always with me, and **all that is mine is yours!** It was proper to throw a party and to be joyful, because this fellow, your brother, was dead, but now is alive again! He was lost, but now has been found!"

This, too, is the Word of the Lord!
Thanks be to God!

FOR US TO GET THE point of Jesus' stories in Luke 15 we need to realize Jesus was trying to reach the 99 sheep who didn't think they were lost or "prodigal" (Luke 15:1-3,7).

Jesus did not tell these 3 stories to try to reach young people going off the deep end, using drugs at raves or runaways who have to turn to prostitution on the city streets to get food to stay alive and feed their addiction. Jesus was trying to reach good suburban, temple-going folk who can pray in public, as the Pharisees did (Mark 12:38-40, Luke 18:9-14), give exact tithes from their net income (Matthew 23:23-24), and knew and could debate in public the right dogmatic answers (Matthew 22:15-40), especially on how to conduct yourselves properly (Luke 10:25-29).

THE POINT OF JESUS' first two stories about the one lost sheep and the one lost loonie is that **God relentlessly hunts down whoever wanders off or gets lost,** the way a **good** shepherd or a diligent housekeeper does it. You don't wait for mixed-up, direction-confused people to pull out their global positioning satellite system gizmo, give you their moral latitudinal-longitudinal coordinates and say, "Okay, please come and rescue me"—

But the first two stories in Luke 15 probably didn't cut much ice with the Pharisee leaders and theological lawyers anyhow, because they didn't think too much, in those days, of rough, low-income sheep herders and domesticated women.

JESUS' MORE ELABORATE THIRD story goes for the jugular vein to correct **the repressive rabbinical idea that human repentance is a condition for God's forgiveness**; God is not out to forgive you until the guilty sinner does something first to atone for his wrong doing.

Not so, says Jesus, with his story about 'the prodigal God': the prodigal God goes extravagantly overboard in loving and forgiving ("electing") undeserving sinners who have lost their way.

God loved God's punished people Israel woebegone in exiled Babylonian captivity (Ezekiel 34:11-16). The merciful God loved us even when we were dead in our sins, the apostle Paul writes to the Ephesians (Ephesians 2:10). God the father in Jesus' story was on the lookout for the forlorn son, undignifiedly ran to him in his long robes to kiss him profusely, and ordered the homecoming feast to begin even before the fellow could get out his full confession (Luke 15:20-24).

THAT'S NOT FAIR, SAID the exiled Israelites. God seems to be partial toward the bad guys who happen to turn around and exacts a more severe code of conduct and judgment against us good guys (Ezekiel 33:17-18). That is precisely what the older son in Jesus' story angrily said to the father too: I've slaved for you (exactly the original Greek word), I **slaved** for you all these years, never went against a jot or tittle of what you prescribed, and you never gave me even a little barbecue to enjoy with **my friends**; and here comes this "other (profligate) son of **yours**" back, and for him you slaughtered the fattened calf! What gives?! (Luke 15:29-30)

IT'S TRUE, SAYS THE LORD God: I will judge each one of you according to the Way you walk (Ezekiel 33:20). But don't think that because you are a good person—do an honest day's work, pay your bills, keep your fingers clean, go to church regularly—don't suppose if you do it all like a routine, thanklessly: don't suppose your "righteousness" will excuse a slip into foolish crookedness. And you will slip, because you are not perfect: don't suppose your do-gooding "slavery," which is really pious self-help pride, will be your salvation. As the apostle James later puts it: anybody who lives by the rule book, O righteous Pharisee and lawyer, who can spot a splinter in the neighbour's eye at 10 meters (Matthew 7:1-15): if you fail in one little legal point, you are guilty before God the law-giver, even if you don't murder somebody or commit adultery (James 2:8-13). **The Way, the spirit in which you do things is what counts—God looks at the heart!** (I Samuel 16:7).

But don't think either that I, God, enjoy punishing guilty wrongdoers, send them packing to Babylon (Ezekiel 33:11). I want the wicked to turn around! Turn around from your little deviations, your self-serving crooked ways, O my captive people—and if you hear my call, says the LORD God in Ezekiel 33-34, and **do what is just till justice flourish, the sins you have com-**

mitted will be wiped off the record, forgotten (33:16)! and you will be liberated to live as my sheep in verdant pastures, unafraid of wild animals and evil enemies (34:16, 22, 25, 28). Don't be duty-bound, grumpy "servants" counting up your spiritual bank accounts and tax credits for heaven: **live gratefully as my protected, anointed feasting flock of sheep.**

SO THAT IS THE first point of Luke 15 and Ezekiel 33-34: **God is prodigal with grace, spilling it over upon sinners even before they are historically ready to receive such deliverance from their captivities.**

THE OTHER MAIN POINT this morning is for us to grasp how Luke 15 fulfills, and goes beyond, the promise God made in Ezekiel to become self the good shepherd of God's people and get rid of the bad shepherds who are messing up the Lord's sheep (Ezekiel 34:7-11). I came, said Jesus, to call sinners at their wits end to turn around, not those who think they themselves are pretty good, law-abiding persons (Matthew 9:10-13).

Story-telling Jesus was indeed the Messiah in David's line; **Jesus Christ was God actually showing up live in person on earth as good shepherd** not only to stop the bullying **sheep** from running roughshod over the weaker ones (Ezekiel 34:17-22, Matthew 5:1-12), but even to invite the bad shepherds among God's people to be turned around into good ones! That is the excessive **merciful** justice of God toward us inflexible, prone to self-righteousness plodding sheep and sheep herders who think we have no need of repentance (Ezekiel 34:16; Luke 15:28,31).

Bad shepherds—the Older Testament often fills out what the Newer Testament focusses down on—bad shepherds provide no protection for their scattered sheep, neglect to be lookouts who can warn of impending disaster, look after their own interests, but do not know how to give their flock nourishing pasture, fresh water, grass to grow on (Ezekiel 33:6, 34:12).

This matter becomes very serious when you realize that not only the elders and deacons and pastor of the congregation, the Sunday School and catechism teachers, the musicians, Youth workers, the leaders in the Alpha program, NeighbourLink, Kingdom Kids, Friendship group, Church committee chairs, parents and grandparents are "shepherds," but every follower of Jesus Christ who claims to be anointed by the Holy Spirit is called to function as a shepherd for our neighbours who may be aimlessly wandering hither and yon, unaware they are meant to be feeding in God's world pasture.

BAD SHEPHERDS HAVE NO idea of what the score is in history, so they cannot evaluate current trends. They may not even know that God's people are living in captivity! Isaiah made fun of the "watchmen of Zion," calling them dogs lying in the sun that don't even know how to bark (Isaiah 56:9-12). Ezekiel describes bad shepherds like ghosts out-to-lunch, playing theological trivial pursuit maybe, nursing their own pet practical projects, but AWOL, absent from tending in their office to the crying needs of the sheep, to exercise the weak sheep to become stronger, to give splints to the crippled sheep so they can eventually walk and maybe even learn to dance for joy, unconcerned about showing the way out of the Babylonian labyrinth or the Pharisaical maze in which some of the sheep have gotten confused and lost their direction, even though they still go through the usual sheeplike motions of nibbling what's available (Ezekiel 34:3-6).

THE CLUE FOR US to understand what to do comes from what the prodigal father God in Jesus' third story said to the angry, uptight older son: "**Everything that is mine, is yours!** my child," inviting the hard-working older son not to hoard the inheritance all to himself but to enjoy it, give it away in celebration of lost sheep becoming found, dead people becoming alive! (Luke 15:31-32).

Older sons and daughters are not just to stand there and find fault with what's wrong in the world. Good prophetic watchmen do not just holler, "The sky is falling! The sky is falling!" **Good** shepherds are more than cultural "whistle blowers"; **good** shepherds go the extra mile and provide organic food and unpolluted fresh water for their fellow sheep. **Good** shepherds know where there is **good** pasture for the flock of sheep to chew on and mature.

EZEKIEL 33:15 HAS A powerful phrase which deftly catches the mark of experienced, wise good shepherds (which you may not have fully gotten from the NIV translation, which says the wicked who are converted "follow the decrees that give life"). The Bible means: **God** structured all creatures in good ways; any human creature who follows those ordinances of the LORD will be blessed with genuine fruitful living. Good shepherds know how to lead sheep to walk in God's ordained structures for family life, for commercial life, for political life, for prayer and congregational worship life, for sport and entertainment life, for school life....

Parental shepherds anointed by the Holy Spirit don't just holler at their teenage youth, "Shape up or ship out!" but spend disciplined love time themselves **bonding with and nurturing the gifts of their offspring.** Employers and labourers convicted to do justice do not merely not cheat, but mind God's economic creatural ordinance for **generous thrifty management and work in supplying wholesome resources with a smile for real needs of neighbours.** Good political shepherds do not only not yield to the temptation to take kick backs and not be opportunistic to seize power, but tend faithfully, persistently, to **caring for the commonweal.** Shepherding schoolteachers in David's line do not play the popularity card or police their classrooms as if it's a jail, but are inventive enough to **intrigue** beginning or post-graduate students **with the wonders of creation and the terrible crimes and surprises found in history,** so students become avid investigators. Such are **God's ordinances of genuine living for us creatures <u>good</u> shepherds come to know.**

Sheep need to pray hard for their shepherds. The Bible says teaching shepherds will receive a much stiffer judgment at the last day than ordinary people (James 3:1). Every time I get behind a pulpit to exhort from God's Word or you dare tell somebody, "This is what the Lord says," if I or you mislead, oversimplify, tempt a little sheep to sin, the sinner gets hurts, say both Ezekiel and Luke, but we who do the misleading get the millstone around the neck (Ezekiel 33:6, Luke 17:1-4). And again, **the Way one shepherds is crucial: with a firmly gentle, searching and forgiving, <u>self</u>-sacrificing holy spirit** lest you train sheep to become stingy, overconfident, libertine, vain, or judgmental bullies in attitude.

LET ME SHOW YOU in closing a parable make-over of Jesus' story, a series of five photographic artworks called *The Return of the Prodigal Son* (1982 by Duane Michals). Like a mirror image of Masaccio's Adam expelled from paradise, the naked son [1] enters from the right into a room where the father is leisurely scanning *The New York Times*. The startled older man [2] looks at the youth bowed in shame. The father

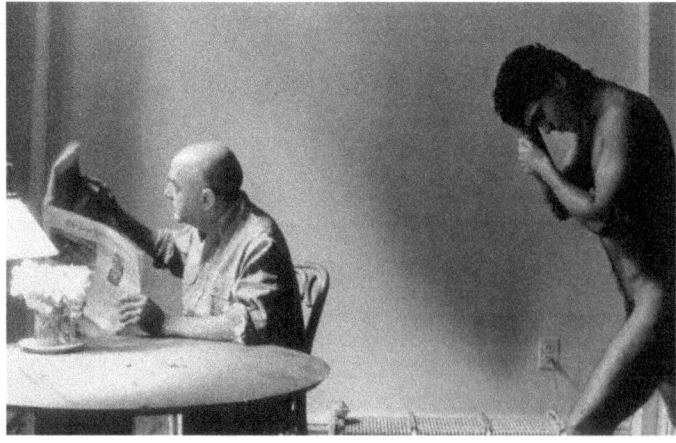

THE LORD GOD IS A PRODIGAL GOD WHO GIVES

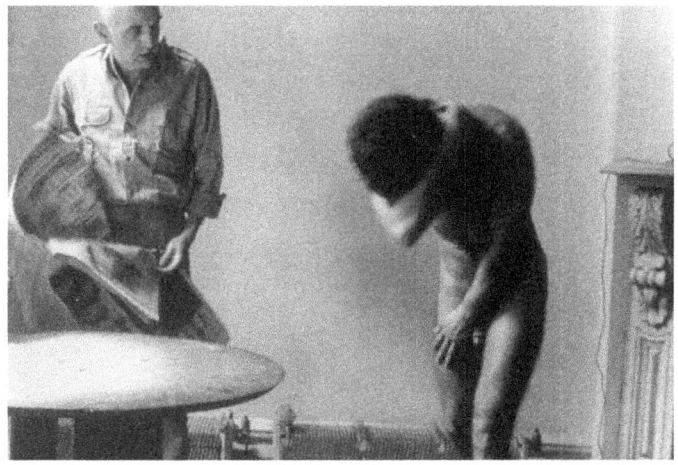

loosens [3] his shirt to protect the other's nakedness, and then thoughtfully removes [4] all his clothes to give them to the younger one. Finally, the naked old man [5] gingerly gives the returned son a hug offering reconciliation.

That's a metaphorical picture of what God did for us human sinners and the polluted world. God went naked in sacrificing God's only begotten son for our sakes, for us

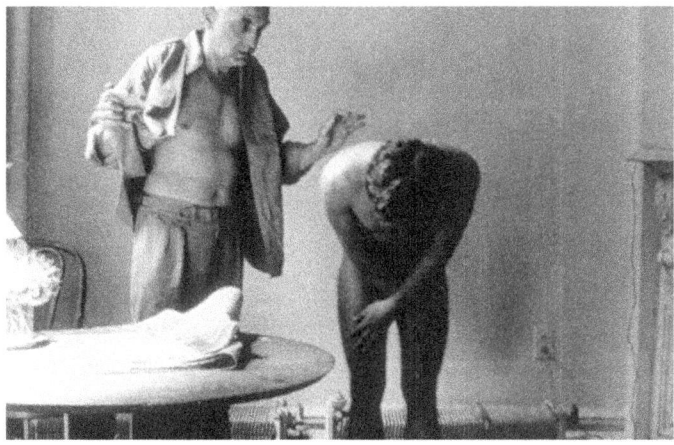

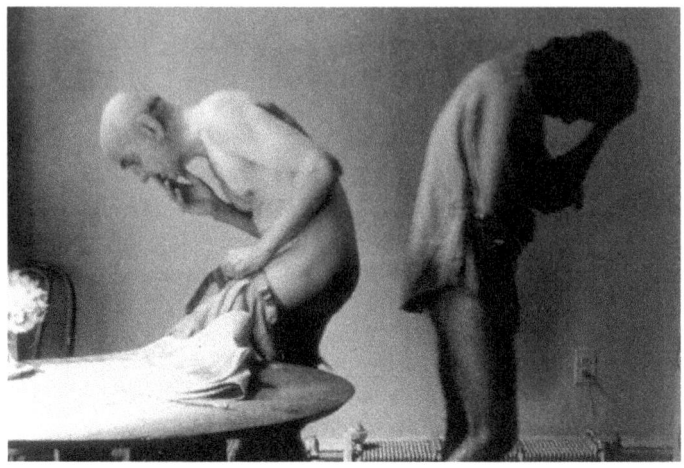

who are the older sons and daughters who have "wasted" our inheritance from God too, our gifts, by keeping them locked up selfishly, without joyful giveaway thanksgiving. The artwork sequence is also a metaphorical picture of how Jesus Christ acted as good shepherd. "I am the good shepherd," said Jesus in the gospel of John; "The good shepherd lays down his life for the sheep" (John 10:1-18, v.11). Jesus

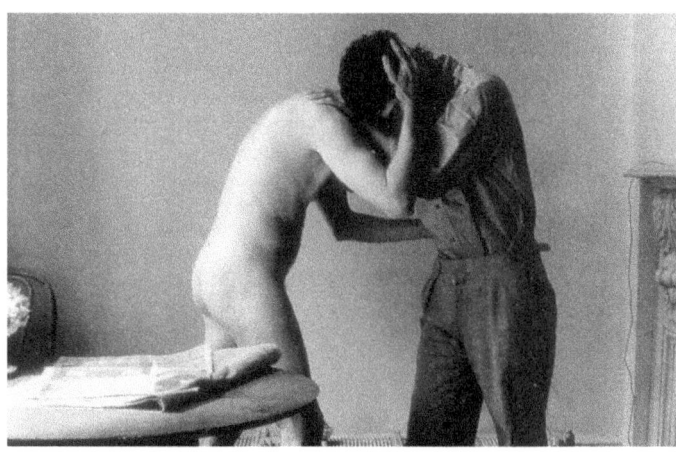

Christ laid down his life, went naked on the cross to give us the redemptive opening to be clothed for deeds of becoming a ready hand and a sure foot, a perceptive eye and listening ear, or a wise mouth for our fellow handicapped sheep (I Corinthians 12).

You can also take the five photos to be a show-and-tell of the holy spirited action in which we who would follow the Good Shepherd are freed to climb down from our spectator tree and do a Zacchaeus with our wealth (Luke 19:1-10), or **nakedly giveaway our life time** to help clothe the poor throughout the world, put a robe of comfort around the elderly or sick in hospitals, send a scarf of a written note to the lonely, share a flower or a wink of a joke with someone needing encouragement (Romans 12:14-21), or **do something just and <u>hopeful</u> in the public square,** fruitful in bearing others' burdens rather than adding to their insecurity (Galatians 5:25-6:2).

And if we do not take the shirt off our backs to clothe the wasted poor hungry children in the world, never pray for the imprisoned locked away and forgotten, do not visit the sick with comfort as well as medicine, or give good pasture to those chewing crud…in classrooms, workplaces, government offices, believers at worship, God self will shepherd "the least of society," says the Bible (Matthew 25:31-46), and find others than us older sons and daughters to care for the bewildered sheep on the city streets.

So the second good news for us to remember this morning—beside the prodigality of God's love—us who may be faulty shepherds, humdrum, inexperienced or disoriented sheep of God's flock, or simply inquisitive beast, is summed up in the verse 31 of Ezekiel 34 and verse 31 of Luke 15—you can underline verses 31 in your Bibles when you get home.

Hear the passionate (post-Easter/post-Pentecost) outpouring love of the LORD God: **O you, <u>my</u> sheep, the sheep of <u>my</u> pasture—you mortal creatures! —I AM YOUR GOD! Everything that is mine, is yours! my child—give it away to your neighbour in my Name!**

IF YOU WOULD BE a good shepherd in the footsteps of Jesus Christ, or simply a sheep in the flock of the Good Shepherd **willing to do acts of justice till it flourish**, it is time to sing a hymn, and also never have to be afraid, come what may.

When You Pass Through Rough Waters

When you pass through rough waters,
Though the out-come seem bleak,
God will do some-thing new,
Thank the LORD for tough love,

when you pass through rough waters,
though the out-come seem bleak
God will do some-thing new.
thank the LORD for tough love:

they shall not o-ver-whelm you,
re-main true to the vis-ion
If you tire on the jour-ney,
re-main joy-ful and pru-dent

THE LORD GOD IS A PRODIGAL GOD WHO GIVES

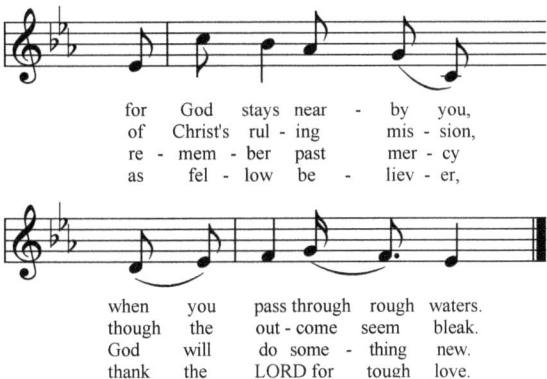

for God stays near - by you,
of Christ's rul - ing mis - sion,
re - mem - ber past mer - cy
as fel - low be - liev - er,

when you pass through rough waters.
though the out - come seem bleak.
God will do some - thing new.
thank the LORD for tough love.

Text: Isaiah 38:10-20 Calvin G. Seerveld, 1998© 66 76 6
Tune: Heinz W. Zimmermannm, 1971, Concordia Publishing House © *Little Flock*

Closing Prayer

Dear Lord, Thank you for your Word of overflowing grace, covenantal mercy, and comfort so amazing to us little sheep and children You call to grow up to become shepherds. Thank you for telling us to have no fear because your Son, **our** Shepherd, has stooped down to rescue us from our wayward, exiled selves. Please lead us, O Holy Spirit, in paths of just doing that follow in the naked footsteps of Jesus Christ, who has shown us how to walk selflessly in the ordinances of genuine living. We pray happily, gratefully, in the Name of the Good Shepherd, Amen.

17 April 2005
Willowdale Christian Reformed Church
Toronto, Ontario

12

The Sorrowful Pottery-Making God Revealed in Jesus Christ and our Psalm 2 Task

Texts: Psalm 2, Jeremiah 18:1-20:6 with Joel 2:12-14, II Timothy 2:11-13

Psalm 2

(we shall read as a chorus of voices)

The wise cantor
1. Why do the peoples of the world rage about [like madmen] Why in the world do the different nations keep on thinking up stupid schemes?
2. Earth kings get together "for a consultation"— important rulers hold conferences all together against the LORD God and against God's anointed one *(mashiach)*. [These earthly rulers say:]
3. "Let us smash the chains of this God that hold us down! Let us throw off the reins of God's 'anointed one'!"

Another liturgist, perhaps a priest
4. The One who sits enthroned in heaven begins to laugh,
    my Lord mimics their foolish bluster;
5. and then God turns to them in (holy) anger,
    stops the upstarts short with God's fierce outrage:
6. "It was I! it is I who have set up my anointed king on Zion,
        my set-apart mountain."

Princely ruler taking official part in the liturgy
7. Yes, I will recite the decisive appointment by the LORD God.
    God said to me:
    "You are my son. Today is the day I have borne you.
8. Ask it of me and I will give you peoples of the world for
        your heritage;
    the most distant nations of the earth will be yours to tend.
9. You may have to break them with a rod of iron.
    You may have to smash them for remolding as a sculpting
        potter reshapes her clay dish—"

[the congregation stands]

Wise cantor again
10. So now, you (small-time little) rulers, you had better wise up!
    You who (only) judge on the earth, hadn't you better get the point?
11. Serve the LORD God with an attentive awe—
    Take joy (in your task only) with trembling—
12. Give homage to this (adopted) son (of God too)—lest he also get
        worked up, and you obliterate any way [for you to walk],
    for God's anger can flash up like lightning....

Congregated chorus
> Blessèd are all those who have run to take shelter with the
>   anointed one.
>
> **Blessèd are all those who have run to take shelter with the
>   anointed one.**
>
> **Blessèd are all those who have run to take shelter with the
>   anointed one.**

Now let us hear the prophet Jeremiah for a couple of chapters[1]

Jeremiah 18:1-20:6

[It is possible that it be Jeremiah's Secretary, Baruch, who writes]

This is the Word which came to Jeremiah from the LORD God: "Get up, and go down to the house of the potter, and there I will let you hear my words."

So (says Jeremiah) I went down to the house of the potter, and Wow! was he industriously working away at his trade on the revolving potter's wheel. But the vessel which he was busy making was messed up by the clay in the hand of the potter. So he did it over, he reworked (the clay) into another receptacle till it seemed goodly formed in the eyes of the potter.

Then this Word of the LORD God came to me:

"Am I not able to do work with you, O house of Israel, the way this potter has done? intones the LORD God. **Do you not realize that like the clay in the hand of the potter, so you, O house of Israel, are in my hand!**

"Suppose I were to declare at one time or another over a folk or over a nation that it be ripped up and broken down and actually destroyed, but if that folk were to turn around (repent!) from its evil doing which I have described, then I would let myself be sorry about the punishing evil which I had intended to do to it. And if

---

1 Here printed is the whole pericope of Jeremiah 18:1-20:6 which I had assigned a week earlier but read only excerpted in the service. One really needs to hear the whole section in order to live fully into the throbbing pulse of God's sorrowful promise about God's people's coming disaster, and to meet the incredibly passionate, angry, cursing prophet who is suffering, jailed, jeered at by the ruling priestly establishment for bringing the LORD's unwelcome message.

at another time I would pronounce over a folk or a nation that I will establish and get it to flourish, but if then it do evil in my sight not listening to my voice, I would let myself be sorry about the good I had promised to do for them.

"So now, please tell the men (and women) of Judah and those who dwell in Jerusalem, Thus says the LORD God: Look out! I am shaping up evil and am thinking up machinations against you all. **Yes! turn around, every person from your evil way of life! Make the Way you do things be genial, let your dealings with others be kindly.**"

But then the people all keep on saying, "Nothing doing! We will carry on, standing behind our own plans. Every man and woman wants to be busily acting in the pigheadedness of their evil heart."

Therefore, thus says the LORD God: Go ask about it among the peoples of the world, Who has ever heard the likes of this?! The virgin Israel has done something extremely appalling!

Does the snowfall of Lebanon let go of the crags of Mount Sirion?

Do the foreign waters of the ice-cold streams dry up?

Yet my people have forgotten all about me—they offer burning offerings to fake deities (Nothings)! They have stumbled in their ways, in their age-old paths, to walk on off-road bypaths, not at all on a sound thoroughfare. They are inducing their land to paralysis, a shame to be tattled about forever. All who pass by will be horrified and shake their heads.

Like an East wind I will scatter them in front of their enemy's face. I will show them the back of my neck, not my face, in the day of their calamity.

But the people leaders said, "Come on! Let's think up counter plots against Jeremiah. It looks as if the *torah* coming from the priest shall not be destroyed, counsel shall not be wanting from the wise, and the Word (of God) shall not be lost to the visionary prophet: so, come on! let's hit Jeremiah with counter charges, and not give a moment of attention to all his talk!"

(Yet, says Jeremiah:) You, LORD God, please give sharp attention to me, and listen carefully to the voice of my opponents. Is evil the recompense for doing good? Yes, they are digging a pit for (taking) my life! Remember when I stood before your face, (my Lord) to speak good things about them, to turn your anger away from them!

Therefore, give their children over to famine; hurl their children out to the power of the sword. Let their wives be childless and become widows. May their men meet death by pandemic pestilence, their young men be executed by the plague of warfare. Let a wailing dirge be heard from their houses, when you bring a marauding band unexpectedly upon them—Yes! they have been digging a hidden pit of a trap to catch me and laid a snare for my feet!

But You, O LORD God, Yourself know all their secret plotting to engineer my death. Do not forgive their premeditated offence; do not wipe out their sin done in front of your face. Let them be tripped up in front of your face—deal with them while You are angry!

About now is the time when the LORD God said (further): Go take a walk, (Jeremiah,) and buy an earthen clay pot finished up by a potter. Take some of the elders of the people and some of the senior priests along. Go out to The City Dumps (Valley of Benhinnon), at the opening entrance to the Potsherd gate (the Pots-broken-into-bits gate, popularly known as the Dung gate, in King James translation). And **there** you will proclaim the Words which I shall tell you to say.

You shall declare: All of you, hear indeed (שִׁמְעוּ) the Word of the LORD God, you rulers of Judah and you inhabitants of Jerusalem! Thus says the LORD God of the angelic forces, the God of Israel: Pay attention! I am going to let such evil come upon this place (=Jerusalem) that all those hearing about it, their ears will tintinnabulate.

Because you people have left me behind and have profaned this place—you allowed burned offerings of incense in this place to other gods which neither you nor your forebears nor the kings of Judah have known of—you filled this place with the blood of (sacrificed) children (=innocents), built up the sacred high places of the Baal [God of authoritarian force, a Militaristic Mentality] to burn up your children with fire, as burnt offerings to Baal—something I never ordered, never decreed, it never crossed my mind [heart].

Therefore, never forget! The days are coming—thus says the LORD God—when this place shall no more be called Topheth (the Place for burning rubbish) or The City Dumps (the Valley of Benhinnon), but shall instead be called Auschwitz (the Valley of Slaughter). In this very place I will dislocate the carefully conceived plans of Judah and Jerusalem, and I will let their people fall by the sword in front of their enemy's face, and by the hand of those ready to snuff out their life. And I will gives their corpses for eating to the scavenging birds of the sky and to the beasts of the earth. I will set this city up to be an astonishing disaster, a joke to be jeered at—everybody passing by it will be shocked, and will jeer at its battered ruins. And I will make this people so that they will eat the flesh of their sons and the flesh of their daughters, and every person will eat the flesh of their neighbour in the stressed pandemic oppression in which their enemies and those out to take their life have stifled them.

Then, (Jeremiah,) you shall totally smash the potter's pot right in front of the eyes of the delegation of fellows on their walk with you, and you shall say to them: Thus says the LORD God of the angelic forces: **I will smash this people and this very (holy) city to smithereens, just as one can demolish a potter's vessel so** it cannot be put back together again. They will bury people in Topheth (the Place for burning rubbish) because there is no other place to bury (the dead). That is what I shall do to this place (Jerusalem), declares the LORD God, and to its inhabitants, making this (holy Jerusalem) city like Topheth (the Place for burning rubbish). The houses of Jerusalem and the houses of the rulers of Judah shall be desecrated like the place of Topheth—all the houses upon whose flat roofs they burned sacrifices to all the power deities of the heavens and poured drinks (libations) to other gods.

When Jeremiah came back from Topheth where the LORD God had sent him, **there** to prophesy (to the leaders of God's people), Jeremiah took a stand in the forecourt of the LORD God's temple. Then Jeremiah spoke out to all the people (gathered), "Thus says the LORD God of the angelic forces, the God of Israel: That's right! I am letting all the disaster come which I have pronounced as coming upon this Jerusalem city and all its surrounding towns, because they have stiffened their necks so that they would not hear my words...."

Now when Paschhur Immerson, the priest and head administrator in the temple of the LORD God, was hearing Jeremiah prophesying on these matters, Paschhur had the visionary prophet Jeremiah beaten, and had him placed in the stocks which were at the Upper Benjamin Gate of the temple of the LORD God.

The next morning when Paschhur had Jeremiah let go from the stocks, Jeremiah said to him, "The LORD God does not (anymore) call your name 'Paschhur' [which means 'Set free'], but 'Ambient Terrorist.'" For thus intones the LORD God: That's right! I will make you to be a fearful terrorist to yourself and for all your dear ones; they shall be cut down by the sword of their enemies while you have to look on with your own eyes.

And I will give all of Judah into the hand of the king of Babylon, so that he shall deport them captive to Babylon and disappear them with the sword. And what's more, I will give away all the cultural wealth of this city (Jerusalem), all its hard-worked-for valuables, all its prized belongings, and all the treasures of the kings of Judah, into the hand of their enemies who shall plunder them, grab them, and carry them off to Babylon.

And you, Paschhur, and all who dwell in your household, shall straggle into captivity; you shall go to Babylon and there you shall die, there you shall be buried, you and all your friends to whom you have prophesied falsely.

This is the Word of the Lord!
Thanks be to God!

WE'VE HEARD ENOUGH SCRIPTURE now, including Psalm 2, to grapple with the show-and-tell news that God is like a potter moulding and remaking us human lumps of clay, sometimes smashing clay pots to smithereens—that doesn't sound like good news—and even our task as God's anointed ones to rule as potters ourselves making pots. I'm fascinated especially by the revelation that God has regrets, remorse, and grieves over defective clay pots God has had a hand in forming—

Historical context of the prophet Jeremiah's recitation of God's Word

THE HISTORICAL CONTEXT OF Jeremiah's prophecies is this: the Ten tribes bulk of God's people, Israel, who split off from David's line after King Solomon's death, and who worshipped idols and foreign no-gods, have disappeared, dispersed through the Assyrian empire, already 130 years ago (722 BC). Three or four generations have gone by with only Judah, the Davidic cream of God's people, left on the earth among enemies, and now (c. 600 BC) facing exiled punishment themselves for their leaving the LORD God behind, and living selfish, greedy, unjust lives.

God has Jeremiah take the leaders of Judah out to the burning, stinking Jerusalem city garage dump to preach to them **there** how bad their punishment will be—so pandemically oppressed and starving they would be driven to eat their own children! According to the Bible that had already really happened with Israel when Samaria was besieged by the Syrians in the days of Elisha (II Kings 6:24-30). No wonder Jeremiah is told in the Bible not to get married and not have children (Jeremiah 16:1-4)! No wonder too that people were out to kill the messenger, Jeremiah, for bringing God's message of Auschwitz atrocities and the imminent and permanent dislocation of the whole country because of their life lived as if the LORD God were absent.

How would you people feel if, as a prophet, I took you away from sanitized tree-laden Willowdale to the Toronto city dumps, in Hamilton's outskirts and there clearly preached: unless we start to house the homeless in our city, end the hunger and derangement of the invisible poor around us, somehow return this land to the custody of the indigenous Haudenosaunee and Anishinaabe peoples, in ten years God will make us fodder for the troops of Communist China? You could well be incredulous and say, "Well, good thing you're not Jeremiah!" But that's precisely what did take place for God's people Judah in 597 and 586 B.C.: not Assyria or Egypt, but the Babylonians massacred Judah, and razed Jerusalem to dust, in Jeremiah's lifetime.

I WILL NOT SPECULATE on what the history of Judah's two-generations Babylonian captivity might imply for our don't-rock-the-boat Canadian Christian community. The Devil is wily and might just trick us into a godless **American** cultural captivity. But we should hear the good news Jeremiah 18-19 and Psalm 2 proclaim about (1) God's clay pottery activity, and (2) God's calling us in Psalm 2 to be following in God's pottery-making footsteps.

God is a remoulding potter

WHEN THE CLAY IS too soft or lacks moisture and is brittle, the potted bowl or jar is likely to be flawed. So a skilled potter reduces the vessel to a clump of clay again, corrects the consistency, and reshapes it into a good-looking, sound receptacle that is serviceable and worth the trouble. That's the way God works with an obstreperous people, says the Bible.

In the cities Cain and his great-great-grandson Lamech built (Genesis 4:17-24), business and night life became so wicked, God was sorry humankind had been created, and gone evil. In the beginning God practically wiped the universe clean of humans with the Genesis flood, even though it grieved and hurt God, gave God a heart spasm (Genesis 6:5-8). So God started over with a Noah and seven person clump of clay. Later in history God formed a special covenanted receptacle with Abraham and Sarah, "cut into the flesh," which God promised would last forever (Genesis 17, v.7). Still later the potter God reformed God's "Golden calf" people with Moses, and then made David the national shepherd. And now comes the crisis with leftover pot Judah, where God's people are unrecognizable from the garbage at the Potsherd, Pot-Broken-to-bits gate rubble steeped in manure.

JEREMIAH RELATES IN CHAPTER 18 God's intense plea to the Judah people of God: Turn around from your evil, godless Way of life that is paralyzing society. Remember my abiding sworn love for you. Be kind to one another rather than hateful and violent, so I don't have to wipe you out as I did the ten tribes of Israel.

But God's Judah people **kept on back-talking**, "No deal! We are doing our thing! WE first!"

Then in Jeremiah 19 God says: I guess I'll have to smash you people all into pieces that cannot be put back together again, nor remouldable into a useable pot.

And God does it! No flood, but Nebuchadnezzar devastated Jerusalem, ended Judah's existence as a nation, and turned the Jewish people into captive exiles.

However, Bible readers know, two-three generations later God used a Persian strongman Cyrus to send a ragtag remnant of Jews back to Palestine under Ezra and Nehemiah to start over as a people keeping covenant with the LORD God of the angelic forces.

Does the potter God never give up?

A clue to God's complicated pots

THE CLUE TO THE pattern of God's pottery activity is in the fine print of Jeremiah 18: if I pronounce judgment over a people, says God, and they stop doing evil, I deeply regret the punishment that takes place, and if I promise blessing over a people, and they start to do evil in front of my face, I'm deeply sorry about the good they have received (18:7-10).

What happens depends upon the clay, even though God as potter wants to/wills/can make a good trustworthy pot out of God's current people.

It is similar for persons. When the Israelites got tired of charismatic judges and wanted a king like the pagan nations around them, God finally gave them the handsome, Spirit-filled (I Samuel 9:1-3, 10:9-13) son of Kish Saul, until later on, because of the Way Saul disobeyed the LORD's instruction, God has to say. "I regret I made Saul king" (I Samuel 15:11). And then God removed the Holy Spirit from Saul (I Samuel 15:14), so Saul had to go to a witch to try to find out what God wanted (I Samuel 28:3-19).

But the Bible says clearly, "God does not change God's mind as humans do (I Samuel 15:28-29 [Numbers 23:19-20])! God uses defective clay, but woe to the pot God regretfully has to remould, or worse, leave to founder at the Pot-Broken-in-Pieces gate of the dumps.

The Good News for us as human clay pots

THE GOOD NEWS, HOWEVER, is that until "the roll is called up yonder" (Revelation 19:11-18), God in Jesus

Christ and the Holy Spirit <u>never</u> gives up on any lump of clay. In the midst of a withering plague around 800 B.C. the prophet Joel told the truth:

Joel 2:12-14

"Yet even now" [in this locust pandemic], intones the LORD God, "return to me with all your heart, with fasting, with weeping, and with laments."

"Rend your hearts (says the prophet), not your clothes,
    and return to the LORD God, your God!
for your God is deeply kind and merciful,
slow to get angry, and overflowing with steadfast love (חסד),
yes, sufferingly regretful of evil happening
    [relents from punishing]
Who knows whether God will not turn around
    and be remorseful,
and then leave behind a special blessing, a present of sorts
and a gift of thanks from the LORD God, God of you people!"
    prophesies Joel.

And the autistic prophet Ezekiel also reports that when the LORD gives God's people a fresh start again, God says to them: "You shall recognize firsthand, O house of Israel, that I indeed am the LORD God when I deal with you for the sake of my name! and not according to what is fitting for your evil ways and your corrupted dealings" (Ezekiel 20:44).

And long after Joel, Ezekiel and Jeremiah's day, when the regenerated Jewish people of God burned itself out again with leader High Priest Caiphas denouncing the special saviour God provided them, Jesus Christ (Matthew 26:57-60), the apostle Paul writes that the failed Jewish clay has no right to challenge the potter God for moulding non-Jewish, non-kosher, uncircumcised *goiim* Gentiles into their Davidic root and clay (Romans 9-11, 9:19-29), **the better to glorify God's worldwide mercy** already promised to Abraham (Genesis 12:3 "all races of the earth will be blessed in you").

II Timothy 2:11-13

AND THE APOSTLE PAUL told Timothy:
"This saying is trustworthy:
If we have (suffered and) died along (with Jesus),
 then we shall also live with him.
If we have persevered (with Jesus),
 then we shall also rule with him.
If we spurn (Jesus), then Jesus himself will disown us:
If we become unfaithful (to Jesus),
 Jesus…shall still remain faithful (to us)
because Jesus cannot repudiate his very nature.

THIS IS THE BIBLICAL truth for each one of us: The LORD God has not given up on you—on Laodicean lukewarm you, on generation-long church-going worshipping you a little stale, on rebellious critical know-it-all you, on discovering sinful you—Come to me all you who work hard and are burdened by stuff, says the Potter God, Jesus Christ and the Holy Spirit, and I shall give you and your loved ones rest, peace (Matthew 11:28).

And to the Willowdale Dutch-Torontonian-Iranian-Canadian congregation in the Reformation faith-thought tradition: your clay is a good mix, ingenious, says the prophet and Psalm 2, so put your hand to the potter's wheel and carry on your ministry while singing the Lord's psalms.

The Call of Psalm 2 today

GIVEN THIS BACKDROP OF God's flexible potter final faithfulness toward the people of God, Psalm 2 gives Christians, the adopted children of God, a tremendous, exciting and sobering imperative: follow my begotten Son Jesus Christ in ruling the nations!—includes the peoples who do not yet know God—"shepherd" the nations of the world in line with the potter God and God's only begotten Son (cf. Revelation 2:27, 12:5, 19:15).[2]

Psalm 2 refers first of all to God's Son Jesus Christ as the ruling Lord of history who in the end will smash evil rulers into potsherds, useless fragments. (Revelation 14:14-20, 16:1-21). But Psalm 2 follows up the apocalyptic threat of verse 9 with an injunction to Trudeau and Trump, Putin, Kohmani, Merkel and industrial CEO's with their million dollar salaries everywhere, in verses 11 and 12: Serve the LORD God with an attentive awe, and honour the Rule of God's Son, or the Lord's anger may flash up like lightning, and there will not be any more remoulding of the clay but simply a discarding of your administration. That's something worth chewing on, in faith!

---

2 Psalm 2:9 is not a simple future tense sentence. My translation keeps רעע ("to break") concessive, Cf. Martin Buber, "du magst mit eiserem Stab sie zerschellen"). The Septuagint reads רעה ("to shepherd"), which underlies the Newer Testament Greek variant of Psalm 2:9, ποιμαίνειν, in Revelations 2:27, 12:5, and 19:15. Cf. "Psalm 2: Linguistic-Literary Analysis & Translation," p.9 n.30, at https://za.pinterest.com/pin/575827502349066755/); C.A. & E.G. Briggs, A Critical and Exegetical Commentary on *The Book of Psalms* (Edinburgh: T & T Clark, 1906) 1:22-23; John Goldingay, *Psalms* (Grand Rapids: Baker Academic, 2006) 1:101.

Psalm 2 also has the carry-over of speaking to the adopted sons and daughters of God, as our Heidelberg Catechism Q&A 32 states: "I am called a Christian because as a Christ believer and follower **I/we share in Christ's anointing (baptized) as caretakers tending God's world.** Therefore, so long as there be night and day, summer and winter, seedtime and harvest (Genesis 8:22) under God's rainbow (Genesis 9:8-17) we apprentice potters are all called to mould our household, our trade or profession, our occupation and leisure, our neighbourhood, society, culture and generation in a genial, kind way that honours the faithful love of God the Lord for our fellow creatures of clay. Psalm 2 calls us to hear and obey Jeremiah 18 ourselves, and to embody the good news of never giving up on faulty pots of our own making, or those we encounter. We are not the potter God, and do not have the power and authority of Jesus Christ, but we adopted children of God do have the gift of the Holy Spirit to quietly, **humbly serve in the constant mending of things, and in forming anew what could be good, acceptable and mature thank offerings to God our Lord** (Romans 12:1-2).

To sum up: Jeremiah 18 and 19 reveal that God has **feelings!** hurts, regrets, gets upset and outright angry. And it is disastrous for persons to grieve God the Holy Spirit (Ephesians 4:25-5:2, 4:30). So be warned against waywardness while still comforted by God's long-suffering patience and desire to provide shalom for us clay jar human creatures (II Corinthians 7, especially v.7).

Psalm 2 is a manifesto for Citizens for Public Justice, for our voting out demagogic and corrupt rulers, and for supporting leaders in society who realize that, as Jeremiah puts it, to know God is (not to wave Bibles for photographers but) to give just well-being to the poor and needful (one could add "indigenous, refugees, handicapped") persons (Jeremiah 22:13-17).

Just a postscript comment about the stomach-turning passages of Jeremiah I did not read in our public worship service, about distraught parents boiling their own children as food to eat (cf. Jeremiah 19:3-9)—why is such horrific, apocalyptic detail in the Bible?

Especially the prophets recount the atrocious evil we humans, including sinful born-again children of God, do, to stop us from settling down as comfortable well-fed and self-satisfied customers of God's bounty, who see no evil, hear no evil, and live as if there be no evil. God's written Word wants to tell us that **true faith in Jesus Christ is gutsy, far-sighted, costly!** (Philippians 1:27-30, v.29).

A prophet would detail the horrendous gasping of a COVID-19 pandemic patient struggling to breathe, as if being water-boarded, in a hospital without enough ventilators, as the Almighty Pantocrator's ironic response to the bluster of a fool, "AMERICA FIRST!" Indeed, "first" in the world in coronavirus deaths!

The Bible is not a manual on how to be "heavenly-minded" and to have "nice sentiments." The Bible is a reality check for us vain people, pointing us to drastic repentance, and to troubled hope and joy in **the God who acts in history** (at Sinai and in the baby birth of Jesus and sending the Holy Spirit) to **save us from ourselves.**

Closing Prayer

THANK YOU, LORD, FOR the exceptional call of the prophet Jeremiah, to be turned around to what truly counts. Help us to feel somehow God's fingers moulding us into pots that can hold water and blessing for others. And give us the energy and insight and courage to form a few educational, societal, churchly, even political weather-beaten clay pots that are worth saving for the next generation to utilize for **loving first your firm compassionate Rule** for us and our handicapped neighbours worldwide. Give us an ear to hear and obey your calling today (Psalm 95) we pray, in Jesus' Name, Amen.

Psalm 2

THE SORROWFUL POT-MAKING GOD, AND OUR PSALM 2 TASK

TEXT: Psalm 2, vers. Calvin Seerveld, 2009, © 10 5 10 5 10 5 10 5
TUNE: Steven Jones, 1879 *Tanymarian*

6 July 2020
Willowdale Christian Reformed Church
Toronto, Ontario

Approximate Times of Rulers and Various Prophets in the Older Testament

Saul (1052-1012) Samuel
David (1012-972) Nathan
Solomon (972-932)

Judah (and Benjamin) David dynasty		Israel (10 tribes) pick-up kings and queens
Rehoboam (9323-915 BC)		**Jeroboam** I (932-911 BC)
Abijah (915-913)		Nadab (911-910)
		Baasha (910-887)
Asa (913-872)		Elah (887-886)
		Zimri (886-886)
		Tibni & Omri (886-882)
		Omri (882-875)
Jehoshaphat (873-840)	Elijah(c. 875-850)	**Ahab & Jezebel** (875-854)
		Ahaziah (854-853)
	Elisha	Joram (853-842)
Jehoram (849-842)		**Jehu** (842-814)
Ahaziah (842-842)		Jehoaz (co 815-799)
Ataliah (842-836)		
Jehoash (836-797)		Joash (799-784)
Amaziah (804-775?)	Jonah	**Jeroboam II** (785-745)
Uzziah (co 786-749)	Amos	Zechariah (745-745)
Jothan (749-734)	Hosea	Shallum (745-745)
		Menahem (745-736)
		Pekahiah (736-735)
Ahaz (734-727)	Isaiah (c. 750-700)	Pekah (735-730)
Hezekiah (728-687)	Micah (c. 740-710)	Hoshea (730-722)

FALL of SAMARIA to ASSYRIA 722 BC

son Manasseh (687-639)
son Amon (639-638)
son **Josiah** (638-608)   Jeremiah (c. 629-570)
Jehoahaz (608-608)   Nahum

Assyrian NINEVEH DESTROYED 612 BC

Jehoiakim (608-597)   Habakkuk & Zephaniah
Jehoiachin (597-597)
Zedekiah (597-586)   Ezekiel (622-570) & Daniel (c.600-520)

JERUSALEM razed by BABYLONIANS 586 BC into EXILE

PERSIAN CYRUS (c. 600-529) conquered Babylon c. 538 BC

REMNANT of Israelites RETURN from EXILE 536 BC with ZERUBBABEL
Darius ruled (521-486); Haggai & Zechariah pro temple rebuilding 515 BC
Xerxes (=Ahasauerus; ruled (486-466); Esther (made queen 478 BC)
Artaxeres ruled (465-424); Ezra and Nehemiah building wall + reform c. 445 BC
Malachi
5 books of edited Psalms completed (?)

13

The Rechabite Alternative and Following Jesus Christ First!

TEXTS: Jeremiah 35, Luke 9:57-62, Mark 11:17-31 and Mark 8:34-35, 38

THIS IS THE WORD from the LORD God to Jeremiah which happened in the days of Jehoiakim, son of Josiah, King of Judah—

Do you know what "the days of Jehoiakim" were like? Give me 4 minutes.

If you read chapters 22-24 from II Kings, you know that Josiah was a good God-fearing king of Judah (c. 638-608 BC) who reformed the worship culture of the nation according to the Moses book of Deuteronomy the High Priest Hilkiah had "found"! in house-cleaning the temple. Josiah held a Passover communion ritual which had not been done for 400 years! not by Saul, David, Solomon, or any leader of Judah or Israel ever.

When Josiah was killed in a battle with the Egyptians, the people put Josiah's son Jehoahaz on the Judean throne (who lasted 3 months). Then Pharaoh Neco appointed Josiah's next son, Jehoiakim, king of Judah (608-597 BC), until the new superpower of the day, Nebuchadnezzar of Babylon, took charge of little Judah (II Kings 24:7) and made Jehoiachin puppet king (a few months of 597) and finally Zedekiah (597-586).

The point we need to hear to understand Jeremiah is that the Bible says: Jehoahaz, Jehoiakim, Jehoiachin and Zedekiah, everyone of these successive kings "did what was **evil in the sight of the LORD God**" (II Kings 23:32,37; 24:9,19) and undid Josiah's Reformation.

FOR EXAMPLE: **EVIL IN God's sight was the promotion and service of idols Baal and Astarte**, the false gods of Violence ("love it!") and Lust ("yeah, man!") in the land, and even **in God's temple!**

That means: suppose this Church building was God's holy temple. Instead of Joanne Sytsma's Advent banners there would be huge full-colour nude pin-up girl photos on the wall; instead of Willem Hart's banners with symbols of the Christian faith praising God's grace, there would be old Rambo movies showing and a heavy metal punk rock band playing gig after gig. The Sunday School rooms in the back would hold beds with charming male and female prostitutes ready for a little business after the coffee. The Fellowship Hall would have an abortion clinic where you could also dispose of unwanted babies. Fortune teller psychic Mona on Finch Avenue would use the Pastor's office to help you plan your relationships and play the lottery. The elders and deacon priests organize frequent Saturday night drunken orgies instead of home visits dealing with the state of your faithfulness and prayer life.

I'm not making this up! I'm reporting what is happening in Judah during the reign of Manasseh, Jehoiakim's great-grandfather he is emulating, documented in the Older Testament Bible, book of the Kings and Chronicles (II Kings 21 and II Chronicles 33), which hardly anybody reads today. That's why we have only a faint idea of what Isaiah and Jeremiah went through who prophesied to God's people, "Stop it! God will punish you like a California wildfire for violating the poor with your well-to-do Baal lifestyle and Astarte indulgences. God is going to level your houses, destroy heavenly fortified Jerusalem, and deport you to Siberia Babylon!"

No wonder Isaiah walked around preaching in his underpants for 3 years (Isaiah 20) trying to get God's people to listen, and Jeremiah wore a yoke for show-and-tell of what's coming if God's people did not accept Nebuchadnezzar of Babylon as God's servant! to punish God's wayward people (Jeremiah 27-28). Then King Jehoiakim cut up God's tough written Word for people to repent which Jeremiah had dictated to his secretary Baruch; and then King Jehoiakim burned the dictated scroll to ashes, and had his soldiers hunt down the hiding prophet Jeremiah and his secretary (Jeremiah 36)....

Jeremiah 35

THIS IS THE WORD from the LORD God to **Jeremiah** which happened **in the days of Jehoiakim**, son of Josiah, king of Judah:

Go to the household of the Rechabites, speak to them, and let them come into the house of the LORD God, to one of the rooms, and offer them wine to drink.

So I took along Jaazaniah, son of Jeremiah, son of Habazziniah, and his brothers and all his sons, and the whole household of the Rechabites. I brought them to the house of the LORD God, to the room of the sons of Hanan, the son of Igdaliah, the man of God (איש האלהים)—which was near the room of the princes which is above the chamber of Maaseiah, son of Shallum, the gatekeeper.

Then I set in front of the sons of the Rechabite household pitchers full of wine, and cups. And I said to them, "Drink some wine!"

But they answered: We cannot drink wine, because Yonadab Rechabson, our forefather set a command over us, "Never drink wine, neither you nor your sons—never! Do not build a house. Do not sow seed. Do not plant and have a vineyard for yourselves. No, you should live in tents all your days so that you may live many days on the face of the earth there where you are sojourners (strangers)."

We have listened to the voice of Yonadab Rechabson, our forefather, in all that he commanded us, "not to drink wine all our days, not ourselves, not our wives, not our sons, not our daughters, and not to build houses for us to settle down in." We do not have a vineyard or a planted plowed field for ourselves. But we have lived in tents and have obeyed (נשמע) and done all that Yonadab our forefather commanded. However, when it happened that Nebuchadnezzar, king of Babylon, came up against the land, we said, "Come, we had better go to Jerusalem in the face of the Chaldean army and in the face of the Syrian army— that's why we are settled down in (the city) of Jerusalem."

At that point the Word of the LORD God came to Jeremiah: Thus says the LORD God of the Army of Angels (Sabaoth), the God of Israel, "Go and say to the men of **Judah** and to the inhabitants of **Jerusalem:** Will you not take disciplining instruction for yourselves, so that you will be hearing/obeying **my** words! says the LORD God. The words of Yonadab Rechabson which he commanded his descendants has been kept, 'not to drink wine'—they do not drink wine to these very days, because they have heard and obeyed their forefather's command. But I have spoken to you all persistently again and again, yet you have not listened to me! I have sent you people all my servants, the visionary prophets (כל־עבדי הנבאים) again and again saying, 'Please! let every person be turned around from your evil Way and set straight your Way of doing things—don't fool around with chasing other gods [like Baal and Astarte] to serve them—then you shall be restored to settle in the cultivated land which I (God) gave to you and to your forefathers (and mothers)....' But you people never listened to me. Yes, the children of Yonadab Rechabson have kept the prescribed tasks of their forefather which was stipulated, but this people have not listened/obeyed me at all.

Therefore, thus says the LORD God, the God of the Angels, the God of Israel: Pay attention! I am going to bring upon Judah and upon all the inhabitants of (holy fortified) Jerusalem all the evil which I pronounced over them, because I have spoken to them, and they have not listened; I have called out to them, and they have not responded."

But to the house of the Rechabites, Jeremiah said: Thus says the LORD God of the Angels, God of Israel (יהוה צבאות אלהי ישראל), "Because you all have obeyed the assigned tasks (מצות) of your forefather Yonadab and have kept all his precepts (מצותיו), and have done all that he commanded you (צוה), therefore, thus says the LORD God of the Angels, the God of Israel, "Yonadab Rechabson shall never lack a person to be standing before my face in all the days (to come)."

This is the Word of the LORD, for today too!
Thanks be to God!

DID YOU MEAN IT? really thanking God for Jeremiah 35? Or did you say it because it is printed out for the proper response?

How are we supposed to understand this Bible? Is God asking you this morning to become a Rechabite? Or is this just "*Old*" Testament, out-of-date stuff? and we could "do a Jehoiakim job" on it, burn it, forget it?

BEFORE WE LISTEN TO the Newer Testament update take on Jeremiah's chapter 35, let me tell just a little bit more about these Rechabites.

Yonadab Rechabson who commanded his followers not to drink wine and to remain desert-like nomads so they would not "settle down" and become part of the Canaanite culture of Baal and Astarte were descendants of Moses' father-in-law Jethro (Exodus 18, I Samuel 15:1-9), the non-Jewish Midianite Kenites who went with the Jews out of Egypt to the promised land of Canaan. Jael, the woman who pounded a stake through the head of Canaanite General Sisera, to help the Jews, was a Kenite (Judges 4:17-22, 5:24-31). The Kenite-Rechabites were teetotalers with a sojourner style of life, thanks to Yonadab their forefather's commands. It's quite like the Mennonites, who followed Mennon Simon's (1492-1561) word never to fight—if you are attacked, just move away—and forever be pacifists. Or like the Seventh Day Adventists who obey Ellen White's (1827-1915) injunction to worship on Saturdays and never eat meat; so they are God-serving abstemious healthy vegetarians to this very day.

THE RECHABITE ALTERNATIVE, AND FOLLOWING CHRIST FIRST

Yonadab Rechabson was renowned for his **zeal** simply to follow the holy LORD God's commands with a single-minded whole heart. That's why he became friends with Israel's "Clean-up King" Jehu in the time of Elisha.

"Climb up in my chariot," said the fast-driving Jehu to Yonadab, "and watch my **zeal** for the LORD God" (II Kings 10:15-17). Jehu had just killed Queen Jezebel who had promoted the worship of the sex goddess Astarte in the Ten tribes of Israel. She had put on her cosmetics to seduce Jehu. "Throw her out the window," said Jehu. A couple servants threw her out; Jehu trampled Jezebel with his horses, and then went in and had a good meal—this is in the Bible (II Kings 9)—That was Jehu's **zeal** for the Lord, killing off **all** the Baal sympathizers of earlier King Ahab.

It struck me that one of Jesus' apostles was Simon the Zealot, mentioned almost last in the lists of the Twelve, just before Judas Iscariot (Luke 6:12-16). Zealots were Jews fanatic about rising up against the Romans who controlled God's people in Canaan. Jesus called the apostles John and James Zebedee "Sons of Thunder"—zealots! (Mark 3:13-19—because they asked Jesus to call down a lightning strike on the despised ethnic Samaritan village who would not give them lodging (Luke 9:51-56)—

THE BEST I CAN tell is: Rechabites, Mennonites, Adventists, Nazarites!—no wine, no hair cut, specially dedicated to the Lord, like Samson! (Judges 13): Rechabites are frugal **pacific** purist **zealots** who keep God's commandments religiously and do not feel at home—nomads—in the sinful world full of violent and lascivious-inducing idols. So the point of Jeremiah chapter 35 is very clear, it seems to me: there will always be a Rechabite standing up for the Kingdom of God in history, now and forever; but God's people Judah were headed for exile like the dispersed Ten tribes of Israel, because they had not listened to the call of God's prophets Isaiah, Micah and Jeremiah....

And the chapter 35 passage faces us too: have we people listened to God's call to **obey the LORD** in how we vote, in what we read, watch, and buy? God's call to **follow Jesus** in this crooked cultural generation? the call proclaimed by God's prophets Slofstra, Tamminga, Westerhof, VanderVelde, van Nyenhuis and Kok? Are we seeking the Kingdom of God and God's merciful just-doing **first** (Matthew 6:33)—just checking—or has some version of the deeply unbiblical mantra "America First!" "Ontario first!" "Me first, and then afterwards maybe the poor and the asylum seekers" got a hold on our conservative innards? Should we better help the Reformational preachers and try on a Jeremiah yoke for size?

LET'S GET A NUDGE from the Newer Testament gospels:

Luke 9:57-62

AS THE COMPANY OF Jesus was walking along the road some fellow said to Jesus, "I will follow you wherever you happen to go." And Jesus said to him, "The foxes have holes, and the birds of the sky have nests (κατασκηνώσεις), but the Son of Man does not have anywhere to rest his head."

Jesus said to another person, "Follow me." But the person said, "Sir, please allow me first to go bury my father." Jesus said to him, "Let the dead bury their own dead; but you go spread the news of the Kingdom of God."

Another person said, "I will follow you, Lord, but first allow me to say goodbye to my family." Jesus said to the person, "Nobody who puts the hand on a plow and looks backward is suitable for the Kingdom of God."

Mark 11:17-31
(parallel, Matthew 19:16-30 and Luke 18:18-30)

AND JUST AS JESUS was starting out on his journey, one fellow running up kneeled before Jesus and asked Jesus, "Good teacher, what must I do in order to inherit eternal life?" And Jesus said to him, "Why do you call me `good'? Nobody is `good' except one, God. You know the commandments: Do not murder, do not commit adultery, do not steal, do not bear false witness, do not withhold something that belongs to another; honour your father and your mother...."

And the (probably Pharisee) fellow said to Jesus, "Rabbi/Teacher, all of these commandments I have kept from my youth on."[cf. Luke 18:18 ἄρχων and see Luke 10:25 νομικός.]

And Jesus, looking intently at him, loved him, and said to the fellow, "There's just one thing you are missing: go, put up for sale whatever you own, and give (the proceeds) to the poor, and you will have treasure in heaven. Then come along, follow me."

Upon hearing Jesus' word the fellow's eyes clouded over, and he went away grievously troubled ("vexed"), because he had a lot of valuable possessions.

Then Jesus, casually looking around, said to his disciples, "My! with how much difficulty it is for those who have a lot of stuff to enter the Kingdom of God."

The disciples were flabbergasted at Jesus' words. But Jesus responding further said to them, "Children, how difficult it is for those trusting in riches to step into the Kingdom of God! Why it is easier for a camel to go through the eye of a sewing needle than it is for a wealthy person to enter the Kingdom of God."

And Jesus' disciples were even more astounded, and kept saying to themselves, "Who then can be saved?!"

But Jesus, looking intently at them, said, "Among humans it is impossible; however, not so with God—with God all things are possible."

Then Peter piped up to say to Jesus, "Remember! **we** left everything behind and have followed you! [The Matthew 19:27 account of this event adds that Peter says, "What's in it for us?"]

Then Jesus said, "Truly I tell you, there is no one who has left behind household or brothers or sisters, mother or father, children or belongings **for my sake and for the sake of the gospel**, who will not receive back 100 times as much **now**, in this very time of opportunity, household, brothers and sisters, mothers and children and belongings [—100 times as much!—] **albeit with persecutions,** and also will receive in the coming age everlasting life. However, many who are first will be last, and the last will be first.

This, too, is the Word of the Lord!
Thanks be to God!

JESUS' WISE WORDS OFTEN seem cryptic, Rechabitish even: if you follow me, you (nomads) won't even have a cheap motel or a camp site to rest your head; if you really walk in the Way of God's kingdom, don't bury your parents? don't even say goodbye to the family? and certainly don't have a paid-off mortgaged house and a good-sized RRSP in the bank! And then this inquiring fellow who could honestly say, "I have kept all of God's commandments since my youth"—some of us might try to say that—and Jesus loved him and his testimony, but the fellow still missed the boat…because he was trying so hard to save himself! What in God's world are we potential nomads supposed to do?!

I've been told I sometimes bring up too much different material in a sermon all at once. I'm sorry about that. But the Bible is not a fast food hamburger without onions. The Bible is a full course Thanksgiving Day feast with meat and wine and dessert. Jeremiah 35 and Jesus' preaching in the gospels complement each other. In fact, when Jesus once asked his disciples "Who do people say that I am?" it was reported some thought he was Jeremiah (Matthew 16:14)!

The whole Bible—Older and Newer Testaments together— is a complicated read, even if its main point is utterly clear for those who have ears to hear: **<u>repent</u> in your gut of your stubborn pride to go your own way to save <u>your</u> face, and <u>live in forgiven thankfulness to the</u> LORD for letting you share in the long-term grace Jesus offers you in a communion of sinful saints till he comes back** (or you go to be with him).

LET ME TRY TO pull these remarks all together:

God's people reduced to little Judah in the days of King Jehoiakim were practically indistinguishable— God's people—from their Canaanite cultural woodwork of deceptive power politics and glittering sex scandals, while not caring to listen to God's voice spoken by the yoked prophet Jeremiah (Jeremiah 27:2, 28:10). Faced with similar circumstances today I'm sometimes tempted by the Rechabite alternative, to want to be an Amish Mennonite pacifist who drops out of the rat race somehow, maybe become a wandering Kuyperian Franciscan monk sworn to poverty, chastity, and unquestioning obedience. It would simplify things, reduce one's responsibilities?

But an isolated itinerant monk, monasteries and nunneries are not perfect islands of peace. Pacifist Mennonite communities, as Rudy Wiebe's novel *Peace Shall Destroy Many* (1962) shows, still find ways to fight to be FIRST, in charge of calling the shots. And Pastor Joel's Rechabite example 6 years ago from this pulpit—when he sees a beautiful woman approaching him on the sidewalk, he looks down at the ground—fine, but that doesn't change how some women half-dress on the street and most of us men keep looking. And the pious young Pharisee of Mark 10, a latter-day Rechabite, who broke Jesus' heart with his earnestness, had to be told it is impossible for humans to save themselves and their society: only God, God's Holy Spirit, can possibly break your stubborn will to do things **your** way, what **you** trust, so that instead, you want to become an **adopted** child of God, a baptized **adopted** brother or sister to Jesus Christ walking in **his** footsteps.

That's what Jesus hard sayings in Mark 10 means: the willingness to accept Jesus' extended hand has to come **first,** before everything else that could stand in the way—repressive government (Baal), seductive pleasure (Astarte), dysfunctional family needing attention, your source of money, addicted you yourself: the willingness to accept Jesus' extended hand has to come **first,** because what comes **first** underlies and informs everything else in your life. And once you say, "I hear you, Lord, I come, just as I am, hang-ups and all," then Jesus Christ promises you 100! loving fellow brothers and sisters, 100! offers of support and encouragement in rough times, like having to have to leave your homeland Iran, 100! **memories** of **enriching** surprise blessings despite being old and feeling forsaken—My yoke fits snug on your tired neck and is gentle, says Jesus Christ (Matthew 11:28-30). I don't want sacrifices from you! Just take me at my word, hold my hand, and walk with me as a companion, and once in a while sing me a song of thanksgiving that you love me, say the Psalms (Psalm 40:6-8, 69:30-33; I Samuel 16:22).

That's how yoked Jeremiah 35 and the gospel of Jesus Christ according to Mark, Matthew and Luke go together: don't be and look like the god-less (Nicolaitan) culture you inhabit, and don't trust your own do-goodingness, but surrender to the gentle piercing call of Jesus in God's living Word, "I want you to be my adopted sister or brother following me—that's all."

I CLOSE WITH THE verses of the gospel according to Mark 8 (the Reflection printed in your order of worship). When Inès and I were counselors at a Billy Graham Crusade in Chicago in 1970, Graham read this passage for his altar call at the end of the service.

Mark 8:34-35, 38

CALLING THE CROWD TOGETHER with his disciples, Jesus said to them, "If anyone wishes to follow in my footsteps, let him or her deny oneself and take up his or her cross, and follow me. Anybody who wants to save one's own life intact will ruin it: whoever loses one's life for my sake and the sake of the gospel, will rescue their life. ...Yes, whoever is ashamed of me and my words in this fast-and-loose and devoutly wicked generation, well, the Son of Man will be ashamed of that person too, when the (victorious) Son of Man comes in the glory of his Father with the holy angels.

ALL OF US WHO are adopted children of God have different crosses to bear—forms of persecution: the childhood trauma of an alcoholic parent, simply getting old and decrepit, being miserably lonely and can't admit it, uncertainty of income, the sad relief of a divorce, an elderly parent with faltering health, children who have forgotten their baptism, a friend who has lost the Way but doesn't know it, prospects of unpleasant repression in your work place, driven from your home by fire or an evil government, submerged doubts about who or what to trust, maybe even a criminal past—

Just pick up your cross, and follow my lead, says Jesus Christ. To "follow Jesus" is not an idea you put into practice that solves all your problems, it's a Way of being alive: **repentant cross-bearing forgiven engaged gentleness unashamed of belonging to Jesus.** If we as a Willowdale congregation are somewhat like that long-ago Ephesus church in Revelation 2:1-7, doctrinally solid but missing the attractive shine of its first Kuyperian/Rechabite love, which Betty Carter articulated a year ago (the immigrants who formed this congregation supported the church and Christian education **first**, and then you bought groceries with what was left), it's time to be captivated again by the simple life-giving exuberant love of Jesus for you, even if you have hurts. Don't be ashamed of Jesus Christ's loving you! Go, tell it on the mountain to a neighbour or stranger; simply show it with a smile. Even if it means you could wear a Jeremiah yoke to work tomorrow morning on the Toronto subway because we too live in the days of Jehoiakim….

Closing Prayer

Dear Lord and Holy Spirit, Help us to take in personally the sober but good news of Jeremiah and Jesus this morning: God in Jesus loves me, this I know, for the Bible tells me so. Protect us Lord, from being ashamed of you to Baal and Astarte devotees. Hold us close in our cross-bearing. And keep giving us the stamina and hope we need to trust and follow **You,** in Your footsteps…**first**. Thank you for the little joyful communion celebration we can share now with a hundred brothers and sisters, and a thousand more all over the world, in Jesus' Name, whether we came in first or at last, Amen.

> 19 August 2018
> Willowdale Christian Reformed Church
> Toronto, Ontario

14

The Beasts in God's World and our daily Psalm 2 Responsibility: Tough Merciful Just Rule Expecting Jesus Christ's Return

Text: Daniel 7:1-18, 27

I READ TO YOU part of Daniel 7 where a dream God gave Daniel is written down; it begins in verse 1 with a hurricane producing a succession of 3 enormous strange-looking animals.

Daniel 7:1-18, 27
IN THE FIRST YEAR of Belshazzar, King of Babylon, Daniel saw a dream envisioned in his head as he lay abed; so Daniel wrote down the dream, reporting the key happenings of the matter.

Daniel said: I saw in the nightmare apparition—look at that!—
the four winds of the heavens [North, South, East, West] were stirring

up a watery hurricane. And four monstrous Beasts rose up out of the agitated sea, each one different from the others.

The first Beast was like a lion which had the wings of an eagle until—as I watched in this vision—its wings were ripped off! and it was jerked up off the ground and made to stand up on its feet like a man; and the centring heart of a man was given to this (lion-like) Beast.

And—good night!—another Beast! a second one, something resembling a bear reared up on one side...three ribs in its mouth between its teeth. And this bearish Beast was told, "Get up! indeed, devour a lot of flesh!"

After that I looked and saw happen—could you believe it!?—another Beast, something like a leopard with four bird wings on its back. And this leopard-like Beast had four heads. **Ruling power was given to this Beast.**

…and after that I saw in the nightmare apparition—Wow!—a fourth Beast, fearsome, terrifying, and monster-strong! It had huge teeth made of iron; it devoured and smashed (things) to bits and stamped what was left over with its feet. This fourth Beast was different from all the other Beasts that came before it—it had ten horns.

I inspected the horns carefully—that's right!—another horn, a little one came up among the ten horns before which three of the earlier horns were ripped up by their roots and—believe it or not!—there were eyes on this little horn! like eyes of a human being! and a mouth speaking boastful crude talk.

As I watched Thrones were put in place. An ages-old hoary Figure was seated—the clothes were white as snow, the head of hair like pure wool. The Ancient Figure's throne was flames of fire, its wheels an incandescent burning! A stream of (holy) fire spewed forth from the hoary Figure's presence. A thousand thousands (of angels) served this Ancient One; ten thousand times ten thousands stood at attention. The Court for Judgment was set in place, and the record books were opened....

I watched very closely now because of the noise of the gross boastful words which the (little) horn kept spouting. And I kept on looking until that Beast was killed, and its body destroyed, given over to being burned by fire. As for the rest of the Beasts: **their violent power to rule had been taken away**, and the length of their lives was prolonged just for a certain time and a bit more.

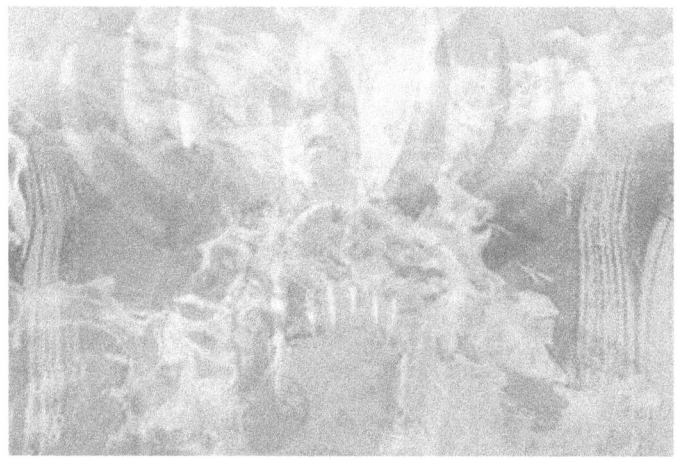

I saw and kept looking at the nightmare apparitions, and suddenly! There on the clouds of the heavens there happened to come "Someone-like-a-human-being" (Son-of-Man), and he was brought before the hoary Ancient One, and was specially presented before the ages-old Ancient One.

To that "One-like-a-human being" was given ruling power, weighty authority, and royal kingdom rule: all peoples, nations, and languages are to serve this "One-like-a-human-being."

His ruling power is an everlasting ruling power which shall never disappear, and his royal kingdom rule shall never be destroyed.

As for me, Daniel, my spirit within me was deeply shaken up, and the visions in my head totally frightened me. I approached one (of the angels) standing nearby, I wanted to know from it something reliable about all of this stuff, and the angel told me, interpreted what had happened:

These four monstrous Beasts are four kingdoms which will rise up out of the Earth-world. But the saints of the Most High God shall receive the (final) Kingdom Rule, shall possess the (final) Kingdom Rule for everlasting, yes, forever and ever and ever and ever....

...the Kingdom Rule (of "The-One-like a human-being"), the governing power and greatness of the Kingdom Rule under the entire heavens **shall be <u>given</u> to the holy people of the Most High God:** their Kingdom Rule shall be an everlasting Kingdom Rule, **and all centres of power shall serve and obey them.**

This is the Word of the Lord.
Thanks be to God!

BOTH DANIEL 7 AND REVELATION 13 talk about Beasts that materialize out of the ocean and the earth-world, which Beasts are terrifying to prince Daniel in Babylon (540 BC) and to apostle John imprisoned on the island of Patmos during the Roman empire (after 70 AD). These Beasts are not normal strong and glorious animal creatures, but are horrifying monstrosities, nightmarish dragonic monsters with 10-11 horns, each one like the dangerous horn of a rhinoceros, and a special little one with piercing human eyes. These imaginary Beasts are scary because the Bible pictures them to represent the belligerent regimes and rulers of Psalm 2 which hold G7-type meetings to show off their godless military prowess and to boast about their cultural power to control hordes of people.

And Daniel chapter 7, Psalm 2, and sections of Revelation (1:12-16, 14:14-16) also tell about a heavenly personage who acts like a "Son-of-Man," a human person born of a woman, who becomes designated by the enthroned ages-old, fiery LORD God (Hebrews 12:29) of the heavens and the earth to receive the authority and power to build up, lead and rule a whole kingdom of people into everlasting joy and shalom. Daniel's dreams and the whole 22-chapter apocalyptic vision of John proclaim that this coming everlasting Kingdom of peace and fruitfulness at the historical end of things will be **given** to God's holy people soon—expect it!—but not yet.[1]

The key verse of the last book of the Bible, 1:9, says God's believing children should follow Jesus' merciful just Way of doing things, patiently suffering persecution which may then happen. You saints might get hurt, says that Revelation 1:9 command, because your Psalm 2 task may include practising like a potter, breaking up evil power constellations which violate the Son-of-Man's gently firm rule

---

[1] The attending angel's explanatory interpretation of the fourth Beast's persecution of God's saints says the saints shall suffer for "a time, two times, and half a time" (7:25; cf. also 7:12). This "3 ½" phase is mentioned in Revelation 11:2; 12:6, 14; 13:5, and is "an approximate visionary designation of a fairly-long-but-shortened time period" (C. Seerveld, *Bewondering God's dumbfounding doings* [Jordan Station: Paideia Press, 2020], 81). That is how long Elijah's prayer stopped rain over Israel, and about how long Jesus Christ's mature ministry lasted on earth. That's the enigmatic long-shortened length of time believers may expect before Christ comes in glory to end our sin and misery.

on earth, because we need such life-experiential knowledge of re-directing and re-forming evil forces, since at the final judgment day, God's company of sinful saints will be called upon to "judge angels" (I Corinthians 6:13), **fallen** angels, and that includes, I believe, "unclean spirits," principalities, powers, thrones (Romans 8:37-38, Colossians 1:16)—the "Beasts"!

THAT IN A NUTSHELL is the message from God's Word this morning. So let me first explicate "the Beasts," and, second, explain "the Son-of-Man," and finally delineate how persons like us who have been baptized into the Name of God the Father, God the Son Jesus Christ, and the Holy Spirit, have promised to act toward the Beasts while we expectantly work and wait for Jesus Christ to come again.

(1) "Beasts" revealed by the Bible are normally vicious, invisible evil forces in the world with a hold over our lives. That's why the Bible, I think, describes the Beasts in such vivid, outlandish detail: ruthless bronze claws, horns with penetrating surveillant eyes that can see right through your innards, and unspeakable iron brute power to control your every move and debilitate you—but you can't see the Beast overwhelming you! So Scripture wants to make us aware that these hideous, malformed invisible Beasts are real!

The cursed COVID-19 novel coronavirus, biblically speaking, is a Beast, invisible but killing millions of people around the world and in Canadian long-term old-folks' homes—like a no-god taking our breath away. A driving communal Spirit of greedy unconscious selfishness is a

Beast afoot in God's world: you can't put your finger on it, but our well-being, being able to buy ripe fruit in winter in Toronto from Chili, Spain and Morocco—there's nothing wrong with that is there!?—contributes to the cartel-produced poverty of hundreds of thousands of families in Africa and the *favelas* of South America. The curse of societal poverty is bigger than you or me; we are in the grip of a systemic Economic stock-marketed Beast that lets us eat vegetables and bread while neighbours out of sight starve and have no drinkable water.

The right to use force and collect taxes which a lawful political government with its police has, according to the Bible (Romans 13:1-7), becomes Bestial when such coercive armed power becomes capricious, and the legal authority enables injustice and criminal gain. Poisonous gas in warfare and megaton bombs dropped from miles up in the heavens upon cities of sleeping civilians are practicably invisible—whether it be the Nazi supersonic U2s headed over Holland for England in the 1940's or the atom bomb made in the USA hitting Hiroshima in 1945—such antihuman measures of murder are the home-made stamping feet of the militaristic Sea-Beast (Daniel 7 and Revelation 13:1-10). When the petty tyrants of Psalm 2 assume superman authoritarian power like an Emperor Caesar Caligula, Louis XIV (*L'état c'est moi*), Hitler, Khomeini or Putin, with secret surveillance that assumes a godlike power over the populace, it stokes a pervasive Fear in the subconsciousness of ordinary people who have a principled integrity.

And a most cruel Beast is the Lie, the subtle Deceit of media communication, crooked distorted reporting that misleads or confuses people, because False Witness quickly can become second-hand anonymous, and therefore an un-located Evil for which no one takes responsibility; IT soon drifts on the air waves into your TV or hides in-between printed sentences in the newspaper (the second Earth-Beast of Revelation 13:11-18).

So there are different Beasts active in world history, **insidious invisible Evil Powers which distort, depress and destroy normal creatural life.** That's what the apostle Paul wrote about to the early church congregations: "our struggle is not against flesh and blood, but against the principalities (ἀρχάς) against the despotic authoritarian forces (ἐξουσίας), against the spiritual influences of wickedness at work in the unearthly realms (πνευματικὰ τῆς πονηρίας)" (Ephesians 6:7-12).

A fatal pandemic viral Disease, everlasting world-wide deadly Poverty, the cruel unending disregarded hidden Violence against women, children, the handicapped and weak persons, the blatant and subtle Lie manipulated by the arch liar Satan employed since Eve and Adam: these are all Beasts violating God's good creatures, which Jesus Christ's ministry on earth in Palestine illustrated needed to be overcome. Jesus cured the Beast of Disease (Mark 2:1-12, Matthew 10:1, Luke 14:1-6), stopped Hunger and Thirst (Mark 6:32-44, John 6:1-14), reprimanded Violence (Matthew 26:44-54, v. 52, John 8:1-11) and countered the Lie (Luke 4:1-13). And the apostle John gave a general warning too: "We belong to

God, but the whole cosmos lies under the power of the Evil One" (I John 5:19).

(2) In contrast to the deadly Earthy-Ocean generated Beasts in Daniel's dream is this mysterious person coming on the clouds of heaven to be presented to the ages-old Ancient figure who represents God. And this heavenly person is named "Someone-like-a-Son-of-Man," better, "One-**like**-a-human-being."[2] That name, "One-**like**-a-human-being," becomes a special Older Testament way of referring to "the Messiah"! who is expected by God's people Israel to come to bring God's Kingdom Rule to fruition on earth. When the high priest Caiphas asks Jesus to answer under oath whether he be the Messiah, the son of **God**, Jesus answered him, practically paraphrasing Daniel 7:13: "You said it! In fact, from now on you will see the Son of **Man** (="Someone-like-a-human-being") seated at the right hand of Powerful Authority (=the ages-old Ancient One, God), also coming on the clouds of heaven" (Matthew 26:64 / Mark 14:61-62).

---

2   The Aramaic text has בר אנוש which in Hebrew would be בן אדם, "son of Adam"! "Adam" as name means "mankind," "humankind." The genealogy given for Jesus by the Greek medical doctor Luke does not stop at Abraham (as Jewish tax collector Matthew does, Matthew 1:1) but goes back to the very "son of Adam" next to "son of God" (Luke 3:38). So "son of Adam" emphasizes Jesus' humanity and special confraternity with God. Daniel 7:13, "son of a human being," recalls 3:25 where Nebuchadnezzar sees the angel as fourth person in the fiery furnace and says, "it looks like a son of the gods" (לבר אלהין).

So "Someone-like-a-human-being" refers to Jesus Christ, especially in his triumphant coming in glory with angels, when he will gather God's "chosen ones" together from the ends of the earth (Matthew 24:29-31; 25:31-32), finally to reap the harvest of world history and end the evil Rule of the Beasts (Daniel 7:27, Revelation 14:14-26).

(3) Meanwhile, how should we baptized people live, surrounded by Beasts in God's world?

> Let me slip in a parenthesis about reading the Bible. Many theological commentaries struggle to identify the Kingdoms described by Daniel 7's four beasts, by using the huge idol of Nebuchadnezzar's dream in Daniel 2: head of gold, chest of silver, thighs of bronze, legs of iron, feet of iron mixed with clay. The statue and the Beasts refer to the Babylonian empire, the Medes and Persian kingdoms, the Macedonian Greek rule of Alexander the Great, and the Roman empire.
>
> Possibly so, I agree. But the thrust and reach of Daniel's interpretation of the dreams and visions, accompanied by Psalm 2 and reinforced by the book of Revelation, goes far beyond hinting at historical data and the fall of the Persian, Greek and Roman empire.
>
> Daniel's prophecies not only certify the large picture of the ultimate failure of all "World powers," worldly empires, **and** the sure advent of the completed worldwide dominion of Jesus Christ's Rule, but the Scripture of Daniel, also says the

> apostle Paul (I Corinthians 10:11), reveals and exemplifies reality for setting and warning our consciousness on how to proceed since Jesus Christ lived, died, was resurrected, and ascended back to God's throne, and the Satan and its Beasts make life difficult for creatures in God's world (Revelation 12:7-17).

The Beasts we have to contend with are vicious invisible evil forces which disturb and disrupt God's blessed Rule of normal creatural shalom. In institutions created by God as havens for us human creatures to prosper within, like a marriage or family or friendship, like a village, city or nation, **there can be a warp hidden in such an institutional bond that damages the woof its inhabitants weave.** For example, *retinitis pigmentosa* which genetically blinds grandchildren may inhibit a couple from bearing the joy of children because of what it means for a next generation. Good coastal real estate near rich fishing waters or habitations near fertile volcanic ash soil may have the killing flaw of easy flood or lava eruptions underneath their daily life.

The wonderful tripartite checks-and-balances of the United States of America government seems to be plagued currently by a pervasive evil spirit of Falsehood that renders public communication, social media, so toxic that "good people" are misled by influential Liars and therefore do not know what political "news" to trust. Canada is a prosperous country with many millionaires and a large middle class, but certain indigenous peoples must still boil pollution out of their water during a lifetime! Can—**how does a person reform systemic evil for which no one seems responsible for doing it?**

Rather than blame the rich, the government, ignorant people or the Devil, and shrug one's shoulders, let me suggest the following:

(A) Recognize that certain Evil is so uncanny that only God can stop it; so pray the psalms, not sitting down but on your knees, like Psalm 74, pleading with God "to break the heads of the dragons—the Beasts!—in the waters of the world (Psalm 74:12-14) as you once did, Lord." You finally had Hitler killed, Nazi leadership, in his German bunker, got rid of Idi Amin in Uganda, so you can also paralyze populist Trumpism, our pious Racism, blinding Greed ruining lives of the weak—hear our prayer, Lord!

And such passionate prayer must be bodily prayer, embodied prayer, that is, involving sacrificial action of some sort on one's part—giving away time, lifetime, or money resources, wise words or encouragement to other more able united reformers. Your friend or neighbour's cancer or dementia that hollows out their lives may not be cured by your deeds, but "you give merciful attention so that God's love (through your ministrations) might be revealed to those needy persons" (John 9:1-4).

And the book of Revelation assures you (6:9-10) that the saints in heaven near God's throne are praying, pestering God too, pleading, "Why wait so long, Lord, to bring things to a good conclusion!"

So, A: pray intently to God as if your life and the lives of others depended on it, because they do.

(B) Enter into communal generational long-term building and healing projects, since Beasts are not problems to be solved or errors to be corrected but are spiritual forces which outlast one's lifetime. The cursed Beast of homelessness cannot be fixed just by building more condos at cheaper prices today, because abusive families, pernicious addictions, and wasteful habits of living are complicating constitutive factors behind forlorn living on the streets. There has to be long-range, organized redemptive efforts to better the plight of derelicts and human misfits. Circles of Care, Medical research hospitals, Shalem, chartered communal groupings like Citizens for Public Justice, Neighbourlink, *Medécins sans frontières*, especially schools, educational institutions, Christian teaching and learning that fosters imaginative insight even more than argumentative toughness, so that not success but service is cherished, as one generation enables the next generation to go beyond past restorative contributions. After evangelical churches preach the gospel convicting people to become dedicated followers of Jesus, there needs to be concerted communal non-church follow-through with formative bands of people dedicated to lead restructuring in our other civil areas of society and our plastic-polluted creatural world.

And such communal work, declares the book of Revelation (14:1-5) as well as the gospel according to Matthew (19:27-30), is not a matter of visible success or failure: long-term generational redemptive contributions are the earthly saints' first fruits Psalm 2 testimony to God's Rule on earth, and training for their sitting on the thrones in glory with the Lamb of God.

So, A: **pray like Psalm 39**; B: **enter into long-term communal pottery-making.**

(C) **Be ready to get hurt in your incremental reform of evil in God's world and human society.** As Psalm 2 anointed ruling citizens in God's Kingdom, you may have to "break mis-formed pottery" in order to re-mould better vessels (Psalm 2:9, cf. Jeremiah 18:1-11); and if that means you need to revamp your own household idols or the warped possessions of your parents or your children, it may be very painful to try. It may be true, as Scripture says, "Resist the devil, and it will flee from you" (James 4:7), but some unhealthy addictions—Beasts!—do not turn tail and disappear easily. Habits of luxury become ingrown; authoritarian enemies to whom you give an inch of good food and drink (Proverbs 25:21-22, Romans 12:20) may take a mile of your possessions; pointing out your neighbour's fault may blind you to your own destructive critique (Matthew 7:1-5).

Human reformers are not immune from doing harm to others as well as to themselves just because they would reform matters in Christ's Name. And as Jesus found out, sound prophets do not always receive honour and a hearing among their own hometown crowd with whom they are familiar (Matthew 13:54-58). Fighting Beasts and reshaping clay pots, even if done wisely, can afford the persecution of loneliness and discouragement.

But the book of Revelation repeats and repeats the encouragement of chapter 1:9: ὑπομονή! Hang in there! Despite mistakes, weakness, regrettable sinful deeds and short comings, persistent working expectation of blessing shall! surprisingly, joyfully overcome the debilitating evil we come to know (2:23b-29, 3:20-22, 21:7).

So, A: pray; B: work out communally your salvation; C: expect hardship.

IN CLOSING LET ME say this: the fact that we are called to fight gigantic Beasts in God's world which Daniel dreamed about, and the book of Revelation confirms—Sea-Beast of evil Coercive Violence and Earth-Beast of Big Lie Media—the Beasts should not make God's children paranoid. Don't become an ingrown toenail, says God through the prophet Jeremiah to the buffeted people of God stuck in Babylon (where Daniel and his friends prevailed! at the court of Nebuchadnezzar and Belshazzar): "Seek the shalom of the city where I have let you people be exiled; pray to me, the LORD God, for them, since in their welfare you will also find peace" (Jeremiah 29:7). "Look," said Jesus to his closest disciples, "I am sending you out as sheep into a pack of wolves. So you all become worldly-wise as snakes, and (remain) as innocent as doves" (Matthew 10:6).

Today I have anointed you all with baptism as my adopted sons and daughters, says God in Psalm 2:7, to the communion of believers. So your life may not always be happy as you obediently follow Revelation 1:9—bringing God's Rule to bear in this world, despite sorrows, expecting Jesus Christ to return soon—but you may be certain and joyful through tears and disappointments, because **the**

Kingdom of God shall be <u>given</u> to you! when the time comes **for you to rest from your labours** (Daniel 7:27, Revelation 14:12-14).

Closing Prayer

DEAR GOD, HELP US to learn to pray bodily, first on our knees, and then on our feet, for your will to be done on earth as it is done in heaven, trusting you can make us crooked sticks straight again, and that You will be hospitable to us (Psalm 39:12-13) who love you with our whole heart, mind, commitment and strength in following Jesus Christ by the care-filled leading of your Holy Spirit, Amen.

Psalm 39

```
Once    I      said,  "I            must    keep    qui - et;
"LORD,  are    You    re  -  veal  -  ing   lim - its,
"Why,   O      Lord,  must         I       be      wait - ing
"But,   my     Lord,  your         heav -  y       bur - den
"Can    You    see,   LORD,        I       am      cry - ing?

else    I      sin    in           harsh   dis  -  pute.
how     my     days   look         in      your    sight?
when    my     hope   is           still   in      You?
wears   me     out    and          weighs  me      down.
Do      not    spurn  my           sore    un   -  rest.

Just    to     see    the          wick  -  ed     near me
Just    a      breath and          fleet -  ing    sha - dow
Keep    me,    LORD,  from         sin    and      trou - ble,
All     your   dis  - ci     -     pline  for      sin - ning
I       pass   by     like         those  be  -    fore me,
```

BEASTS IN GOD'S WORLD AND OUR PSALM 2 RESPONSIBILITY

TEXT: Psalm 39, vers. Calvin Seerveld © 87 87 7
TUNE: Evan Morgan, 1846-1920 *Llwyn*

11 April 2021
Willowdale Christian Reformed Church
Toronto, Ontario (and on Zoom)

15

The Older and Younger Generation of Christ's followers may expect the Wisdom of Moses and the Energy of Elijah to unite them in service during the last days

Texts: Malachi 3:13-4:6, Luke 1:16-17, Jude 24-25

I BRING YOU THE comfort of the Lord tonight, but it comes through the crucible of the prophet Malachi.

Malachi brought this Word to God's people when Nehemiah was writing down chapter 13 of that book by his name, around 420 BC. This is the same time when Socrates over in Greece lived in Athens (469-399 BC). Persia, however, ruled the Near Eastern world and had let the Jews return to their plundered land from which they had been deported several generations before by Babylonian Nebuchadnezzar. Prophets Jeremiah, Ezekiel and Daniel have all been dead and gone now for more than 100 years, about as long ago before Malachi as Abraham Kuyper (1837-1920) has been dead and gone before us today.

The hardy Jews back in Jerusalem had expected the millennium to come, a new era, a *new* year was going to break through all their miseries of exile. Instead, they faced the episode of Queen Esther, Hamaan, Mordecai and Ashasuerus-Xerxes; they had struggled to build up a dinky second temple under Ezra, prophets Haggai and Zechariah; and they were trying to get the city administration and its protecting walls in working order again under Nehemiah amid fierce animosity from the surrounding Samaritans and local Canaanites. God's people were disgruntled, the priestly leadership had no vision, and many respectable citizens made a practice of short-changing and blaming God for their troubles. This is the time of Malachi.

THE END OF GOD's Malachi book (2:17-4:3) is about the Day of the LORD coming. Since most of us think this is *Oude Jaars Avonddienst* (Old Year's Eve) and tomorrow is New Year's Day, it could be reforming tonight for us to let Scripture help us face not just the end of a calendar year but realize this is a service for our facing the end...of the world. Some of us people right here in this room will do that in the year 2001; we will meet God face to face. It could be me (aged 70). It may be you (aged more or less than three score years and ten).

The change of date from 31 December to 1 January has never meant much to me. It's an old pagan ritual to think if you have a blow-out of a party, you can start your life over the next day utterly "new." It's simply not true. There is nothing "new" under the sun except what God's Holy Spirit does in converting us from the dead end of sin to a life of troubled joy in following Jesus Christ. Malachi can save us from the trivia of thinking a chronological change from 2000 to 2001 A.D. is significant by moulding our memories of the recent past into the prospect of the Day of the LORD acoming.

WHAT DOES THE PROPHETIC good news of Malachi say to us tonight, surrounded by Nehemiah, Psalm 90, Psalm 16, Psalm 126, Revelation 21-22 and Psalm 150: how are we to live, with what kind of focus, as we literally face the end…of the LORD's awesome Day coming, very soon.

Let me read aloud for you to listen—God's Word should be **heard**—Malachi 3:13 to the end of the book. We can open the NIV Bibles to the text after hearing the reading. Listen in now on how God interacted with God's people then, as Malachi tells it.

Malachi 3:13-4:6

YOUR CONVERSATION TOWARD ME is impudent, says the LORD God, and then you say, "Why, what have we been saying against You?"

You have so much as said, "To work hard for God is a farce! What does it profit a man or a woman to keep on standing guard for what God cares about? Why should we walk along, bent over before the face of the LORD God of the army of angels? From now on let's face the facts: Blessed are the domineering guys who push for what they want, because those who run roughshod over limits not only get ahead but even dare God, so to speak, and get away with it!"

Then those who stand in awe of the LORD began to speak together, each person with the neighbour: but the LORD God is listening with pricked ears and hears [such crooked talk]. A Commemorative Book is being written in to remind God, as it were, [the names and deeds] of those who stand waiting for the LORD, who [anticipate action] respecting God's Name.

These [last] are the ones who belong to me, says the LORD God of the army of angels. They will be my special possession on the Day when I act, for I will take responsibility for them as a father and mother take responsibility for a son or daughter who works hard for them. The time is coming when you shall once again discern the difference between a right-doing man or woman and a wicked person; you shall be able to recognize the difference between one who works hard for God and one who is slaving away all right but does not really serve God.

Yes, that's right! The Day is coming, burning like a refiner's blast furnace, and all the domineering persons who pushed to get ahead and kept on running roughshod over limits as if God were absent, shall now become worthless burnt-out cinders. That Day coming shall burn them to a crisp, says the LORD God of the army of angels, and leave behind for them no root, no offshoot.

But the sun of redemptive right-doing shall rise [like a meteor] and shine down on you who really know me by name and patiently wait expectant, shine down with restorative, health-giving power in its rays, so that you all shall break out, stampede like young bulls [released] from the stockade, to trample the wicked—they will be like ashes under the soles of your feet: that's what happens on the Day when I finally act, says the LORD God of the army of angels.

Keep on remembering, all of you, the *torah* [the Guidance] of Moses who worked hard for me, the ordinances and regulations for justice I commissioned him at Mount Horeb to set up for all Israel to keep.

And look! I will send you the seer Elijah before that great and awesome Day of the LORD breaks, so that that prophet shall make the hearts of the older generation reverberate again with the hearts of the younger generation, and foster the hearts of the youth to jibe again with the hearts of the elderly ones, so that I do not have to come smash the earth with a curse of utter destruction....

This is the Word of the Lord!
Thanks be to God!

THE TEXT THIS EVENING, the last three verses of the Older Testament, in the English Bible, Malachi 4:4-6 deals with Moses, Elijah, and the union of the older and the younger generations of faith.

(1) Moses and God's law sums up much of the Older Testament and is God's injunction for us today too: love God above everything! and your **neighbour** as you would take care of yourself (Romans 13:8-10, Galatians 5:25-6:2).

Keep on remembering that, says Malachi 4:4, not because it'll get you credit in the heavenly bank, but because that is the LORD's merciful way of giving you well-being, of leading you to a taste of shalom in your earthly life of 70/80 years.

To not cheat, as Ananias and Sapphira did in church with their offerings (Acts 5:1-11), to not push yourself forward officiously as was the practice of the leaders in the temple in Jesus' day (Luke 11:42-44, 18:9-14), to not take advantage of those weaker than yourself—single mothers, street kids, homeless persons, refugees (mentioned by name in Malachi 3:5, James 1:26-28); that is, to live a peaceable, generous daily life with the realization that the LORD God of the army of angels is a terrible refining fire (Malachi 4:1, Hebrews 12:28-29) who takes the side of the meek, those who don't and can't stick up for themselves (Psalm 37:8-11, Matthew 5:5): that is the wisdom Moses stands for, being at home with your neighbour in the way the LORD ordered the world.

Tonight, our Scripture says: remember Moses and God's hug of giving love rather than trying to get more of whatever for yourself.

(2) The Elijah mentioned in v.5 as herald of God's final Judgment Day is someone the Jews expected to show up on earth.

"Who do people say the Son of Man is?" asked Jesus. "Some say, 'Elijah!'" said his disciples (Matthew 16:13-20). When Jesus hollered on the cross, "Eli, Eli, lema sabachthani!" bystanders said, "See, he's calling for Elijah to come" (Matthew 27:45-50). The Pharisees sent priests and Levites from Jerusalem to ask John baptizing across the Jordan river, "Are you Elijah?" "No," said John, "I am not Elijah the Tishbite; I am the voice of one crying in the wilderness, 'Prepare ye the way of the Lord!' who Isaiah prophesied would come" (John 1:9-28).

However, when Jesus was transfigured on the mountain so that "his face shone like the sun," Peter, James, and John saw Jesus talking with Moses and Elijah! who had appeared. Later, as the disciples walked down the mountain after the experience, they asked Jesus, "Why do the teachers say, 'Elijah must come first'?" Then Jesus explained, it says in Matthew 17:1-13, that John the Baptizer was "the Elijah" who was to come, the forerunner to the coming of the Lord who would make all things well again, restored!

So the "Elijah" of Malachi 4:5 is the rough-hewn Baptizer John who "in the spirit and power of Elijah of old" —that's what God's angel told disbelieving Zechariah, the father of John, in the temple—Baptizer John **is** the "Elijah" who announces the birth of the Messiah, and prepares the Way of the Lord by preaching, "Repent of your proud selfishness, people, and be forgiven, so you shall bear **good** fruit" (Luke 3:1-9).

That's the way the overlapping horizons of the Bible try to tell us how God works in history: Elijah, Baptizer John, whoever prepares the Way of the Lord today. Preachers true to Scripture, parents who read the Bible in faith to their children, the women of this church who lead the young in Sunday worship, who lead Sunflowers, shepherd Friendship Club, **are** "Elijahs" in Malachi's sense, preparing hearers to face the coming "Day of the LORD."

The "Day of the LORD" in Scripture also, like "Elijah," both will come and has already come, **is acoming**. The Day of the LORD's judgment came for Israel when God's people were sent into exile, gone with the wind (II Kings 25:1-21). The Day of the LORD's judgment came with the birth of

Jesus! says Scripture, when the Light came into the world, and some said, we prefer to do our deals in the dark, and so became blind, condemned liars, even though they pretended to see (John 3:16-21, 9:35-41; cf. I John 1:5-10). The "Day of the LORD" comes for whoever has his or her life breath taken back by God who first gave it to us through our mothers and fathers (Ecclesiastes 12:1-7), and that day will be either a celebration of the LORD's tender, everlasting merciful power that George Vandervelde preached about from Isaiah 42, or an utterly sad ending. I'll come to that in a few minutes for the conclusion, but first v.6 in Malachi 4.

(3) Your NIV/RSV translation says that the Elijahs "will turn the hearts of fathers to their children and the hearts of children to their fathers."

It's a mistake to read that verse as if it cuts out mothers. It is also a mistake to think that Malachi is referring simply to blood relations, to restore family ties that have become strained. I can say this because in Luke 1:16-17 the angel talking to Zechariah about his son John's coming mission quotes and expands on Malachi 4:5-6 in a way that shows the **generations** of God's people are involved, especially with regard to doing what is right on the earth, in being faithful to the LORD's calling throughout the ages until…the Day of the LORD comes.

Luke 1:16-17
Says the angel Gabriel to Zechariah:
(Your prospective son) will turn many sons of Israel
    around to the Lord their God;
and your son will go before the Lord in the spirit
    and power of Elijah

to turn the hearts of fathers to children, that is
the disobedient to the wise counsel of those
    who do what is just,
(in order) to make ready for the Lord
    a well-equipped/well-prepared/ready people.

So, in the epilogue to Malachi's booked prophecy v.6, God promises to bring the older and younger generations of God's people in line with one another, to reconcile the X-generation which grew up displaced in pagan urban Babylon now back in shell-shocked Jerusalem with the old saintly leadership of Jeremiah, Ezekiel and Daniel. Or it would be more correct to say, in the light of Luke's commentary on Malachi, God promises to tune the hearts of an older wayward generation which deserved exile and has come back to Jerusalem in nostalgia for the good old days, tune their hearts to those younger ones faithfully rebuilding the walls of the "holy city" under Nehemiah's leadership.

THIS IS THE KEY point of our text: God wants the generation steeped in Moses' wisdom, which like an Elijah fervently realizes the Day of the LORD is at hand! to buoy up the generation of God's disaffected people, those older or younger believers who are listless, whose faith is full of holes, as Jesus puts it, and are just perverse, who dislocate just-doing (Matthew 17:14-21), who have the form of godliness but fake its actual power (II Timothy 3:1-5).

It is important for us to understand that neither the older nor the younger generation of believers has a corner on obedience to God because they are older or younger.

Psalm 78 epitomizes this truth: teach the coming generation, says Asaph in Psalm 78, the Great Deeds the LORD has done in history and the marvels God has created so that the next generation and their children **not** be like their stubborn forefathers and mothers whose heart was not steadfast, who just wanted a good job for their kids, whose spirit was not faithful to God (Psalm 78:1-8), so that the generation walked around in circles for 40 years in the wilderness, wishing they were back as slaves in Egypt! (Exodus 16:1-3, Numbers 11, Psalm 78:9-72).

Don't let anybody put you down because of your youth, Paul told Timothy: you set the believers of any age an example by your speech, conduct, loving, faithful purity of action (I Timothy 4:12), seeking God's Rule **first** rather than second.

So, v.6 in Malachi 4 asks everybody who expects the Day of the LORD to come tonight or tomorrow in 2001 A.D., as unexpected as your death or a thief in the night, to unite with those older and those younger than yourself—we are all always both following and preceding a generation—unite in remembering what God wants done, and be intently busy preparing the Way of the Lord's return by doing what is just together, loving to keep our promises, and walking humbly as a congregation with God (Micah 6:8).

How should we as a congregation get ready tonight ... for the Day of the LORD acoming?

You probably have heard that apocryphal story about Martin Luther who is reported to have said, "If Jesus Christ is actually coming back tomorrow, I'd plant a tree today."

Johann Sebastian Bach would have said, "If Jesus is coming back tomorrow, choir practice tonight!"

That is, you don't drop everything and start praying: you carry on your normal God-thanking work with intent anticipation, for tomorrow the tree you planted today will no longer become polluted, and the children you mentored in catechism this past year will never again forget who is their only comfort in life and in death, and the person you have been trying to console because of an abusive relationship will soon have every tear wiped away from her face forever (Revelation 7:13-17).

Nehemiah, because he expected the LORD to come back for a final accounting of his stewardship as mayor/governor of rebuilding Jerusalem: Nehemiah wrote in his diary at different times the last words of chapter 13: "Remember me for good, O my God, all the trouble I went through for this people of yours!" (Nehemiah 5:19, 13:14,22,31). Write it down in the Commemorative Book of Life You are keeping, Lord, the one Malachi mentions in chapter 3:16, that I persuaded the Jewish bankers to cancel the impossible debts of the poor (Nehemiah 5:1-13); that I got people to tithe again, so we could pay the temple musicians (Nehemiah 10:32-39, 13:10-14); I outlawed commercial buying-and-selling on the Sabbath so the city could enjoy the restfulness you instituted as a blessing (Nehemiah 13:15-22). Please remember me, O Lord, that I respected your Name and tried to have your will be done on earth as it is done in heaven, even though nobody else around seemed to notice—

If our congregation means to follow God's Word of Malachi about having the younger and older generations active together facing the Day of the LORD coming soon, which the last chapters of Revelation celebrate, then our worship services (like the one Pauline put together last Sunday evening) will liturgically practice such intergenerational worship of our Lord. So a Senior believer will read Psalm 90, and younger believers will profess our faith in the "New Creation," showing a natural united witness: experienced Moses' wisdom and expectant Elijah energy, from whichever generation, when focussed by the light of God's Word, will bring the comfort and hope God's people need to make disbelievers jealous and want such ongoing life too.

Marie Roeleveld, John, and family may be the first among us in the year 2001 to experience the awesome Day of the LORD nearby—please pray for them to keep their strength through the ordeal. How their grappling with "the last enemy" exactly fits together with the cosmic, cataclysmic Final Coming Day of Jesus Christ's return (Revelation 22:3-5) is not so clear. But this is certain: when the transfigured Christ, shining like the sun, returns in glorious tender power, the faithful meek, like Marie and John—can you imagine it!?—will stampede like young bulls released from the stockade, trampling under their dancing feet (this is Malachi's image) the warlords of the earth! all the aggressive, domineering figures who make the existence of the weaker in God's world miserable. That's the incredible but sure promise for every child, young person and adult here whose name is noted in God's Commemorative Book of Life.

All we need do tonight is hear God's Word of Malachi to realize we are returned exiles from sin, no longer captive to Babylon's strategies in its city malls and media. It's true, somewhat as an alcoholic who has given up the constricting habit of strong drink is always a **recovering** alcoholic, so a redeemed sinner is always a **sinful** saint. But we pray intently as older and younger generations of God's faithful people covered by the blood of Jesus (Ephesians 1:3-10, Colossians 1:15-20), pray to the Lord with Psalm 126 (breathed by God into human language at the time of Nehemiah and Malachi): we pray God give us new beginnings to prepare the Way of the Lord in the land.

Psalm 126

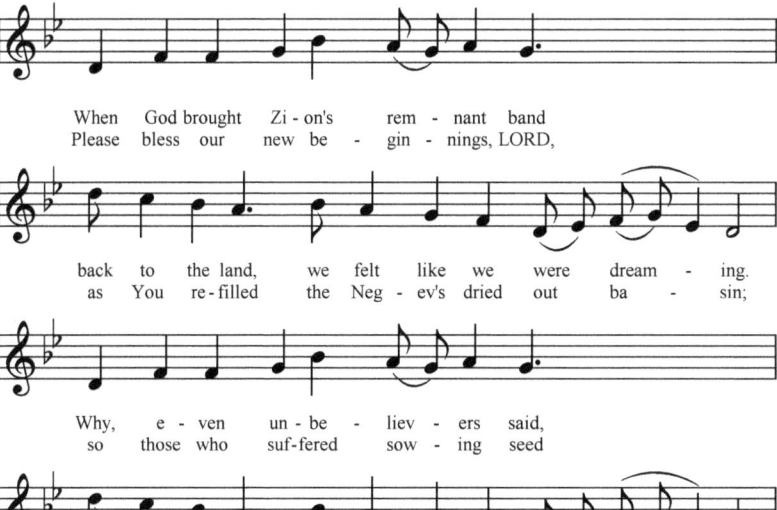

TOUGH STUFF FROM THE BIBLE, TENDERED GENTLY

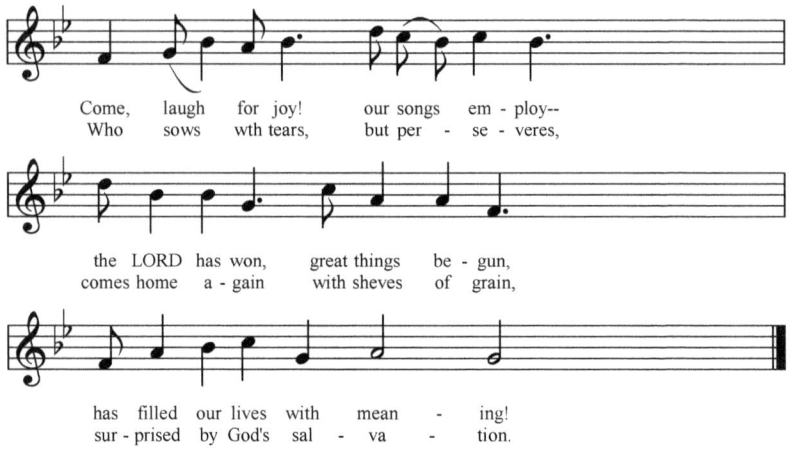

Come, laugh for joy! our songs em-ploy--
Who sows wth tears, but per-se-veres,
the LORD has won, great things be-gun,
comes home a-gain with sheves of grain,
has filled our lives with mean-ing!
sur-prised by God's sal-va-tion.

TEXT: Psalm 126, vers. Calvin Seerveld, 1985 ©   847 847
TUNE: J. Klug's Geistliche Lieder, 1535   *Mag Ich Ungluck*

RECEIVE GOD'S BLESSING for the pandemic week ahead from Jude, verses 24-25.

Jude 24-25

NOW TO THE ONE who is able to keep you from disbelieving, and is able to present you without blemish! before the presence of God's glory, even with triumphant joy: to the only God, our Saviour through Jesus Christ our Lord, let there be glory, majesty, almighty ruling power and final authority before all time, and now, and forever and ever more, AMEN

> 31 December 2000
> Willowdale Christian Reformed Church
> Toronto, Ontario

Index of Scripture passages freshly translated

Older Testament

Psalm 2	223-224
Psalm 33:12,18-22	164
Psalm 115	197-198
Isaiah 11:1-10	13-15
Isaiah 28:1-22	30-35
Isaiah 28:23-29	49-50
Isaiah 30:1-3, 8-21,31	63-66
Isaiah 30:15-18	46-47
Isaiah 31:1-3	66-67
Isaiah 32:15-18	67
Isaiah 36:11-15	88-89
Isaiah 37:7,14-20, 37-38	89-90
Isaiah 38:1-6, 9-20	83-85
Isaiah 39:1-2, 5-8	85-86
Isaiah 42:18-43:21	105-109
Isaiah 53:2-5	121-122
Isaiah 54:1-3	132
Isaiah 59-60	157-164
Jeremiah 18:1-20:6	225-230
Jeremiah 35	245-247
Ezekiel 18:1-5,9,19b-20,26-32	184-186
Ezekiel 33:1-20	201-203
Ezekiel 34:1-16, 20-25, 28-31	203-205
Daniel 7:1-18, 27	259-270
Joel 2:12-14	235
Malachi 1:10d-13	122
Malachi 3:13-4:6	287-289

Newer Testament

Matthew 20:1-16	188-189
Mark 8:34-35, 38	255-256
Mark 11:17-31	251-252
Mark 11:20-26	97-98
Mark 14:1-11	122-123
Luke 1:16-17	292-293
Luke 9:57-62	250-251
Luke 15	206-209
Romans 4:4-8	192-193
Philippians 4:4-7	79
II Timothy 2:11-13	236
Hebrews 5:4-6:12	133-135
Jude 24-25	298
Revelation 5	15-16

Heidelberg Catechism

Question/Answers 61 & 65	195

Psalms and Hymns

"I said, 'Must I now disappear under the ground,'" 86-87
Hezekiah's prayer, Isaiah 38:10-20
(2011) Calvin Seerveld
tune: Calvin Seerveld, *Hezekiah* (2011)

"Magnify the Lord" 154
(1985) Bert Polman, Luke 1:47
tune: Jacques Berthier, *Magnificat* (used with paid permission)

"When you pass through rough waters" 220-221
(1998) Calvin Seerveld
tune: Henry W. Zimmermann, *Little Flock* (1971)

Psalm 2, "Why do the nations rave like madmen?" 240-241
(2009) Calvin Seerveld
tune: Steve Jones, *Tanymarian* (1879)

Psalm 39, "Once I said, 'I must keep quiet'" 282-283
(1983) Calvin Seerveld
tune: Evan Morgan, *Tyddyn Llwyn* (1846-1920)

Psalm 126 "When God brought Zion's remnant band back to the land" 297-298
(1985) Calvin Seerveld
tune: J. Klug's Geistliche Lieder, *Mag ich Ungluck*, 1535

List of Illustrations

2   Peter Smith, **Working Late**. 1986, wood engraving, 76x102 mm.

56-57   **Vacant field filled with yellow dandelions** (*taraxacum officinale*) to cheer up passers-by, Finch avenue, Willowdale, Toronto, c. 1994? [English "dandelion" has French source, "*dent de lion*," because of the shape of the leaves]. Photo by Calvin Seerveld

84   Johanne Vollenhove, **Emblem of bed-ridden Hezekiah's life being extended 15 years** (1734)

180-181   Brochure cover for City of Toronto Reformation Festival **Art, Worship, and the City**, organized by Bert Polman, 29-31 October 1976.

216-218   Duane Michals, **The Return of the Prodigal Son** (1982), 5 gelatin silver prints, 13x18 cm, Henry L. Hillman Fund

242   Chronological table relating ancient Israel and Judah's Kings with certain of the prophets composed by Calvin Seerveld, arranged by Peter Enneson

260-268   **Beasts** and **The Ancient One** imaginatively reported in Daniel's nightmarish dream which the prophet then interpreted Unknown, PD, from various sources on the internet

269   Detail of Mathias Grünewald, **Reurrection panel of the Isenheimer** (c. 1516), Musée d'Unterlinden, Colmar, France (represnting "Son of Man" in Daniel's dream)

Note: Earnest attempt has been made to track down permission from the proper source of each artwork. If there be matters needing rectification, please contact the author.

Praise for
Tough Stuff, Tendered Gently

THE BIBLE'S BROAD SWEEP tells the story of a Creator who refuses to let this beloved and good creation go. This refusal grounds Calvin Seerveld's reading of the prophets. Their call remains unvarnished in the face of humankind's defacing of life on earth. It is a call to repent and to hope. 'Turn, return to a Creator who lives to bring restoration.'

This collection of talks challenges cynicism about the power of corporate greed and political grift. Seerveld reiterates the prophets' brisk understanding: the powers-that-be, then and now, are held accountable for how they helped or further crippled the vulnerable on earth. This includes the complex and delicate ways that spell life to humans and the natural world.

The call in these talks goes beyond structural repentance. Seerveld's translations zero in on each reader/listener, inviting us to consider our individual ways of life. Ground your hope; our Maker notes and honors every small daily shift to line up our talk with action. That realignment in the heart and the imagination towards a desire to see the Realm of God's shalom come now, come here: that bit you try to do? Those attempts count. The prophets are tough. At the same time, theirs is an invitation, "tendered," to sift through the sand until we find solid ground.

These talks are dense in places. If they bog you down, try reading them slowly and out loud.

Agnes Hamstra is Professor of English Literature, emerita, St. Stephen's University, New Brunswick, Canada, and member of Freechurch, Toronto

WE BECAME ACQUAINTED WITH Cal at the 1992 Greenbelt Festival (England) and were immediately captivated by his artistry to paint descriptive word pictures in the mind, particularly through inventive compound adjectives and sentence structures that cause you to slow down and chew the words thoroughly before moving on to the next paragraph. His compelling weaving together of Older and Newer Testament Scriptures and their context, together with a broad perspective of the arts, challenges us to "take seriously the embedded life of God's people in the socio-political culture of our day." His participation in several Arts Gatherings in Spain have left a deep imprint on all who attended, as well as the Poblenou evangelical church.

Joyce & James Phillips are Arts Manager/Voice Actor in Barcelona, Spain

TOUGH STUFF FROM THE *Bible, Tendered Gently* is vintage Seerveld. The eminent aesthetician, philosopher, theologian and sometime preacher stacks phrases and images to expand our vision while simultaneously zeroing in on the Christian scriptures. This collection of speeches and sermons are best read individually, like short stories, and then pondered as

Seerveld leads us into an understanding of just how wide and deep is the kingdom of God in Christ. I find his writing best read aloud as if it were the lilting poetry of "Fern Hill" to savour Seerveld's unique writing/speaking style. From Isaiah walking about in his underwear to a cosmic Christ bleeding redemption onto a wounded world, Seerveld is worth reading and re-reading.

Calvin Seerveld's scriptural insights are rich, rich, rich: not so much biblical exposition as it is musical meditation complete with complex chords and contrapuntal variations. Although his style is his own—as one professor noted, "It is his style, not exactly English, but it works" through lilting combinations of phraseology that surround and embroider and expound biblical passages.

In a world of label-laden theology in my opinion only two scholars stand out as above theological ideology: Eugene Peterson and Calvin Seerveld. Not scholastic, not liberal, not dogmatically Reformed or Lutheran, not modernist nor fundamentalist, not post-modern nor progressive, both in their quite different styles show that the Christian scriptures are alive and active, sharp as swords, and soothing as balm, exhilarating and painful as love.

Curt Gesch is a retired school teacher, farmer, hymn lover, journalist and poet (*A World of Small Things, Poems from Iqaluit*, 2018). He attends St. John Divine Anglican Church in Quick, British Columbia, Canada, where he plays the hamonium for worship services; he also plays piano for various United, Anglican and Lutheran congregations in the area.

www.ingramcontent.com/pod-product-compliance
Lightning Source LLC
Chambersburg PA
CBHW062056290426
44110CB00022B/2610